Purchased at H.....
S⁺ Petersburg, FL
26 Dec 1997

WARRIORS OF THE STEPPE

Warriors
of the
Steppe

A Military History of Central Asia, 500 B.C. to 1700 A.D.

By
ERIK HILDINGER

SARPEDON
New York

Published by
SARPEDON
166 Fifth Avenue
New York, NY 10010

ISBN 1-885119-43-7

Library of Congress Cataloging-in-Publication Data

Hildinger, Erik.
    Warriors of the Steppe : a military history of Central Asia, 500
B.C. to 1700 A.D. / by Erik Hildinger.
        p.   cm.
    Includes bibliographical references and index.
    ISBN 1-885119-43-7
    1. Asia, Central—History, Military.   I. Title.
DS329.4.H56   1997
355'.00958—dc21   97-25574
                                                            CIP

10 9 8 7 6 5 4 3 2 1

Contents

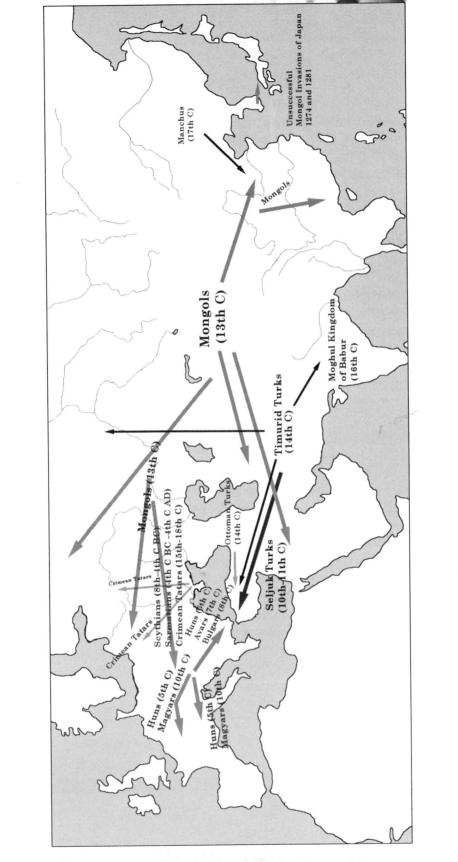

Chronology

451	Attila raids Gaul and is stopped by a combined Roman-Visigothic army near Troyes
452	Attila raids northern Italy
453	Attila dies
454	German subjects revolt and defeat the Huns at the Battle of the Nedao River; end of Hunnish Empire
ca. 557	Avars appear in the Russian steppe and establish themselves in the Hungarian plain
587	Avars begin to raid Byzantine territory
601	Byzantine general Procopius defeats Avars
626	Avars unsuccessfully besiege Constantinople in concert with the Persians
634	Bulgars gain independence from their Avar masters and begin to raid Byzantine territory
762	Avars unsuccessfully attack Constantinople
788–796	Charlemagne's army defeats Avars and captures their capital, the Ring
811	Byzantine emperor Nicephorus I is killed campaigning against the Bulgars
899	Magyars establish themselves on the Hungarian plain
899–954	Magyars repeatedly raid France and northern Italy
955	King Otto I of Germany defeats Magyars at the Battle on the Lechfeld and puts an end to their raiding
1055	Seljuk Turks consolidate hold on Middle East
1071	Byzantine emperor Romanus Diogenes defeated by Seljuk Turks at the Battle of Manzikert; most of Byzantium's Asian territory is lost as a result
1098	Western knights of the First Crusade take Antioch and Jerusalem, defeating Seljuk Turkish armies
1187	Crusader knights defeated at Hattin by Saladin and an army containing Turks
ca. 1160	Temujin born
1205–1209	Temjun subdues Xixia

1206	Temujin becomes "Khan of All Who Live in Felt Tents," controls all of Mongolia and takes the name "Chinggis Khan"
1219–1221	Chinggis Khan and the Mongols attack and subdue the state of Khwarezm
1223–1224	Mongol generals Subotai and Jebe conduct a reconnaissance in force through the Russian steppe, defeating Russians and Kipchak Turks
1209–1227	Chinggis Khan conducts wars against Kin Dynasty China
1227	Chinggis Khan dies
1236–1238	Mongol conquest of Russia; establishment of the Golden Horde or Kipchak Khanate and of the Tatar Yoke
1240–1241	Mongol campaigns against Hungary and Poland
1250	Mamluks (slave soldiers of Turkish extraction) seize the Egyptian government
1258	Mongol conquest of Persia
1260	Egyptian Mamluk army defeats Mongols at Battle of Ayn Jalut in Syria
1276	Mongol Great Khan Kubilai moves his capital to Peking and Mongols establish the Yuan Dynasty
1279	Mongol conquest of China complete
1336	Timur Lenk (Tamerlane) born
ca. 1360	Kipchak Khanate breaks up into smaller khanates: Kipchak, the White Horde, the Little Horde
1368	Mongols driven from China by Chinese; Ming Dynasty established
1380	Prince Dmitri Donskoi of Moscow leads Russians to victory against Khan Mamai of the Kipchak Khanate
1381	Khan Toktamish of the White Horde defeats the Kipchak Khanate and reunites the two
1381	Khan Toktamish defeats the Russians and burns Moscow; reimposition of the Tatar Yoke
1395	Timur defeats Khan Toktamish of the Kipchak Khanate and destroys its capitals

1398   Timur conquers the Sultanate of Delhi

1400   Timur defeats the Egyptian Mamluk Sultanate in Syria

1402   Timur defeats Sultan Bayazet of Turkey

1405   Timur dies

1435   Khanate of the Crimea separates from Kipchak Khanate

1445   Khanate of Kazan separates from Kipchak Khanate

1480   Stand-off at the River Kalka frees Russia from the Tatar Yoke

1552   Ivan IV the Terrible destroys the Khanate of Kazan

1556   Ivan IV the Terrible destroys the Khanate of Astrakhan

1613   Nurhachi unites the Jurchid (Manchu) tribes

1636–1639   Manchu raids into Chinese territory

1644   Manchu seizure of Peking and establishment of the Qing (Ch'ing) Dynasty

1771   Russia formally annexes the Khanate of the Crimea

1912   Fall of the Manchu Dynasty

WARRIORS OF THE STEPPE

Introduction

No people in history have been so "naturally" expert in war as the nomads of the Eurasian steppe. Many civilized, settled peoples have been accomplished at war; among the ancients, the Romans come foremost to mind, with an army that performed as a successful institution for hundreds of years. However, the Roman army, like those of many nations that followed, was the product of conscious development. The Roman army underwent a deliberate evolution from a citizen militia to a professional force, its tactics changing from Greek-style phalangite fighting with spears to sword fighting in looser formations, after casting javelins to disorder the enemy and make their shields useless. With its formal training, fatigue marches, regular division into legions and cohorts, and professional officers, doctors, clerks, blacksmiths, veterinarians, as well as weapons and armor produced by state factories, the Roman army resembled a modern one and, viewed in this perspective, its steady successes for over five hundred years are not a surprise.

Nonetheless, the Romans were not "natural" warriors. Instead, they were civilized men who, as soldiers, were taught the craft of battle, formally acquiring the skills needed to fight. It was in fact the purpose of the soldier's training to do more than imbue skill in the use of arms: it also served to make him fit for the rigors and hardships that settled, civilized life normally blunts in its citizens. It follows, then, that the more barbaric a people, the better they are as fighters. Carl von Clausewitz stated this clearly:

War is the realm of physical exertion and suffering. These will destroy us unless we can make ourselves indifferent to

1

them, and for this birth or training must provide us with a certain strength of body and soul. If we do possess those qualities, then even if we have nothing but common sense to guide them we shall be well equipped for war: it is exactly these qualities that primitive and semicivilized peoples usually possess.[1]

Napoleon put it more bluntly: "The first qualification of a soldier is fortitude under fatigue and privation. Courage is only the second; hardship, poverty, and want are the best school for a soldier."[2]

This book is about certain peoples schooled in want and hardship who, as a result, were excellent warriors. What is more, not only were these peoples toughened into hard fighters by a harsh environment, they were molded into warriors with a distinct and peculiar style of fighting well suited for use against the settled peoples whose lands bordered theirs: they were the nomads of the steppe. This book will examine a number of these people and show the consistent character over time and distance that made them akin to a natural force, and it will examine the troublesome, often brutal treatment they meted out to others.

Consider the first whom we know anything about: the Scythians of the sixth century B.C., a nation of nomadic horsemen who plundered and briefly subjected Persia. When, years later, the Persian king Darius I led a large punitive expedition into the steppe north of the Black Sea he could do no more than follow them for weeks across the trackless plains, never able to close with them, always subject to their constant harassing attacks until, in the end, he was forced to retire, his aims completely unfulfilled.

Around the turn of the first century A.D. Roman armies began to encounter fully armored warriors on armored horses who fought with heavy lances. These Sarmatians, another nomadic people from the steppe, were to fight Rome for four hundred years and signally influence shock cavalry warfare in the West for a thousand more.

At the turn of the fourth century another horse people appeared on the fringes of the empire: Huns. These people alternately served and attacked the empire for two hundred years, even riding their ponies south across Roman territory to attack the heart of the Persian Empire and west as far as Gaul, where they sacked such cities as Tours. In 451 A.D., on a plain near the modern French city of Troyes, a combined Roman-Visigothic army fought the Western Empire's last great battle against barbarians, stopping the Hunnic army of Attila and forcing its withdrawal to the Hungarian plain, that westernmost outcrop of the great Eurasian steppe.

Avars and Magyars followed, coming off the steppe into the Hungarian plain between the sixth and eighth centuries. They ravaged the infant states of Europe for two hundred years, pillaging Germany, riding west into France, where they ravaged the region of Lorraine and heading into northern Italy. All central and western Europe was subject to their incessant raids.

These were followed two hundred and fifty years later by the Mongols, known in the West as Tatars or Tartars, who swept into central Europe and annihilated a series of knightly armies as they sought to annex Hungary to an empire stretching from northern China across all of Central Asia, Russia and the Ukrainian steppe. Even the breakup of the Mongol Empire did not spell the end of the Tatar threat; it lingered on in the form of separate khanates and kingdoms that troubled the Middle East, China and Central Europe. Only gunpowder tilted the scale permanently in favor of settled peoples during the seventeenth century.

While this book explores why these nomads were so effective, another brief quote from Clausewitz might not be out of place: "Four elements make up the climate of war: danger, exertion, uncertainty and chance."[3] This observation might equally apply to the life of the horsemen of the steppes and account for the ease with which they waged war; it did not present difficulties so very different from their quotidian existence.

NOTES
1. Carl von Clausewitz, *On War*, trans. and ed. M. Howard and P. Paret, Princeton, NJ, Princeton University Press, 1976, Book I, iii.
2. Napoleon Bonaparte, *The Military Maxims of Napoleon*, trans. G.C. d'Aguilar, London, Greenhill, 1987, Maxim 58.
3. Clausewitz, op. cit., p. 101.

1

Nomads

To understand why the armies that swept off the steppe to attack sedentary people were such a terrific threat, and so often unbeatable, one must understand something of their origins. It is simply not enough to describe how they fought and how their fighting differed from that of, say, the Europeans. What follows is not an exhaustive description either of the steppe, or of the peoples who lived there. It should, however, supply enough background to appreciate the innate strengths, and weaknesses, of these people.

The steppe forms the heart of Eurasia, comprising land along the borders of China, all of Central Asia, the Ukraine and the area surrounding the Black Sea to north of Afghanistan. Its westernmost outcrop is the Hungarian plain. Modern regions with all or part of their territory in the steppe are China, Inner Mongolia, Outer Mongolia, Russia, Kazakhstan, Turkestan, Turkmenistan, Uzbekistan, Tadjikistan, Afghanistan, Ukraine and Hungary. The steppe is thus a vast place and, accordingly, not uniform in feature. It is not, for example, one vast sea of grass, although there are such places. There are mountainous areas, deserts such as the Gobi, and a forbidding subarctic forest belt, the taiga. Climate is severe, even in the better areas which are generally found in the West. In the central belt of the steppe—the land of the Turks and Mongols—temperatures may vary between winter and summer by 80 degrees centigrade; it is a climate for the hardy and it has historically been the home of the nomad.

The term nomad, in the popular imagination, suggests a people wandering aimlessly from place to place. In fact, however, such a practice would be deadly for those, like the steppe dwellers, who have traditionally lived on the very edge of subsistence. Instead, the true nomad is a migratory creature shifting his home twice a year between summer and winter pastures which are recognized by the tribe, and by neighboring tribes, even though they may be hundreds of miles apart or found at different altitudes. He travels as he does because he is a pastoralist, a keeper of sheep, goats, cattle or horses (depending upon the tribe, a combination of any of these) from which he gets or makes the mainstays of his existence: meat, milk, hides, felts, horsehair for bridles, dung for fires and even an alcoholic beverage—koumiss, or fermented mare's milk. However, the steppe will not feed the flocks and herds all year round in a single spot. Hence the inexorable need to shift his home twice a year. And hence so much else that characterizes his life.

Something has been said about how hard the life of the nomad is. His life is so hard, in fact, that he cannot live it entirely from his animals; there can be no "pure nomad"; the anthropologists agree upon this. The animal products—meat, milk, hide and hair, used for food, clothing, felt and other necessities—are insufficient to keep him alive. The nomad, as it turns out, needs agriculture. He may even practice it somewhat; there is evidence of Scythian and Sarmatian and even Hunnic agriculture on the steppe. The nomad, however, does not concentrate upon it. That is for settled peoples and the degree to which the latter practice it is what distinguishes them from the nomad; they do not have to wander between two homes. Thus, the nomad, whether he wants to or not, must deal with settled people to some degree. His condition drives him to it the more he approaches the "pure" type of nomad, and as he approaches the "pure type," survival depends upon either trade with or predation upon settled peoples.

This dependence means that historically nomads have tended to live in appalling poverty, at the very margin of life, and this poverty can be mitigated only by contact with settled peoples. The need to move twice a year, often great distances, means that they are almost incredibly hardened—toughened to a degree difficult for sedentary people to appreciate. Thus, there is a natural spur acting upon the nomad to trade with or plunder settled peoples. The domestication of the horse made the latter quite practical, and the use of the horse, coupled with archery, made for particularly successful plundering.

Nomads could cover great distances to attack settled people, the distance protecting the nomads from settlers and at the same time allowing them to surprise their opponents. Archery was a perfect skill to allow fighting without coming to close quarters, and its effects could be enhanced by the natural mobility of the horsemen. And the nomads were the best horsemen because they rode every day to manage their herds.

It is observed that as nomads become more skilled and successful at raiding they tend to give up whatever agricultural activities they may have maintained—agricultural products and the luxuries of the settled peoples can more easily be gained as tribute and plunder, though the abandonment of agrarian activities ties the nomad more firmly to the settler from whom he must get what he needs by trade or war. War is therefore a natural consequence of successful nomadism and like any skill needed for survival it will be practiced to proficiency.

Their natural situation, then, tends to make nomads inclined to war, and at the same time very good at it. As noted, both Clausewitz and Napoleon recognized that hardness and stamina are the first prerequisites of any soldier, and there were no steppe tribesmen who lacked these qualities. Those who were weak or frail as children simply never reached adulthood.

Toughness aside, what tends to make any group of nomads skilled at war (as opposed to being merely strong enough to endure it) are those traits they share with other nomadic people whom they resemble in way of life and war over amazing stretches of time and distance. It would be fair to say that the Hun of the fifth century A.D. would have had marked affinities with both the Turco-Mongol Crimean Tartars of the seventeenth century and with the Scythians of the fifth century B.C. He might have allied with either of them without a second thought, and he would have found nothing unfamiliar in their lifestyle: all were pastoralist horsemen fighting as mounted archers.

Because Central Asian nomads have no fixed abode they have tended to live in *gers*, drumlike felt tents with an internal wooden structure. These have doors and a central hole in the roof to allow in light and air and to exhaust smoke. These structures can generally be assembled or disassembled in about an hour and are taken with the nomads wherever they go. They vary in size, the largest being of a more permanent construction and mounted on carts drawn by oxen—either a handful of animals or, in the case of the gers of great men, perhaps as many as twenty. The Mongols, Turks and Tatars were seen to use these wheeled gers from the twelfth to the seventeenth centuries A.D. and Scythian and Sarmatian artwork from the fourth century B.C. shows that these Iranian-speaking nomads of the Black Sea steppe did so as well. As for the more usual ger, disassembled and packed upon animals for transport, they persist today in Mongolia and among Mongolians living in China, and they were used on military campaigns by the Crimean Tatars into relatively modern times, as reported by the seventeenth-century French traveler Guillaume Le Vasseur de Beauplan.

Modern census takers dealing with nomads generally assume about five people to live in each ger, or tent, though of course this must vary, now as in the past, especially as the gers themselves must have varied more in size then, when the nomad was frankly more important than he is now. Because the pastoral life is hard, a group of gers will be gathered to divide labor and form a camp called a *yurt*, a term often misapplied to the individual gers making up the camp itself. The camps of the medieval Mongol khans and other powerful Mongols were, of course, much larger and known as hordes. This word has passed into our speech to signify a Mongol army itself, although the proper use of the word was known in the thirteenth century by such as Giovanni di Plano Carpini, who traveled among the Mongols and explained the word "horde" in a report.

Central Asian nomads have historically belonged to three main groups: the Turkic, Mongolian and Iranian. The Turkic branch is the most widely spread; in fact the Turks are one of the most widely dispersed peoples in the world. There have been scores of Turkish nations: Huns, Kangali, Seljuks, Kipchaks (or Cumans), Uigurs, Kazakhs, Uzbeks and others. Of the Mongolian branch, the Mongols are the best known, but there were Merkits, Naimans and Tatars too, the last being perhaps the largest before their defeat and amalgamation into the Mongol nation by Chinggis Khan. The Iranian branch, which tended to be centered on the steppe surrounding the Black Sea and the environs of Persia (the Persians are their cousins) during the centuries before and immediately after the birth of Christ, has as its most important representatives the Scythians and Sarmatians, each made up of a loose group of tribes. Of the Sarmatians the best known were the Alani, Roxolani and Iyazges.

Each of these peoples had some influence upon Western history, a few of them a more devastating effect upon the history of the Middle East and China. Each of these peoples was different, of course, but the picture of the nomad remains curiously similar across time and space: clad in trousers (which he bequeathed to the ancient Germans and to the Chinese) and tall, soft boots, he wore a tunic, or in the east where the steppe is higher and the weather more severe, a long belted coat, often quilted or lined with fur. On his head he wore a fur cap, or perhaps a felt one if he were a Scythian, or a turban against the sun of the hot summer steppe. He rode a small horse, a pony actually, which is tougher than a horse and hardier, and he fought from horseback with a powerful and efficient bow. The bow he kept in a case hung from the left of his belt while the arrows were held in a quiver on the right. If he were well-to-do he might have other arms—a sword perhaps or a saber—but we must not be distracted by such things: the bow is the primary and distinguishing weapon of the steppe nomad and it is due to the bow that he won his victories.

The Mongols and Turks are related, if no longer closely. Their languages are of the same broad family, the Tungusic-Altaic, but they are not mutually intelligible. Chinggis Khan had his sons learn Turkic because, in the western *ulus* or appanages their subjects were primarily Turkic. In time the Mongol khanates of Russia, the Ukraine, the Black Sea steppe and Transoxiana became Turkic-speaking and their people were generally known as Tatars or Tartars. The Turks and Mongols were anciently divided into numerous small tribes who, from time to time, joined each other in confederations which often, as in the case of the Mongols, took the name of the leading tribe.

Their relationships were fluid and marked by warfare. As the chief of a tribe was generally called khan in the Turkic-Mongol tongues, the leader of a number of tribes was known as ka-khan or kaghan, and tribes willingly joined one another as the leading men sought successful chiefs to follow, even differences of language being no obstacle. The Mongol Chinggis Khan began his rise to power as a follower of the Turkish khan Toghrul of the Keraits, and this amalgamation of lesser tribes could result in a steppe conqueror's army actually growing in size over the course of a successful campaign.

The political organization of such a confederation was little if any more sophisticated than the organization of any of its constituent tribes. Scholars draw some distinctions between Turkic and Mongol social organization, but it is enough here to observe that they were similar and primitive and that any confederation or polity depended for its existence upon the force of the leader's personality, so that his death often ended the state. A son did not necessarily follow his father as khan; on the contrary, the nation was often divided into ulus or appanages, territories and populations given out to each of the khan's sons, or at least those of the principal wife. The entire nation was simply property to be divided as the khan saw fit. This meant, of course, that a steppe state was inherently unstable.

The custom of lateral succession, whereby a ruler might be succeeded by his brother, or a series of brothers, is observed on the steppe and might have arisen to temper the instability of the state since it would tend to delay the breakup of the nation—though, of course, it could not do so for very long.[1] The steppe custom of having many wives also increased the number of young men of noble or royal descent (illegitimacy was no bar to inheritance and did not affect status) and might from time to time cause problems as well. It is interesting to note that Clausewitz in his treatise *On War* uses the term "Tartar nation" to describe a state riven by internal divisions and with no strong constitution to hold it together.

Poland was his case in point and he believed its dissolution through partition between its neighbors was directly related to Tartar influence across Polish history. However this may be, it is true that Poland's disappearance was the result of nobles who judged their personal interests more important than the survival of the nation.[2] The point here is not whether Poland was really a Tartar state in the midst of Europe, but rather that it exhibited characteristics found in steppe or "Tartar" states: incipient divisions waiting only for the death of the leader to work their ways. It will be seen that this political fragility, something less often suffered by sedentary peoples, has been one of the most important checks upon the power of steppe tribes.

Why were their polities so primitive? Nomads live dispersed and, one may suppose, do not have any more political baggage than they need. Ferdinand Lot in his book *L'Art Militaire et les Armées du Moyen Age*[3] pointed out that the population of Mongolia in the first half of this century (when it must have been almost entirely nomadic, which is no longer the case) was estimated at seven hundred thousand. There is no reason to suppose that it was much different in the Middle Ages, though some reckon that Mongolia then supported a population of about a million. Neither figure is high and would follow from the low density of population found in a pastoral society that needs much land. Other areas subject to pastoralism at various times, such as Transoxiana, the Ukraine, Russia, Siberia, Afghanistan, Turkestan and the Crimea, would likewise have had relatively sparse nomad populations.

In spite of their relatively low numbers in contrast to settled peoples, they were able to field highly effective armies and control vast areas. Clausewitz said of them that if they could have developed a high degree of civilization, nothing would have stopped them.[4] The implication is that the nomad (or "Tartar" as Clausewitz called it) state could not do this, and there is some truth to this. Clausewitz thought that nomads moved in search of new territory with their wives and children, thereby outnumbering other nations. Sometimes nomads move in entire nations; the Huns did so when they came to Europe, as did the Avars and Magyars. The Mongols, on expeditions of conquest, however, did not—they sent only the army, and even the Huns did not invade the Roman Empire with their whole people. They were satisfied with raiding, as were the later Crimean Tatars of the Black Sea region.

Therefore Clausewitz was incorrect in this regard, or perhaps considered only the example of the Huns in Hungary or the Mongols in Central Asia, where the situation supported his theory of war as an extension of politics—that is, the triumph of one state over another in a primarily political sense. In fact, however, while steppe peoples could and did engage in wars of conquest, as we shall see, more often they operated on the fringes of civilization, simply sweeping in on freebooting expeditions, sometimes small, sometimes huge. Timur of Samarkand (better known in the west as Tamerlane) operated on a very large scale indeed, conquered powerful states and sacked great cities, but did not actually extend his dominions much. His operations were different from the eighth-century Magyar raids into eastern France in degree but not in kind. They were little more than gigantic raids. However, it was this very propensity for raiding that made the steppe peoples very difficult indeed to deal with. From a strategic standpoint, of two evenly matched forces, the one in retreat will outstrip or evade its pursuer. This will only be exaggerated where, as in medieval Europe, heavy horsemen formed the great strength of national armies.

Where it was difficult for a heavily armored knight to catch a fleeing knight, he could have no real hope at all of overtaking a light cavalryman such as the steppe produced. This was of course true on a tactical level too, the level of the battles. But where the steppe warrior engaged in raiding (as most were wont to do), making incursions not for the purpose of invasion or the annexation of territory, but rather as a purely economic exercise—in short, where he raided for booty—the advantage normally accruing to a force in retreat accrued to him instead. He was most difficult to catch, and it was nearly impossible to tell where he might strike, because he would seldom have any generally recognized strategic targets. It could not be said by what route he might fall back to his own country, and he could not generally be forced to fight if he was unwilling. And, as we shall see, he did not generally desire a fight unless he were assured of victory; and then it was dangerous indeed to fight him.

Another way in which these people were able to control large populations while they themselves were not particularly numerous was that, in nomadic societies, as in most primitive or simple cultures, a much higher proportion of the male population can be mustered for war. Thus, given equal populations, nomads will field a larger army than a sedentary people, and this, to some degree, will offset a settled people's advantage in numbers.

A second, and psychological, advantage has been the fear and revulsion that the nomad has so often induced in the settled: a product of the nomad's cultural and often racial difference. This has sometimes caused sedentary peoples to openly question whether such people (the Huns are an example) were in fact altogether human. One finds an echo of this feeling as late as 1635, when the

French traveler Guillaume Le Vasseur de Beauplan returned from a journey to the Ukraine where had encountered, and even been attacked by, Crimean Tatars. He repeats what must have been a widespread tale among the Poles and Ukrainians of the area, that Tatar babies were born with their eyes closed like dogs, and did not open them until several days after their birth.[5] The implication is clear: the Tatar, like the dog, is a lower creature than the civilized European, a point that must have seemed obvious to the people of the Ukraine, victims of their raids for centuries. And the terror was, in some cases, cultivated. Mongol generals used wholesale slaughter in tandem with selective sparing of small numbers of prisoners induced to flee to other parts in order to spread panic. The Mongols knew the value of calculated terror; as a campaign progressed, more and more cities and towns would surrender to them without a fight. The momentum of the war would shift in their favor, allowing small armies to dominate large areas. Timur of Samarkand is still notorious for pyramids of severed human heads and displays of greater-than-Mongol cruelty.

Finally, the nomad lifestyle taught the steppe dweller to shift camp and move in an organized manner imparting a certain basic and almost military discipline that would carry over to a nomad army on campaign. The Englishman Captain John Perry remarked on the regularity with which Siberian Tatars shifted their encampments around the year 1700:

> . . . some later spread the Country in Parties, from 8 or 10, to 15, or sometimes 20,000 of them or more in a Body and pitch their Tents in Streets and Lanes, in the same regular Manner as in a Town or Village, and every one knows their due Place and Order; so that I have seen Cows stop at their own Tents, when they drive them home to milk them.[6]

This description would apply to any band of nomads, and any band of nomads would have been served by the sort of discipline needed to shift such a camp with all of its people and its huge number of animals.

All of these points combined to make the nomadic steppe warrior an extremely dangerous opponent for sedentary people. He was a supremely good soldier, trained in the most effective pre-industrial weapons and techniques, naturally somewhat disciplined, easily tougher than his opponents, and favored by elementary rules of strategy when he chose to use the initiative to raid instead of to conquer.

NOTES
1. Chinggis Khan was succeeded by his son Occodai, but Occodai was in turn succeeded by two of his brothers: Guyuk and Mangu.
2. Clausewitz asks, reasonably enough, how a nation can survive if only its neighbors wish it to exist. Carl Von Clausewitz, *On War*, trans. and ed. M. Howard and P. Paret, Princeton, NJ, Princeton University Press, 1976, p. 375.
3. Ferdinand Lot, *L'Art Militaire et les Armées du Moyen Age*, Paris, Payot, 1944.
4. Clausewitz, Book VIII, chapter 3, p. 586.
5. Guillaume Le Vasseur de Beauplan, *La Description d'Ukranie*, Ottawa, Les Presses de l'Université d'Ottawa, 1990, p. 61.
6. John Perry, *The State of Russia Under the Present Czar*, London and Edinburgh, Thomas Nelson, Ltd (reprint of 1716 edition), pp. 83–84.

2

Horse and Bow

Two things in combination define the steppe warrior more than anything else: the horse and the bow. Many peoples have used one or the other with devastating effect in warfare, but only the steppe peoples have consistently used them together. Everything else about them of a military nature follows this as a matter of course, as we shall see, and to appreciate this, one must appreciate the horse and bow, and their combination.

The horse was first domesticated in the steppe in the fourth millennium B.C., where it was used as food. Selective breeding led to larger animals and the horse's consequent importance by the second millennium B.C. was in drawing the chariots which, for hundreds of years, became the mainstay of Near Eastern armies such as those of Egypt, Babylon and Assyria. The chariot spread further afield to such places as Greece, where the terrain did not suit it—a testament to its prior reputation in places where it had large, flat areas to operate. The chariot's most famous appearance in Western literature is in Homer, where it is a Mycenean holdover.

The Egyptians have left us paintings of their chariots and they seem to have learned their use from the Hyksos, a barbaric people who used them to briefly conquer and rule Egypt. However, the chariot is probably a product of the borderlands between the steppe and the civilized Mesopotamian area, whence it spread to both civilized and nomadic peoples.

It is the Middle Eastern peoples who have given us the first surviving pictures of men riding on the backs of horses. Seventh-century Assyrian wall carvings show soldiers sitting toward the haunches, rather than on the back, because the animal was otherwise too small to bear the weight. Horses were selectively bred for size, however, and over time they could be ridden as we do today. Riding horses probably occurred first on the steppes, and much earlier than it did in Assyria, though it is in the art of the sedentary peoples that we see the first pictorial evidence of it.

The steppe horse should probably be considered a pony rather than a horse, and the distinction between pony and horse is recognized by horsemen today, even if that distinction is not precise.[1] Ponies are generally smaller than horses, usually no more than fourteen hands high, and in the common view this is their principal distinction. However, there are other equally significant differences between ponies and horses, and these are important in considering the effectiveness and threat posed by the steppe peoples who rode them.

Ponies are tough, often stockier than horses, and surprisingly strong. Some modern ponies, such as the halflinger, while not as tall as a horse, may be as heavy. As a rule their proportions are different—their legs may be relatively shorter and thicker and their heads proportionately larger. Their manes and tails are often longer and their hair more coarse. Their generally smaller size may account for the fact that they live longer than horses and require less food, and food of lesser quality. All of these factors, along with some Paleolithic evidence, suggested to a Scottish scientist at the turn of the century that ponies and horses were distinct "races" in ancient times and that size alone might be a rather arbitrary distinction.[2] Clearly the two are very close and are often interbred, but the question of their lineage is not so much a concern here as are the pony's excellent qualities of strength, stamina and ability to subsist on little food. All of this was well known in antiquity. In the fifth century the Roman author Vegetius wrote of Hun horses that they were ugly and small, but rated them as best for warfare because of their toughness and obedience.

The steppe pony's ability to find food in the snow is mentioned by the thirteenth-century papal emissary Giovanni di Plano Carpini in the account of his journey to the Mongol Khan in Central Asia:

When we arrived there [in Kiev], we consulted about our route with a millenarius [Mongol officer] and other nobles

who were there. They told us that if we led the horses we
had into Tartary, they would not know how to dig grass
from beneath the snow when it was deep, as Tartar horses
do, and it would not be possible to find anything else for
them to eat because the Tartars have neither straw nor hay
nor fodder, and they would all die. So, we talked among
ourselves and told the two boys who looked after them to
send them away.

This text will refer to the steppe horses as horses rather than
ponies since they are not in fact distinct species, but the differences
noted here should be kept in mind when considering the effectiveness
of the various steppe armies.

Finally, steppe peoples used great numbers of horses while on
the march, often three or four per man. This allowed them to ride a
different horse each day and thus cover great distances without
exhausting their animals. Speed is important in war. The Romans
knew this and built an outstanding network of roads throughout the
Empire to allow their armies to march from one frontier to the other
most efficiently. A Roman army might march twelve to sixteen miles
a day or, on a forced march, something over twenty—a good distance for an infantry force, especially one that dug field fortifications
every night upon arrival. With the collapse of Rome, however,
medieval armies could hardly have hoped to do as well, let alone any
better.

Not so, however, with the steppe nomad. His armies, entirely
mounted and furnished with spare horses, could cover much more
ground. The Mongol army was known to cover forty miles in a day
and even sixty if need be. This kind of strategic mobility requires of
a defender a much larger army to deal effectively with the threat than
would otherwise be the case. The enemy can be everywhere and it is
difficult to garrison every place. One of Napoleon's maxims deals
with this very situation: "The strength of an army, like the power in
mechanics, is estimated by multiplying the mass by the rapidity; a
rapid march augments the morale of an army, and increases all the
chances of victory."[4]

Of course, the matter is not quite as mathematical as Napoleon's
statement might suggest, but there is a good deal of truth in it.

Imagine an army of steppe warriors such as the Mongols able to move three or four times as fast across the countryside as their opponents, even if they were outnumbered. The steppe warrior, mounted on his tough pony and trailing a string of remounts, could effectively threaten a significantly more numerous enemy by relying on his speed alone, and his speed was only one of several advantages he held over sedentary peoples.

Steppe peoples rode geldings and mares. Stallions are aggressive and difficult to control and so it was only natural that they were few in number and kept for breeding, not riding. Grave finds in which horses were buried as well as observations of tribes in the steppe in modern times confirm this. The more docile geldings and mares would be more easily handled in battle, and the general absence of stallions resulted in less disruption of the horse herds which accompanied the steppe warriors. Stallions tend to fight among themselves and will try to lead groups of mares away from the herd, something steppe warriors did not need to deal with, either in their home territories or on the march.

Horses on the steppe were generally marked by cuts in the ears or by branding on the shoulders or rear flanks. The former method is the more primitive, but branding was clearly used by the Mongols, as reported by Marco Polo in the thirteenth century, and earlier by other peoples, such as the Alani, as suggested by a mosaic from Carthage.[5] The Alani were a Sarmatian people first conquered by the Huns, and then later largely absorbed by the Vandals, who seized North Africa from the Romans in the fifth century. There are *stelae* dated between the first and third centuries A.D. from the Crimea showing Sarmatians with branded horses.[6]

The domestication of horses leads naturally to the development of horse furniture. The Scythians are generally credited with making the first saddles with any real support. Finds of bronze fixtures for saddle bows make it clear that the Huns had saddles built up on wooden trees or frames. During the Battle of Locus Mauriacus, Attila is reported to have built up a pyre of saddles to be set alight if the Romans broke into his camp. That they were the fuel for such a pyre is consistent with their having wooden frames. The Sarmatians, given their methods of fighting, must have used them too; they were the first people to fight with complete armor from horseback. By the time of the Mongols, at least, the steppe saddle had a high saddle-bow and an even higher cantle, both of which were built up at a steep, almost vertical angle from the seat. The Huns, emerging from central Asia, probably used one of similar design.

All of this leads to the issue of stirrups. There is no solid evidence of their use by steppe people, at least in the West, until the Avars seem to have introduced them in the sixth century. As a result, the Byzantine or East Roman cavalry adopted them at this time, which must have been a great help, particularly in using the lance and broadsword and in keeping a seat while wearing armor. Some argue that the Huns must have had stirrups, but there is no pictorial or literary evidence of it and no grave finds to support the theory. It is possible that they did use them and that they were made of a perishable material—they might have been leather loops—but on balance it seems unlikely.

The Romans had a long history of borrowing military equipment from others: chainmail from the Celts, the classic "Roman" helmet from the Gauls, the short sword or *ensis hispanicus* from Spain and later the helmet called nowadays by the German name *spangenhelm* from the East, probably from Persia. When it became advantageous to greatly increase the number of their cavalry and to incorporate new kinds, such as the *clibanarius* or *cataphractus* (adopted from the Sarmatians), they did so. It does not seem credible that the Romans would not have taken up the stirrup as well, if the Huns had them; after all, Huns had served in Roman armies and fought against them for a hundred years. The stirrup would have suited the Roman heavy cavalry even more than the Huns, and the East Romans did later adopt it in the sixth century.

When stirrups did come into use, they were set rather short, betraying the steppe warrior's preference for agility and use of the bow. Western knights, by contrast, rode with their stirrup leathers long to allow them to sit with their legs fully straightened. This was more useful for keeping a seat while swinging a broadsword or wielding a lance. This difference in setting the stirrups caused the French traveler Beauplan to comment on the horsemanship of the seventeenth-century Crimean Tatars: ". . . they are very skillful and dangerous when mounted, but they are badly seated because they have their legs folded up and ride very short; they are mounted on the horse like a monkey on a greyhound. . ."[7]

More prosaically, Richard Chanceler had noted the same thing a century before after observing Russian cavalry which had been influenced by two hundred years of Mongol rule: "They ride with a short stirrup after the manner of the Turks."[8] Russia was practically unknown to the English in Chanceler's day. He was one of the first Englishmen to visit the country and he naturally attributed the Russian style to Turkish influence instead of Mongol, but the difference is insignificant: the Turks, like the Mongols, were steppe people with the same mode of warfare. The short stirrup, or "forward seat," puts the rider's weight over the horse's shoulders rather than square on its back and is easier on the animal. This is why such a posture has been adopted somewhat in dressage and much more so in horse racing, where the jockey's posture reminds one of Beauplan's description.

Horseshoes, another useful device, were never generally used by steppe peoples. They were common in Europe (where they were invented) by the early Middle Ages, and the later Mongol ambassadors and nobility appreciated them as gifts. However, they were not particularly necessary where, as in the steppe, the rider was not heavily burdened with armor and the ground was not generally too hard. As a result, Beauplan noted that the Crimean Tartars in the seventeenth century rode unshod horses: ". . . their horses are not shod because the snow protects their feet, which is not true if the ground is not covered with it."[9] He went on to add that the Crimean Tartar nobles sometimes used rather ineffective leather stockings to protect their horses' feet if needed.

The steppe warrior had wonderful mobility that he took from the pony. He had a wonderful weapon, too: the bow. This quintessential weapon of the steppe warrior differed, however, from those commonly used in the West. Steppe bows have, over history, come in a variety of sizes and shapes, but are of composite construction and are recurved in shape. Bows in the West are generally known as "self" bows and have historically been made of a single, straight stave of wood. The better staves are cut so that the heartwood, which can withstand compression, is found on the belly of the bow (the side facing the archer as he draws). By contrast the sapwood from the outer part of the tree, which can better withstand tension, is used for the back of the bow (the side away from the archer as he draws). The best examples of this are the English longbows of the Middle Ages and Renaissance, used to such effect against the French at Crécy and Agincourt during the Hundred Years War.

The composite bow, which seems to have developed independently in the Middle East and Central Asia some four millennia ago, takes the idea of using different materials to withstand tension and compression a step further. Instead of using a stave cut to employ the different parts of a single piece of wood, the composite bow uses entirely different materials to withstand tension and compression: sinew and horn.

The composite bow is of three-part construction: a thin central stave of wood is laminated with sinew on the back and horn on the belly. A study of old texts on archery as well as the dissection of various surviving examples has told us a great deal about their construction which, despite differences in the size and shape of individual bows, is relatively uniform. Their production was elaborate.

First, a central bowstave was cut from wood. The wood chosen was often maple, cornus or mulberry, selected because they absorb glue well. Some bows used bamboo. The wood was in five sections joined together with fishtail splices about three and a half inches long. There was a central section for the grip, which was joined to a pair of bow arms, and a pair of tips was fixed to the ends of the arms. Horn from long-horned cattle was glued to the belly of the bow and it was tied into an arc against the shape it would be drawn into. This was to create the recurved shape. This gluing was done in the winter when the weather was cool and the humidity higher, in order that the drying process should be gradual. The bow was left to dry about two months. Persian composite bows used strips of horn bound together with sinew since they were generally wider than other bows and it was difficult to find strips of horn both wide enough and long enough that a single piece could be used for each bow arm. Some Korean composite bows are also made with strips of horn rather than with a single piece for each limb. It seems likely that many bows were historically made this way where good single pieces of horn were generally unavailable.

Next comes the application of the sinew which, according to W.F. Paterson, is more important for the bow's performance than the horn.[10] This sinew is taken from the legs of cattle or deer. Some old texts state that tendons from the neck should be used, but Paterson states that in practice they are too elastic for this purpose. These sinews are beaten into fibers that are then soaked with glue and applied on a warm day. A bow may have more than one layer of sinew, flight bows (special sporting bows for shooting long distance) generally having two such layers. After the sinew is applied, the bow is tied again into an even more extremely recurved shape with a cord holding the tips together; this is in turn tied to the handle of the bow. This is to ensure that, when the bow is later drawn, the sinew will be exposed to a good deal of tension and the bow will function efficiently. Tied down in this way the bow is left for another two months to dry.

When the bow is tied in this extreme way, the horn plates of the two limbs that meet at the center of the handle separate slightly. A small shim called a *chelik* in Turkish is inserted here. The Arabs, who also used composite bows, called this shim an *ibranjaq*. Surviving bows show them made of ivory, though on the steppe they were probably more often of hard wood or bone.

When the bow has dried, it is unstrung, warmed and then strung in the direction in which it will be shot. Now comes the tillering, or adjusting of the bow so that the limbs curve uniformly when drawn. The bowyer would draw the bow slightly and observe how the bow arms bent. Where one is too stiff he would file it carefully at the edges. He would then draw the bow somewhat further and repeat this. The process continues until he has adjusted the bow arms to bend evenly at full draw. Failing this, the bow would not shoot accurately.

Strips of bark or thin leather were applied in diagonals to cover and waterproof the sinew. Some bows also had the horn covered, though this is not the case with Mamluk, Mongolian or Sino-Tatar bows. Turkish and Persian bows, at least, had horn inserts in the tips where the bowstring was looped. Now the bow was finished and would exhibit the qualities that made it superior to the self bow. First, of course, it was mechanically superior. Sinew has a tensile strength four times that of wood and horn has a compressive strength about twice that of a hardwood.[11] This means that a composite bow can be made relatively shorter than a self bow with the same draw weight, and more energy is transferred to the arrow rather than lost to a set of long, heavy bow limbs. Thus, given equal draw weights, the composite bow will shoot an arrow faster and further than a self bow. The fact that composite, recurved bows are generally shorter than self bows of any power means that they are handier, especially for men on horseback.

The recurved shape has other advantages over a straight staved or "simple" bow. The tips of the recurved bow are generally inflexible and in some bows are angled away from the bow arm toward the back of the bow somewhat. This inflexibility helps in the draw of the bow by allowing the tips to function somewhat as levers. Therefore, as the bow is drawn further back, the draw weight does not increase proportionately, as it does in a self bow, where the weight "stacks" suddenly at the end of the draw. This means that the recurved bow is easier to shoot accurately since it is easier to draw; minute changes in the length of the draw do not result in markedly different draw weights and consequently different arrow velocities. The design also gives a smoother and more efficient shot without the kick associated with self bows. In short, the composite, recurved bow is a markedly better weapon than the simple self bow.

The recurved composite bow took a good deal of work to make and was a valuable weapon. It is not surprising therefore that when bow pieces are found in Hun graves, they are not from a single bow; they are the mismatched pieces of different, broken bows. Serviceable bows were not buried with their dead owners.

This same difficulty in production may account for the fact that Western Europeans did not use the recurved composite bow, although it should be remembered that during the Middle Ages the Europeans did make the prods or bows of crossbows from composite materials. Paterson suggests the reason for the exclusive Eastern and steppe use of this weapon is that there were no cattle in Europe with sufficiently long horns to make the bows from. This ignores the fact that there are examples of composite bows made from strips or plates of horn joined along the bow arms—the Persian and Korean examples mentioned above, for instance.

A more plausible explanation for the lack of conventional bow development in the West was the widespread use of the crossbow. This weapon had certain distinct advantages over the hand bow: a heavy draw weight which is not so dependent for its use on the strength of the bowman, who usually spans it with a foot in the stirrup and two hands, or else with a belt claw or even a mechanical device such as a cranquin if the bow is extremely heavy. Certainly the crossbow is much slower to use than a conventional bow, and not so practical on horseback (although there have been mounted crossbowmen), but in any case the West had no tradition of mounted archery, and the ease of use of the crossbow could more than make up for its slower rate of fire. While shooting a conventional bow accurately takes years of practice, a man can be taught to shoot a crossbow fairly quickly. By analogy, a modern soldier is expected to be reasonably competent with a rifle in a matter of weeks and a crossbowman could probably be trained at least as quickly.

Even the slow rate of shooting may not have been a real problem. While a windlass-drawn crossbow with a steel prod might only be shot once a minute, this weapon appeared in the High Middle Ages and was then used into the Renaissance. During the period when Europe faced steppe nomads the bow was lighter and was drawn by hand with a foot in the stirrup or by reversing the bow and hooking the string over an iron hook hung from a belt around the waist. The crossbowman then put a foot in the stirrup at the end of the bow and straightened his leg, thus drawing the bowstring up to the catch. Either method is quick and should allow a crossbowman, if necessary, to shoot three or four times a minute.

Even so, as Ralph Payne-Gallway indicated in his definitive treatise on the weapon, it is unlikely that a crossbowman (or any archer for that matter) would have shot as quickly as he could have, for he would soon have found himself without ammunition.[12] Still, the effect of, say, five hundred crossbowmen each shooting once or twice a minute could be murderous: they could easily send out a steady hail of more than twelve bolts a second. While not impressive by the standards of modern weapons, it would be something not lightly faced. Indeed, the Mongols did not like this weapon; Giovanni di Plano Carpini, a thirteenth-century papal emissary to the Mongol khan, related: "Whoever wishes to fight the Tartars [Mongols] should have these weapons: a good bow or strong crossbow (which they fear), and enough arrows . . ."[13]

In fact, the crossbow's effect and ease of use led to its inclusion in the first known weapons ban. By order of the Lateran Council of 1173 neither bows nor crossbows were to be used against Christians. An interesting contemporary appraisal of its effects is found in *The Alexiad*, the account by the Princess Anna Comnena of her father Alexius Comnenus' life. His reign as Byzantine Emperor (1081–1118) coincided with the First Crusade, during which the Greeks, or Byzantines, first saw the weapon.

> The cross-bow is a weapon of the barbarians [i.e., Franks], absolutely unknown to the Greeks. In order to stretch it one does not pull the string with the right hand while pushing the bow with the left away from the body; this instrument of war, which fires weapons to an enormous distance, has to be stretched lying almost on one's back; each foot is pressed forcibly against the half-circles of the bow and the two hands tug at the bow, pulling it with all one's strength towards the body. . . . They [the bolts] are short, but extremely thick with a heavy iron tip. In firing, the string exerts tremendous violence and force, so that the missiles wherever they strike do not rebound; in fact they transfix a shield, cut through a heavy iron breastplate and resume their flight on the far side, so irresistible is the discharge. An arrow of this type has been known to make its way right through a bronze statue, and when fired at the wall of a very great town its point either protruded from the inner side or buried itself in the wall and disappeared altogether. Such is the cross-bow, a truly diabolical machine. The unfortunate man who is struck by it dies without feeling the blow; however strong the impact, he knows nothing of it.[14]

One should remember that Anna is here describing the effect of a simple hand-spanned crossbow, not one drawn by the mechanical contrivances. Thus, the crossbow was fairly quick, extremely powerful and easy enough to master quickly. In fact, crossbow bolts, because they are shorter and usually slightly conical in cross section, are more aerodynamic than arrows, thus losing less of their force to drag.[15] It was the perfect weapon for a sedentary people and likely the reason why conventional bows were not highly developed in the

West. For all its undoubted advantages from the standpoint of the soldier from a sedentary society, however, the crossbow was not suited to the highly mobile mounted warfare of the steppe. It was in this style of fighting that the quick-shooting recurved composite bow could be put to its most deadly use—as settled people found for more than three thousand years.

How accurate and effective was the recurved composite bow? Attila's successes and those of the Mongols at the battles of Liegnitz and Sajo suggest that they were indeed very effective. Let us look at something more specific, though. Stories abound of the incredible accuracy at long distance of steppe warriors, which are just that: incredible. René Grousset in his monumental *Empire of the Steppes* states that Mongol horsemen could strike their targets at distances as great as four hundred yards. This cannot be true because that distance is much greater than a bow will commonly shoot.

It is true that the Ottoman Turks developed specialized and fragile flight bows of heavy draw to shoot special arrows that were lighter and shorter than war or hunting arrows. Because these arrows were so short they were shot with the aid of a guide or trough resting on the left hand. This way an arrow could be shot that was actually shorter than the length of the draw of the bow. These special flight bows could, it seems, shoot the special flight arrows great distances, sometimes up to eight hundred yards, but their performance should not be confused, as it so often is, with the performance of a war bow shooting arrows long enough and with enough weight to serve as weapons. For arrows to be effective in war they must be relatively heavy.

When dealing with the bows actually used in battle we should consider the reports of such as the Frenchman Beauplan, who was attacked by Crimean Tatars while traveling across the Ukraine in the 1630s. He wrote that the Tatars could shoot accurately to sixty or a hundred paces, which is very good shooting.[16] We may presume that his pace equaled about a yard since they are generally regarded as equivalent. Beauplan made another comment later in his work that has additional military significance:

> I have encountered them many times in the country to the number of a good five hundred Tartars who wished to

attack us in our tabor [wagon laager] and even though I was accompanied by only fifty or sixty Cossacks they could do nothing to us nor could we best them because they would not approach within the range of our weapons; but after making numerous feints to attack us and trouble us with clouds of arrows on the head because they shot in arcade easily at twice the range of our weapons, they retired . . .[17]

Shooting in arcade is to shoot at a steep angle of about forty-five degrees to achieve the greatest possible distance. This results in the arrows dropping almost vertically on the target. Though inaccurate, it could be effective against a massed enemy and is, in any case, the natural effect of shooting to the extreme limit of a bow's range.

Further, a sixteenth-century Arabic treatise on archery states that the extreme range for a bow, while shooting accurately, is forty-five bow lengths, or somewhat over eighty yards. The treatise goes on to state:

The soundness of this theory of a range of forty-five bowlengths has been established and its superiority and excellence have been proven. Its advocates do not permit shooting beyond that distance. As a matter of fact, it is less than half the limit of possible effective range, although, according to the experts, no accuracy is sure beyond it.[18]

A modern recurved hunting bow of wood and fiberglass will cast an arrow something over two hundred yards, but the range at which it may be shot accurately is much shorter.[19] All of this should dispel the illusions spread by writers who have no practical experience with the bow.

The skill to hit moving targets was very important, especially other horsemen. The medieval Arabic treatise quoted above gives specific instruction for shooting horsemen:

If the horseman be galloping toward you, aim at his saddle bow. Should the arrow swerve high it will hit the horseman's chest; should it fall low it will alight in his belly. If, on the other hand, the horseman be running away from you, aim at the back of his saddle. Should the arrow swerve high it will hit the horseman's back; and should it fall low it will alight on the back of his mount.

If one of the two be standing still and the other rushing against him to run him down, the former should aim his arrow at the neck of the horse. It will alight either in the rider's chest or between the eyes of the horse. In the event of the horseman's running away, the archer who is standing stationary should aim at the horse's head. Should the arrow swerve high it will alight between the horseman's shoulders; should it fall short it will hit either the base of his back or the mount itself. All this requires practice and perseverance.[20]

This passage explicitly takes into account the movement of horse and rider, no doubt formalizing what a steppe warrior learned from his fellows.

In sum, a review of texts coupled with practical experience suggests that "a trained archer, on foot, should hit a man every time at about 60 yards."[21] Paterson estimates accurate shooting from horseback to be limited to a mere ten yards. None of this explicitly takes into effect the reduction in motor coordination that accompanies great fear or excitement, a factor nowadays recognized and discussed as it bears upon the use of firearms in self-defense. Nonetheless, this standard of accuracy would be effective even at a much greater range against a massed enemy. In view of these accounts and in light of experience with modern recurved composite bows it is clear that, in skilled hands, it was a deadly weapon indeed: faster and more effective than the crossbow, it was an ideal weapon for use from horseback where mobility enhanced its deadly qualities. All of this, however, depended upon the skill of the archer, though by all accounts steppe nomads were universally accomplished with the weapon.

The draw weight of war bows was in the range of sixty to seventy pounds and horse archers probably used somewhat lighter ones as they had to shoot from the saddle, which is more unsteady than shooting on foot. Again, writers with no practical experience claim draw weights in excess of one hundred or even of one hundred and forty pounds for such bows, ignoring the obvious fact that they would be virtually impossible to draw, let alone shoot with any accuracy at all, not only for men of modern stature but still less for men of pre-industrial times who, though no doubt wiry and tough, were generally much smaller.

While the bow varied somewhat across time and area, its recurved shape and composite construction were constant. The Scythian bows were rather short and tended to an extreme recurved shape, resembling cupid's bows; Mongol and Tatar bows were quite large, over five feet in length, even though this length is actually too great to make proper use of the composite construction—they are not the most efficient of the composite bows. Studies and finds suggest that the Hun bow was between 130 and 140 centimeters long and asymmetric: the upper limb was somewhat longer than the lower and the string was fixed permanently to the longer limb, being slipped into the knock of the shorter limb before shooting. A design incorporating limbs of uneven length, though unusual, is not unknown; Japanese bows, while much longer, also have the upper limb longer than the lower. This asymmetric design does, however, appear to be limited among the steppe peoples to the Huns. The most efficient composite bows are generally regarded as those developed by the Turks in the fifteenth and sixteenth centuries, which acquired a shape like that of a modern recurved hunting bow.

In the West we draw bows with three fingers in the "Mediterranean draw." In the East, by contrast, bows were drawn with the thumb, locked under the first three fingers. The thumb was protected by a ring of bone, horn, ivory or even stone. As a result, in the West the arrow is shot from the left side of the bow, while in the East it is shot from the right.

Arrows, as might be expected, also differed from time to time and place to place. The Scythians used small trilobate arrowheads and later adopted larger ones, still trilobate, probably to pierce the armor of the Sarmatians with whom they came increasingly into conflict before being displaced from the Black Sea area by the second century B.C. Hun arrowheads are leaf-shaped as were those of the Mongols. There are also persistent reports that steppe warriors used bone arrowheads across the centuries—something we might expect given the steppe economy, where metal was scarcer than among sedentary populations and the means of working it rarer still.

Ammianus Marcellinus, writing of the fourth-century Huns, says: "What makes them the most formidable of all warriors is that they shoot from a distance arrows tipped with sharp splinters of bone instead of the usual heads . . ."[22]

There is a similar account of the Magyars using bone arrowheads during their campaign in Hungary in 889.[23] Such arrowheads would be sufficient for hunting and, if needed, could be used against unarmored men and horses. The arrowheads of steppe tribes were generally attached by a tang sunk into the arrow shaft rather than by a socket fitted over the end of it as was done in the West, though early Scythian and Sarmatian arrowheads used sockets, and later changed to the tang. Some have suggested that this was to ensure that the shaft split after striking a target to prevent its being shot back. It seems extravagant that such poor people as steppe tribesmen would produce arrows good for a single shot. It seems more likely that this method of attaching arrowheads with tangs was adopted because it is simply easier to produce arrowheads with tangs and this may have been suggested by bone or horn arrowheads, which had to be affixed this way.

The combination of the horse and bow gave the steppe warrior a devastating combination of speed and maneuverability coupled with the most effective missile weapon of the day. On the steppe horse he could travel long distances quickly, maneuver on the battlefield, resist charges and reform, and kill from a distance. He was not a practitioner of hand-to-hand or shock warfare. Because the steppe warrior had great mobility on the battlefield and such an ability to cover distances in a short time, the military style of these peoples was one of wide-ranging, quick conquests and an unwillingness to come to grips with an enemy until victory was certain. This was in contrast to Western armies, which preferred to fight at close quarters and rely on the shock of their attack to decide the issue.

This Western tradition is explored in detail in Hansen's *The Western Way of War*,[24] where he shows that this military approach was first institutionalized by the Greeks in their hoplite phalanx warfare. The Romans followed suit and the western barbarians, chiefly Germans, seem to have acquired the habit from them, probably through prolonged conflict with the Romans and extensive service in their armies. The Western knight's actual technique harkened back to Sarmatian methods learned on the steppes of southern Russia—the mailed rider charging with a heavy lance—but this steppe technique fit in well with the Western preference for shock combat. Still, when this style of warfare met that of the nomad horse archers the effect could be terrible.

NOTES
1. The following comments apply to ponies rather than dwarf horses such as the Iceland pony.
2. J. Cossar Ewart, "The Multiple Origin of Horses and Ponies," in *The Smithsonian Institution Annual Report, 1903–1904.*
3. Giovanni di Plano Carpini, *The Story of the Mongols Whom We Call the Tartars,* trans. Erik Hildinger, Boston, Branden Books, 1996.
4. Napoleon Bonaparte, *The Military Maxims of Napoleon,* trans. G.C. d'Aguilar, New York, Da Capo Press, 1995, Maxim 9.
5. Otto Maenchen-Helfen, *World of the Huns,* Berkeley, University of California Press, 1973, pp. 211–12. Maenchen-Helfen states that this mosaic is now in the British Museum.
6. Ibid.
7. Guillaume Le Vasseur de Beauplan, *La Description d'Ukranie,* Ottawa, Les Presses de l'Université d'Ottawa, p. 63, translated by author.
8. *The Discovery of Muscovy,* from the collections of Richard Hakluyt, London, Cassell and Co., 1904, p. 39.
9. Beauplan, p. 65, translated by author.
10. F. Paterson, "The Archers of Islam," in *The Journal of the Economic and Social History of the Orient,* Vol. IX, Parts I–II (November 1966), pp. 69–87.
11. Edward McEwen, Robert L. Miller, and Christopher A. Bergman, "Early Bow Design and Construction," in *The Scientific American,* June 1991, pp. 76–82.
12. Ralph Payne-Gallwey, *The Book of the Crossbow,* Dover, New York, Dover, 1995; reprint of 1903 edition.
13. Giovanni di Plano Carpini, p. 89.
14. Anna Comnena, *The Alexiad,* trans. E.R.A. Sewter, Hammondsworth, UK, Penguin Books, 1982, pp. 316–17.
15. Vernard Foley, G. Palmer, and W. Soedel, "The Crossbow," in *The Scientific American,* January 1985, pp. 108–109.
16. Beauplan, translated by author.
17. Beauplan, translated by author.
18. *Arabic Archery: An Arabic Manuscript of About A.D. 1500—A Book on the Excellence of the Bow and Arrow and the Description Thereof,* trans. and ed. by N.A. Faris and R.P. Elmer, Princeton, Princeton University Press, 1945.
19. A very practical expression of this is a statement by Fred Bear, the famed

bowhunter and bow manufacturer, in a standard work in the field: "For the average bowhunter 35 yards is about the limit for accurate shooting, and few bowmen can claim many big-game kills beyond 50 yards." Fred Bear, *The Archer's Bible*, rev. ed., Garden City, NY, Doubleday, 1980, p. 98.

20. *Arabic Archery*, pp. 147–48.

21. Paterson, p. 84.

22. *Ammianus Marcellinus*, Book 31, trans. Walter Hamilton, Hammondsworth, UK, Penguin, 1986, p. 412.

23. Statement of Abbot Regino quoted in Denis Sinor, "The Inner Asian Warriors," in *The Journal of the American Oriental Society*, October 1981, p. 139.

24. Victor D. Hansen, *The Western Way of War: Infantry Battle in Classical Greece*, New York, Alfred A. Knopf, 1989.

3

Scythians and Sarmatians

The Scythians and the related Sarmatians are the first steppe nomads of whom we have any real knowledge, although the Romans had long contact with the Parthians, another related people who came off the steppe to found an empire in what had been Persian territory. The Greek historian Herodotus mentions an earlier steppe tribe, the Cimmerians, whom the Scythians displaced, but today they are little more than a name (a familiar one, in fact, to those who follow the fictional exploits of Conan the Barbarian). Herodotus had apparently met Scythians on travels to the Black Sea and up the rivers that debouched into it, so he could write with some authority about them. The Sarmatians, who became important about two centuries later, were the object of contemporary comments and fought against and sometimes in the Roman army in the second and third centuries A.D. Herodotus clearly found the Scythians both important and interesting; he devoted an entire book of his *Histories* to them, and describes in some detail the unsuccessful punitive campaign that the Persian ruler Darius I undertook against them in the fifth century B.C.

The Scythians and their cousins the Sarmatians differ from the other steppe tribes that affected the West in one significant way: they were Indo-Aryan in extraction and spoke an Iranian language closely related to Persian and Median. The Scythians were, in fact, rather closely related to the Persians, who referred to them as Saka, probably the name of a leading tribe. By contrast, most steppe peoples are of the Turkic language group, or related groups such as the Tungusic or Altaic groups like the Mongols. Their customs, however, were not different from those of their eastern Asiatic neighbors and some assert that they are the source of much Asiatic steppe culture. Herodotus records that they worshipped three major deities, whom he associated with the Greek Gods Hestia, Zeus and the Earth. But there were also secondary ones, a number of whom he tried to reconcile with other, familiar Greek gods. The Scythians also worshipped a war-god (Herodotus calls him by the Greek name "Ares") in the form of an old sword thrust into an immense pile of sticks to which animals were sacrificed in great numbers, and occasionally prisoners of war.

Upon the death of a great man the Scythians would kill horses and gut them and place them on frames so that they appeared to be standing. Grooms could suffer the same treatment and have their bodies supported by vertical poles thrust through them to support them on the framed horse carcasses so that they appeared to be riding, thereby ensuring that the dead man had a troop of horsemen in the next world. The Scythians made goblets from the skulls of their dead enemies if they were particularly bad. They were known for adorning the bridles of their horses with the scalps of their enemies,[1] and this sanguinary practice must have made them the object of some horror among the Greeks.

These gruesome customs are not mentioned merely to illustrate the character of the Scythians in isolation, but to place them in the context of the culture of the steppe. For example, the Mongols practiced horse burials nearly two thousand years later. The papal emissary Giovanni di Plano Carpini mentions the custom in the report of his embassy to the Great Khan in Central Asia in 1247–1248. In describing the burial customs of a prominent man, he states:

> Furthermore, there is buried with him a mare with a foal and a horse with a saddle and bridle, and they eat another horse and fill the skin with straw and mount it on two or four poles up high, so that in the next world he may have a tent where he may stay, and a mare from which he may have milk and by which he may increase the number of his horses and the horses he may ride.[2]

The custom of killing, gutting and then stuffing a horse and mounting it on poles persisted among people in the Altai region of the Central Asian steppe into modern times. The ninth-century Bulgars also made goblets from the skulls of their conquered enemies, including that of the unfortunate Byzantine Emperor Nicephorus I when he fell in battle against them. What we have then is a people clearly in the mainstream of steppe culture which, because it is born of pastoralism and a difficult life, transcends even the barriers of language and race. The proof of this is in the persistence of remarkably similar cultural traits over time and area. It will not come as a surprise that we see a great similarity among steppe peoples when we examine their approach to war.

The Scythians not only appear in Greek literature but also on Greek pottery and goods made by Greek artisans for sale on the Black Sea steppe. They are shown in these illustrations wearing the Scythian cap, a felt hat that came to something of a point which usually fell forward. It covered the back of the neck and the ears, the sides often extending down on either side to the shoulders to provide protection against cold and wind. This cap is commonly shown not only on Scythians, but on vase paintings of Amazons in mythical scenes because it was considered exotic. The Scythians wore flowing tunics, loose trousers and sometimes capes.

The Scythians were known as great archers, and vase paintings and contemporary bronze sculptures show them shooting their bows, often directly backwards over the horse's tail in the famous "Parthian shot."[3] They are seldom if ever depicted using any other weapons although in practice of course they did not rely on the bow alone.

As secondary weapons they often carried a peculiar sort of battle-axe called a *sagaris*. Whereas the blade of an ordinary axe or hatchet is in line with its handle, the sagaris's blade was at a right angle to it, "like a modern ice-axe," according to the classicist A.M. Snodgrass.[4] They were known as well for a short, often curved sword, the *akinakes*. Still, the Greeks thought of them purely as archers and for a brief period the Athenians hired them as mercenary soldiers for this skill. Vase paintings show them on foot shooting from the cover of a hoplite's shield instead of from horseback. Perhaps the terrain in Greece was thought too inhospitable for Scythian warfare, though it may be that the Athenians simply did not want to modify their tactical system to accommodate a handful of specialists.[5]

The Scythian bow was one of the smaller used on the steppe and took a graceful and extreme shape, the arms curving sharply forward from the handle and then back in the shape of a cupid's bow. The tips apparently did not have the stiffeners, or "ears," at the ends common to later bows such as the Hun and Mongol varieties described earlier, and the bow was probably flexible close to its tips. The Scythians carried their bows in bow cases hung from the left side of their belts. These cases were in the shape of half a strung bow, and the bow was put into it strung, half of it extending out. Arrows were kept in a quiver hung from the right side of the belt.

This pattern was repeated among all of the steppe peoples up to the turn of the last century, as shown by an old French photograph of a Mongol warrior with the same equipment. Grave finds show that the Scythians used jackets of scale armor, although Greek pottery illustrating them does not show this. Because armor is always an expensive proposition, particularly in ancient societies, this may reflect no more than that armor was used only by the nobles. The Scythians carried round and oblong shields of wickerwork covered with leather, shapes that can be handled easily from horseback, and they also fought with lances. It is fair, however, to regard the Scythians primarily as horse archers and not as close-combat fighters.

This is made abundantly clear by Herodotus, who narrated the course of the Persian king Darius' less than successful war against the Scythians. In describing the people himself, he says:

> The Scythians, however, though in most respects I do not admire them, have managed one thing, and that the most important in human affairs, better than anyone else on the face of the earth: I mean their own preservation. For such is their manner of life that no one who invades their country can escape destruction, and if they wish to avoid engaging with an enemy, that enemy cannot by any possibility come to grips with them. A people without fortified towns, living as the Scythians do, in wagons which they take with them wherever they go, accustomed, one and all, to fight on horseback with bows and arrows, and dependent for their food not upon agriculture but upon their cattle: how can

such a people fail to defeat the attempt of an invader not only to subdue them, but even to make contact with them?[6]

Herodotus had posed a fair question; he recognized the basic character of steppe warfare, a character that would vex Western armies whenever they met it. Recall that Herodotus, as a Greek, was the product of a culture that had chosen the hand-to-hand pitched battle as its means of settling conflicts between states and had developed a peculiarly Greek institution to put this choice into effect: hoplite phalanx warfare. Victor Hansen has shown in his *The Western Way of War* why the Greeks made this choice and what the ramifications were. One of them was an intolerance of light-armed or irregular troops, particularly missile troops who harassed and tried to kill but would not close, in contrast to the heavily armored Greek with helmet, shield, cuirass and spear who willingly fought to the death, face-to-face against similarly armed men. In asking how such a people could "fail to defeat the attempt of an invader not only to subdue them, but even to make contact with them," Herodotus is the first observer to record in words the distinction between the Western and steppe ways of warfare. However, it was not any Western power that directly challenged the Scythians, it was Persia.

Sometime between 514 and 512 B.C. the Persian king Darius, later to attempt the invasion of Greece, decided upon a punitive expedition against the Scythians for raids and conquests they had earlier made against the Medes, who formed part of the Persian Empire. Herodotus was himself from Halicarnassus, a Greek city of Asia Minor under Persian sway, and he wrote of the expedition in minute detail.

Despite his brother Artabanus' warning against the expedition because "the Scythians were such difficult people to get at,"[7] Darius had a pontoon bridge built across the Bosphorus, a remarkable engineering feat for the time, and one suggestive of the resources Darius had to commit to his war.[8] Darius marched from his capital at Susa to Chalcedon on the Bosphorus, and then across the strait into Europe, probably in the neighborhood of Byzantium. A contingent of Ionian Greeks sailed into the Black Sea to the mouth of the Danube and bridged it for the passage of the Persian army. Darius and his forces marched through Thrace and crossed upon the bridge;

they were now in Scythia.

True to form, the Scythians did not choose to meet the Persians in a pitched battle. Instead they broke themselves into two forces. The first, and smaller, contained Scythians and Sauromatae, or Sarmatians, while the second was made up of Scythians and certain of their other allies: Geloni and Budini. Their tactics were simple: to retreat before the huge Persian army while it advanced, and to attack if it retreated. At first, of course, Darius advanced, and the Scythians retreated ahead of him, constantly drawing him further west.

At one point, near the Oarus River, Darius began the construction of eight forts which were left half done when the Scythians he had been chasing disappeared to the north. Unable to find them, Darius headed further west, thinking they must have gone that way. In so doing he came upon the other division of the Scythian army, which then proceeded to lead him on a chase. Darius eventually grew tired of this and sent a messenger to Idanthyrsus, the Scythian king, inviting him to battle and chiding him for constantly fleeing. Idanthyrsus sent a reply stating that he had never run in fear from anyone, but that he was only continuing to live the sort of life he always had. He went on, "If you want to know why I will not fight, I will tell you: in our country there are no towns and no cultivated land; fear of losing which, or seeing it ravaged, might indeed provoke us to hasty battle."[9] No set battle was joined; the Scythians contented themselves with skirmishing against Persian foraging parties and driving them back to the protection of their infantry with which the Scythians would not close.

The Scythians used a second technique to keep the Persians in their country where, over time, they would be made destitute. They would abandon their positions and leave behind a few cattle for the Persians to snatch. The Persians would count this a minor success, though in the long run it was dangerous for them to remain on the steppe. This method was quite consistent with the steppe warrior's desire to wear the enemy down without closing—to fight, if possible, with stratagem.

His untenable position finally became clear to Darius and he pulled back to his bridge over the Danube, still held for him by the Ionian Greeks. The Persian army passed out of Scythia without having accomplished a thing. The king did, however, manage to escape without suffering the destruction of his army through attrition on the steppe—which was clearly the intention of the Scythians. Steppe warfare at its purest is one of travel across great distance, missile warfare and, if it is advantageous, strategic retreat before the enemy until attrition, exhaustion or isolation have made his defeat inevitable. The Persian king was fortunate not to have extended his campaign further or he might have suffered the kind of disaster the Romans did a few hundred years later when they fought the Parthians at Carrhae.

While the Persian king had tried to fight against the Scythians, their cousins the Parthians were already his subjects. These Iranian-speaking nomads had come off the steppe to settle on the Iranian plateau in the eastern regions of what would become the Persian Empire. They were known for their horsemanship and their facility with the bow, the two trademarks of the steppe warrior, and they took their name from the province of Parthava where they had set-tled some time before 250 B.C. The Persian king Cyrus the Great probably conquered this area when he took over Media in the sixth century B.C. and so it was as subjects and allies of the Persians that the Parthians fought Alexander the Great at Arbela during his con-quest of Persia.

Upon the death of Alexander the Great in 323 B.C. his empire was dismembered and shared among his generals, who made of it a series of Hellenistic kingdoms. The general Seleucus' lot encom-passed the eastern satrapies of Persia including Parthia, which revolt-ed under the brothers Arsaces and Tiridates at some time before 247 B.C. Arsaces was crowned the first king of the Parthians and spent his reign consolidating his gains as he struggled to take what territories he could from Seleucus II. The early history of Parthia consists chiefly of its struggle against the Hellenistic Seleucid kingdom until, by the second century B.C., the Parthian kingdom included not only Parthia itself, but also Media, Mesopotamia, Persis, Babylonia, Hyrcania, Assyria, Elymais, Taporia and Taxiana. In short, it con-tained essentially the territories of the former Persian Empire and it represented the only state whose military power could approach that of Rome.

Rome was of course the preeminent military power of antiqui-ty, a state that fielded an organized, disciplined army fighting with carefully considered tactics. The Roman army had bested Gallic and German barbarians in the north, while in North Africa and the east it had defeated Carthaginian and Greek armies organized on the pattern established by Alexander the Great.

The Roman army was essentially one of heavy infantry. The soldiers were organized into legions—administrative units like regiments—which were each tactically subdivided into ten cohorts. In theory a legion contained 6,000 men, although in practice it would number about 4,500, every cohort then containing about 450 men. Each soldier belonged to one of sixty centuries, nominally of one hundred men though in fact numbering between sixty and eighty. The men were commanded by professional soldiers called centurions, who, like sergeants, had the power of corporal punishment over them and who had won their position through experience and steadiness.

Most civilized armies of this period fought on the Greco-Macedonian model in a deep phalanx of soldiers wielding pikes of fifteen to twenty feet in length. The first several ranks marched with spears leveled to produce an apparently impenetrable hedge of spear points to drive back the enemy or hold it steady while cavalry tried to attack the enemy's flanks. Barbaric warriors from northern Europe like the Gauls or Germans tended to rush on foot with spears or long swords in an effort to drive back and disorder opponents by their shock. A few might ride horses into the fray.

The Romans, who had originally fought in phalanx like the Greeks, developed a markedly different system. They retained the heavily equipped footsoldier as the basis of the army, but used him differently. Each legionary wore a jacket of chainmail[10] and an iron helmet. He carried a strong, convex rectangular shield, called a *scutum*, about four feet long and two and a half wide, that covered much of his body, including the legs. It was made of plywood covered with leather or canvas with an iron binding on the top and bottom edges and a boss in the middle. The shield was brightly painted and had the number of the legion and the soldier's name and century number painted on it.

While the Greek heavy infantryman relied upon his spear, the Roman soldier was a swordsman and in this way distinct from his enemies. The Roman sword was short—merely two feet long with straight edges tapering gradually to a sharp point. The grip was of hardwood or bone with a small cross-guard and a simple round pommel. The weapon was not fancy—only practical—and the soldier was taught to use it by experienced instructors, *lanistae*, the men who drilled the gladiators for the arena. He was taught to prefer the thrust to the cut as it exposed his body less to his enemy and produced a much more dangerous wound.

The soldier carried a dagger as well, should he need it, but his next most important weapon was the *pilum*, or heavy javelin. This weapon was made of a solid wooden stock about three feet long, to which was joined a soft iron shaft of the same length. The shaft ended in a barbed head meant to lodge in an opponent's shield if it struck. The legionary carried two of these pila and was taught to cast them one after the other as he ran at the enemy line. When fixed into the enemy's shield it weighted it down and made the shield impractical to use.

Furthermore, the barbed head made the javelins extremely difficult to remove and the shafts bent upon impact so they could not be hurled back. After throwing these weapons the legionaries would find numbers of men who had had to cast off their shields and fight unprotected or who kept shields that were now too clumsy to be effective. The Roman might try to step on the shaft of the javelin that hung down and force his opponent's arm downward. Whatever the precise outcome, he would close with his short sword and stab his opponent, causing lethal wounds. A barbarian was at a signal disadvantage with his long sword in a close fight. This was even more the case with those who fought in the Greco-Macedonian style; once the Romans got beyond the pike points either by turning them aside with their shields or darting below them, or by taking advantage of the gaps which tend to open in a phalanx on the march, the short sword could cause terrible harm while the phalangites could do nothing with their long spears.

As a result of these developments, the Romans tended to fight in looser formations and the Roman battle line advanced not in a solid block or phalanx, since gaps would naturally appear in the formation as the men advanced across the field and gaps in a phalanx are often fatal. Instead, the Romans deployed in a checkerboard formation: the front line was made up of cohorts separated from each other by a gap the width of a cohort. Behind this gap marched another cohort. Gaps in this second line were covered by cohorts behind it. This was called the *acies triplex*, or "triple battle line." Once the Romans were prepared to meet the enemy, the gaps in the front line were closed by the cohorts behind them and the remaining cohorts formed a reserve. The Romans marched with gaps and then repaired them. It was a brilliant system and shows how well the soldiers were drilled in maneuvering.

The flanks were protected by light infantry, often barbarians armed with sword and spear who carried flat oval shields and wore iron helmets and leather jerkins. There might also be archers or javelineers. The purpose of these auxiliaries was to keep the enemy off the flank until the legionaries had won the fight. Cavalry were not numerous and consisted either of small squads of Romans or troops of barbarians (often Gallic or German) also posted on the flanks.

It is not surprising that this army had won victories everywhere it went: Spain, North Africa, Asia Minor, Gaul. And it was with this army that Marcus Crassus marched against the Parthians in 54 B.C. Crassus was reputedly the richest man in Rome, having made money in real estate and speculating in goods seized during political unrest. He was a popular man and politically powerful too; he, Julius Caesar and Pompey formed the first Triumvirate and ruled Rome during the decline of the Republic. Well off as he was, though, he was apparently envious of Julius Caesar's military fame, and particularly that of Pompey, who was known as the Great. Pompey had had the signal honor of having a triumph[11] bestowed upon him by the Roman senate while he was too young even to be a senator.

Crassus had had military experience, being one of Lucius Sulla's lieutenants, and he had later defeated Spartacus and his slave army after it had beaten numerous Roman forces and ravaged the Italian countryside. Still, he had not been awarded a triumph, but merely an ovation, because he had won this victory against slaves and peasants. Accordingly, when he was awarded the governorship of Syria at the age of sixty, he likely regarded it as his last opportunity to win military fame. Instead, he suffered one of the greatest defeats in Roman history. Carrhae would rank with Cannae, Trasimene and Adrianopolis. Fortunately for Rome she was resilient enough to tolerate the misfortune, something not true of Adrianopolis four hundred years later.

Crassus sailed to Syria, whence he meant to set off on his expedition. The Roman ally King Artavasdes of Armenia informed Crassus that he would furnish him with several thousand horsemen if he wished, and he advised the Roman to enter Parthian territory from Armenia, which would allow an approach through hilly country unsuited to the cavalry that constituted the entire Parthian army. Crassus declined the offer and marched away with a force of seven legions supported by about four thousand light troops and four thousand cavalry. As he saw it, the difficulty with the Parthians was to come to grips with them and nothing more; he did not realize that the difficulty of grappling with them was the greatest danger.

Crassus stopped at Zeugma on the Euphrates and then marched along the river. An Arab in Parthian employ who was trusted by the Romans because he had had earlier dealings with Pompey persuaded them to march out into the plains after the Parthians. This Arab led them into the wilderness and through difficult ground and then into a sandy plain, until they reached a stream called Balissus. Crassus' officers wished to establish a camp at the stream, but he insisted they press on. Finally, however, some cavalry scouts pulled up to say that they had skirmished with the enemy and their fellows had been killed. Crassus was shaken, apparently surprised that the enemy was near, and he had difficulty deciding how to range his forces. At first he put them in a long line with cavalry on the wings, hoping that this extended formation would discourage encirclement. He then reconsidered and ordered his men to form up in a hollow square, each face made up of twelve cohorts and each cohort with its own squad of cavalry. The army then advanced in this formation.

Eventually they came upon the Parthians under the command of their general, Surena. There were fewer of them than the Romans had expected, though this was because Surena had hidden many of his troops away. Upon being seen, the Parthians disclosed their armor, which they had covered with cloaks and furs, and they began to beat kettledrums—the military instrument of the steppe which the Parthians had retained. They had retained steppe clothing too: the common Parthians wore loose tunics and baggy pants, high boots and Phrygian caps like their Scythian cousins. Like the Scythians too, they fought from horseback with the composite recurved bow. The nobles wore armor and fought with heavy lances. They were no doubt impressive, although it was to the archers that their victory was largely due. In fact, the lancers thought better of charging the Romans because of the strength of their formation and instead pulled back. Crassus sent light troops out to skirmish, but they were driven back by arrows to the protection of the legionaries.

The Parthians then encircled the Romans. The Greek historian Plutarch, who wrote a splendidly detailed account of the battle, said this about the Parthian shooting:

> But the Parthians now stood at long intervals from one another and began to shoot their arrows from all sides at once, not with any accurate aim (for the dense formation of the Romans would not suffer an archer to miss his man even if he wished it), but making vigorous and powerful shots from bows which were large and mighty and curved so as to discharge their missiles with great force. At once, then, the plight of the Romans was a grievous one; for if they kept their ranks, they were wounded in great numbers, and if they tried to come to close quarters with the enemy, they were just as far from effecting anything and suffered just as much. For the Parthians shot as they fled, and next to the Scythians, they do this most effectively; and it is a very clever thing to seek safety while still fighting, and to take away the shame of flight.[12]

Because they could do nothing about the shooting, the Romans decided to endure it. The men were disciplined and armored and though they suffered losses from the shooting, eventually the Parthians would discharge all of their arrows and, if the Romans could not catch them, at least the enemy could do them no more harm. However, it was learned that Surena had a camel train bringing in more arrows. The archery would continue indefinitely.

Crassus then sent his son Publius at the head of 1,300 cavalry, 500 archers and eight cohorts of legionaries to attack the Parthians. As the Roman cavalry raced forward (leaving the infantry behind), the Parthians retreated. Encouraged, the Romans chased them quite a distance. It was, however, a trick—a feigned retreat. When the

Romans had been drawn sufficiently far from their main body the Parthians turned about and encircled the disordered soldiers. As they rode about them they made clouds of dust which must have caused the Romans to feel isolated. The lancers sat at a distance forcing the Romans to keep together while the light horsemen sent arrows into them.

In desperation Publius himself led a charge and his horsemen, for the most part Gauls, contended with the Parthian lancers bravely. They grasped their enemies' heavy lances and dragged them to the ground where their heavy armor made them clumsy, and they crawled beneath the Parthian horses and stabbed them. Nonetheless, they took a harsh beating and soon most of them were unhorsed. Publius himself was wounded by an arrow and carried by his men to a hillock where the Romans made a defensive stand. The hill might have given them some protection against the lancers, but they were still showered with arrows. Publius thought his situation was hopeless; he and some of his officers committed suicide.

The Parthians now closed in and most of the Romans were killed. Publius' head was cut off and the Parthians returned across the plain to Crassus. Before his death, however, Publius had dispatched messengers to his father to inform him that he needed help. One of these men succeeded in making it to Crassus and informed him of his son's need for rescue. Crassus advanced, but the Parthians now returned from their battle with his son and paraded before his troops with Publius' head on a spear. The sight demoralized the Romans and deeply disturbed Crassus.

The Parthians resumed the tactic they had used on Publius' forces: the lancers stood at a distance, advancing as necessary to keep the Romans together while the horse archers circled and shot incessantly into the crowded soldiers. The fight lasted until nightfall, when the Parthians pulled back. Two of the Roman officers, Octavius and Cassius, determined to withdraw to the walled town of Carrhae after darkness fell. Crassus himself had apparently become too distraught to decide much of anything. The army marched, disordered and fearful, and reached Carrhae during the night. The Parthians, though they knew of the Roman retreat, did not harry them. This may have been because they did not wish to shoot in the dark, where targets were less certain, and defeated as the Romans already were, the Parthians probably had no desire to close with them and fight hand-to-hand; no one was better at this than the Romans. Instead the Parthians rode to Carrhae the next day, contemplating a siege. The Romans, however, were not eager to submit to one and preferred to retreat to the hills of Armenia nearby. But just as they had been guided by a Parthian agent into the plains of Mesopotamia, so now they took as their guide a Greek named Andromachus, who was also allied with the enemy. He took the Romans out, but led them hither and yon through difficult terrain until Cassius and Octavius, at least, grew disgusted. Cassius headed back to Carrhae with a number of troops and Octavius led five thousand men with other guides into the hills. Crassus, however, continued to lead four cohorts and a handful of cavalry until he was again attacked by the Parthian cavalry.

Crassus was not far from the hills where Octavius had taken his men—only about three miles—and Octavius brought his force down from his protected position to support his commander. Together they made a stand on a hill and were just preparing for another Parthian onslaught when Surena approached on horseback, unstrung his bow and announced that the Parthian king wished to treat with the Romans and make peace. Crassus was disinclined to leave his troops and go with the Parthians for these talks, but was ultimately coerced by his men. He and Octavius walked out to meet the Parthians and then were killed, possibly as the result of high tensions and misunderstanding, or possibly as part of a Parthian stratagem to eliminate the Roman leader. The disaster was complete: the remaining Romans were taken prisoner and settled in the far eastern reaches of the Parthian Empire. Only about a fourth of the Roman army made it back to Roman territory; it was a military disaster unparalleled since the days of Hannibal almost two hundred years before.

What is particularly striking is the horrific effect of mounted archery even upon a disciplined, well-equipped and professional infantry. At almost no time were the Romans permitted to do what they did best: come to grips with the enemy and fight hand-to-hand. Carrhae is an almost perfect example of steppe tactics: shooting from a distance, shooting while retreating, the feigned retreat to draw and disorder an enemy, and encirclement to maximize the effect of archery by allowing as many horse archers as possible to have a target. Against these tactics on an open plain, the excellent close-fighting Roman infantry was completely unsuited to reply.

Meanwhile other Scythian cousins had remained on the steppe. When the Persian king Darius had invaded Scythia, a people known as the Sauromatae had helped defend against the Persians; today these people are usually referred to as Sarmatians. These were another Iranian-speaking people who seem to have originated near the base of the Ural mountains.[13] Like the Scythians they were nomadic horse archers, though certain of their tribes developed a method of fighting quite distinct from that of the Scythians and gradually drove them out of the Black Sea area, apart from a small enclave.

The Sarmatian language is considered a related dialect of Scythian; nonetheless, they were a heterogeneous people broken into a number of tribes. For quite some time they resembled the Scythians in their way of life, customs and culture: they were mounted archers and worshipped a sword as the emblem of the god of war. They may have been a more warlike people than the Scythians, however, as is reflected from the burials of a number of Sarmatian women with armor and weapons.[14] It is difficult to imagine Sarmatians using women in actual combat, but Herodotus' tale that the Sarmatians were descended of Scythian men and roving Amazons[15] on the steppe, in addition to his report from the fifth century B.C. that Greeks had met (and defeated) an army of females in the Black Sea region, may reflect some actual tradition of women warriors among the Sarmatians.

Of interest from our perspective, however, is the approach to warfare adopted by certain of the Sarmatian tribes, especially the Roxolani, Alani and Iazyges: the fully armored horseman on an armored horse who fought with a heavy lance and a broadsword. This approach is utterly different from that of the Scythians, or indeed any of the later steppe warriors. In a sense, it is a dead end on the steppe, although Sarmatian influence, as we shall see, lingered for centuries in Europe. Their approach to warfare was one of shock combat, in stark contrast to that of the Scythians. Their equipment and methods resembled those of the Parthian lancers, who were probably patterned after them.

For armor the Sarmatians wore a long-sleeved mail coat and trousers, so that not only their torso but also their arms and legs were protected. Illustrations show this armor usually to have been made of scales. This kind of armor is probably the earliest used on the steppe (aside from padded or fabric armor), and was made by cutting out scales of bronze or iron and riveting them onto a fabric or leather backing so that each row overlapped the one below it. This armor was therefore flexible, which was of particular importance in riding a horse. Sometimes the armor was made with overlapping scales of horn instead, or even sections of horses' hooves. The third-century A.D. Greek traveler Pausanias wrote about such armor, saying that the Sarmatians:

> . . . collect the hoofs of their mares, clean them, and split them till they resemble the scales of a dragon. Anybody who has not seen a dragon has at least seen a green fir cone. Well, the fabric which they make out of the hoofs may not be inaptly likened to the clefts on a fir cone. In these pieces they bore holes, and having stitched them together with the sinews of horses and oxen, they use them as corselets, which are inferior to Greek breast-plates neither in elegance nor strength, for they are both sword-proof and arrow-proof.[16]

The Sarmatians were impressive figures, and representations of them (probably of the Roxolani tribe) can be seen on the Roman Emperor Trajan's Column dating from the early second century, a memorial to his campaigns in Dacia, where he encountered these barbarians. The Sarmatians wore conical metal helmets not unlike medieval European helmets of the eleventh and twelfth centuries, often with the noseguard common to such helmets. What is more, the Sarmatians often armored their horses too, with scale armor like their own.

By the second century A.D. many Sarmatians took up wearing chainmail, probably something they learned from the Romans, among whom it was a favorite armor—although, as we have seen, Pausanius in the third century refers to them as still wearing scale armor. The Romans in their turn had probably adopted chainmail from the Celts, though it became associated with them at an early stage. In 165 B.C. the Hellenistic tyrant Antiochus IV reviewed his army of five thousand men ". . . armed in the Roman fashion with corselets of chain armor."[17] As Sarmatians fought in and against the Roman armies, it is not surprising that they should have taken up chainmail. While it is more difficult to produce than scale armor, it is more flexible. Furthermore, the difficulty of producing chainmail may be exaggerated,[18] as its persistence into the seventeenth century in areas such as Poland, Turkey and the Middle East suggests.

The Sarmatians fought with a heavy lance called a *kontos* by the Greeks and *contus* by the Romans. There has been a good deal of discussion about the effectiveness of this method of warfare before the introduction of stirrups, but the empirical evidence is that it was effective: the Sarmatians dedicated themselves to it for centuries and it was taken up by the late Roman army. The Romans did not adopt military practices from others that they thought ineffective. The Persians also fielded this kind of soldier, probably modeled on the Sarmatian. In Latin the term for such a heavy horseman was *cataphractus*, or *clibanarius*, the latter term referring to an oven and probably a reference to the heat and discomfort of wearing full armor. Also, although they are not generally depicted with them, the Sarmatians apparently carried small shields.

The effect of a troop of mailed cavalrymen on armored horses charging would have demoralized any but disciplined infantry such as the Romans fielded. A horse will not charge into a body of men who stand firm; it will draw up suddenly a few feet away, and this can be used to advantage by foot soldiers with the training and confidence to stand fast. However, the Romans could easily see the advantage of such cavalry against undisciplined footsoldiers, such as the Germans and Dacians they faced over the Danube. It is not surprising that in time they incorporated such troops into their army.

Meanwhile the Sarmatians were a significant power in the Barbaricum, the world beyond the Roman Empire. By the second century B.C. they had achieved control of the steppe around the Black Sea, and began to influence the Bosphoran Kingdom, a protectorate of the Roman Empire made up of Greek cities founded centuries before. The Bosphoran Kingdom became progressively more Sarmatized, its nobility fighting as heavy cavalry in the Sarmatian manner and even bearing Sarmatian names; the Greek ruling house died out during the second century A.D., to be replaced by a Sarmatian one. Bosphoran clothing was no longer Greek: long-sleeved tunics, trousers and soft shoes came into fashion. As well, the trade goods produced by craftsmen in the cities of the Bosphoran Kingdom became decorated in ways more to the Sarmatian taste. When the German Goths and Gepids (a related people) later appeared on the steppe during their migrations from the north they adopted these styles and carried them to Western Europe, where they became the basis of much early medieval European art. In the meantime, however, Sarmatians and not Germans were the power around the Black Sea and north of the Balkans.

Rome first faced Sarmatians during the first century B.C. Iazygian tribes had allied with King Mithridates VI of Pontus, and Rome fielded a punitive expedition north of the Danube against them in 78–76 B.C. These Sarmatian people tried to raid across the Danube, which now formed a border of the Roman Empire, in 6 A.D. and 16 A.D. The Romans successfully stopped them and the Iazyges headed west into the Hungarian plain, where they settled.

When the Roman Emperor Trajan crossed the Danube to conquer and annex Dacia at the beginning of the second century he found Sarmatian cavalry opposing him, allied with the Dacian king Decebalus. These men appear on his monumental column in Rome covered in scale armor from head to foot, both man and horse. His predecessor, the Emperor Domitian, had fought Sarmatians across the Danube before him. They were to be one of many threatening barbarians against whom the Romans had to contend while the pressures increased upon the Danube frontier.

Marcus Aurelius, known for his tireless campaigns against the Marcomani and other German tribes along the Danube, fought and defeated a force of Sarmatians in 169 A.D. and then again in 172 or 173. During one of these battles a force of Roman soldiers pursued a band of Iazyges across the frozen Ister. Dio Cassius, the contemporary Roman historian, wrote of the fight:

> The Iazyges, perceiving that they were being pursued, awaited their opponents' onset, expecting to overcome them easily, as the others were not accustomed to the ice. Accordingly, some of the barbarians dashed straight at them, while others rode round to attack their flanks, as their horses had been trained to run safely even over a surface of this kind.

The Romans upon observing this were not alarmed, but formed in a compact body, facing all their foes at once, and most of them laid down their shields and rested one foot upon them, so that they might not slip so much; and thus they received the enemy's charge. Some seized bridles, others the shields and spearshafts of their assailants, and drew the men toward them; and thus, becoming involved in close conflict, they knocked down both men and horses, since the barbarians by reason of their momentum could no longer keep from slipping.[19]

The fight took on something of the character of a wrestling match, according to Dio Cassius, and the Iazyges were worsted because they were unused to this sort of engagement and had lighter equipment. Certainly the Iazyges must have worn complete armor; still, the Romans wore armor produced by the state factories and it was probably sturdier than that of barbarian manufacture. The encircling tactic used was common to nomads and will be seen again and again. However, steady trained infantry can resist the charge of horsemen, as these Romans proved; if foot soldiers do not break, the horses will balk and the immobile horseman is then easily assailed.

A peace was drawn up with the Sarmatians in 175 A.D. under terms of which they were to furnish the Roman army with eight thousand cavalrymen. Marcus Aurelius sent 5,500 of these soldiers to Britain, where they guarded Hadrian's Wall in troops of five hundred. Traces of these Sarmatian troops have been found there.[20]

The fort at Chesters on Hadrian's Wall produced a horse's eye shield and some beads of Hungarian Sarmatian style, and the Notitia Dignitatum, a fifth-century Roman list of military commands, lists a squadron of Sarmatians at the fort of Morbium and at a fort near present-day Ribchester. It also lists a force of Sarmatians serving in Egypt in the fourth or early fifth century: Ala VII Sarmatarum at Scenas Mandrorum on the west bank of the Nile, not too far distant from the city of Thebes on the east bank.[21] It is hardly surprising that we find Sarmatians serving in Egypt a century after Marcus Aurelius sent thousands of them to Britain. The Romans had come to appreciate them as soldiers; the Emperor Galerius (293–311) even had a Sarmatian bodyguard. The heavily armored horseman had come to the West to stay: between 264 and 268 A.D. the Emperor Gallienus had greatly increased the number of heavily armored horsemen in the Roman army—he had seen their usefulness in both Sarmatian and Persian guises.

Meanwhile, Germans were moving down from the north into the steppe in what is now the Ukraine. The most powerful were the Goths, who by the third century A.D. had established a kingdom on the steppe that intruded into the area about the Black Sea. By the fourth century they were across the Danube from the Roman provinces of Moesia and Thrace. These Goths, or their nobility at least, had learned from the Alani of that area their method of fighting: going armored on horseback and fighting with the lance. They were also no doubt mixing with the Alani, as we see from the occasional presence of Alani names among the Goths.

The problem for the Alani, however, was not displacement or assimilation by the Goths. Their greatest difficulty came from another steppe people heading west from central Asia: the Huns. With the Huns we return to the classic incarnation of the steppe warrior: the mounted archer. When we hear of the Huns in the Roman sources, they had already taken over the Alani and were driving the frantic Goths before them. The sources refer to them as Hunni et Halani, and different as the two people are, it is quite clear that the Huns had conquered the Alani and incorporated them into their horde in typical steppe fashion. There is no question, however, that between the two the Huns were preeminent. Many Goths and Gepids were caught up in the Hunnic whirlwind, and those who could fled west to the Danube and the Roman border where they petitioned for entry into the Empire for protection.

In spite of the huge numbers of Goths, Emperor Valentinian I (ruled 364–375 A.D.) reluctantly agreed and the Romans ferried them across, no doubt expecting to induct the men into various units of the Roman army, something that had been going on for a century. Unfortunately, the officials in charge mishandled the Goths, and they revolted, ravaging the Balkan provinces between 376 and 382. Because of their number they presented a grave threat, and armies from both the eastern and western halves of the Roman Empire converged upon Thrace to crush them, each led by an emperor: Valens, Emperor of the East, and his colleague and nephew Gratian,

Emperor of the West, who advanced with an army taken largely from Gaul.

Valens encountered a force of rebellious Goths on the outskirts of Adrianopolis (modern Edirne in European Turkey) on August 9, 378, and was informed by his scouts that they numbered only about ten thousand men, a figure that the army of the East could easily have handled without Gratian's assistance, although his imminent arrival had been announced by messenger. Estimating an enemy's numbers, however, is always difficult, and the scouts were mistaken; there were probably twice as many Goths as estimated, and perhaps a few more than that.

All the same, the Goths were under no illusions about the strength of the Roman army and they temporized by negotiating their surrender, probably in bad faith, to gain time until a force of mounted Goths under the leaders Alatheus and Saphrax might return. During the parley, the Roman left wing began to engage and the battle began before Valens intended. As the Goths had hoped, Alatheus and Saphrax did return with their men, to whom were attached a number of Alani as well, and these were able to drive off much of the Roman cavalry, thus denying the infantry important support that it needed in fighting with a much more numerous enemy than expected.

The Romans sustained a tremendous defeat. Ammianus Marcellinus states that only a third of the army escaped, while the Emperor Valens was killed on the field. He was said to have fallen amid the *lancearii*, a troop of elite infantry, though his body was never recovered. The Gothic heavy horseman, patterned on the Sarmatian lancer of the steppe, was the catalyst for this defeat, and he would remain a powerful figure on the battlefield long after the disappearance of the Roman Empire. He would become, in fact, the sole effective military agent on the Western battlefield for eight hundred years, as the knight.

NOTES
1. Herodotus, *The Histories*, Book IV, trans. Aubrey de Selincourt, Hammondsworth, UK, Penguin, 1972, p. 291.
2. Giovanni di Plano Carpini, *The Story of the Mongols Whom We Call the Tartars*, trans. Erik Hildinger, Boston, Branden Books, 1996.

3. An expression since corrupted to "parting shot."

4. Anthony M. Snodgrass, *Arms and Armour of the Greeks*, Ithaca, NY, Cornell University Press, 1967, p. 84.

5. These archers, according to. Snodgrass, were a brief innovation by the Athenian tyrant Peisistratos and their use was discontinued by the time of the Persian wars. See Snodgrass, op. cit.

6. Herodotus, Book IV.

7. Herodotus, Book IV.

8. The bridge was designed by Mandrocles of Samos.

9. Herodotus, Book IV.

10. There has been a good deal of discussion lately about Roman legionary armor. Surviving reliefs are sometimes ambiguous and it may be that instead of chain mail some legionaries wore cuirasses of hardened leather instead—what the French called *cuir bouilli* during the Middle Ages, a very stout defense. Others probably wore scale-mail, a defense that became progressively more popular during the second and third centuries A.D. In any case, it was their policy to be well protected.

11. A triumphal procession through Rome accorded to a successful commander and his troops. It was an honor conferred after a vote by the Senate.

12. Plutarch, *Lives*, Vol. III, trans. Bernadotte Perrin, London and New York, Loeb Classical Library, 1916, p. 389.

13. Or perhaps in the area around the Sea of Azov.

14. Tadeusz Sulimirski, *The Sarmatians*, Southampton, UK, Thames and Hudson, 1970. Sulimirski states: "The relatively large number of graves of armed women, especially in Sauromatian cemeteries, is usually looked upon as evidence of the survival of the ancient pre-Sauromatian social order based on a matriarchy," p. 34. On February 25, 1997, *The New York Times* reported that of the many Sarmatian remains of armed women found, particularly along the Russian-Kazakhstan border, few appear to have died violently. This suggests that although women may have been armed for hunting, or protecting the herds, they were not commonly exposed to combat. "Ancient Graves of Armed Women Hint at Amazons," p. C-1.

15. Ibid.

16. Quoted in Otto Maenchen-Helfen, *World of the Huns*, Berkeley, University of California Press, 1973, p. 244.

17. Polybius, Book XXX, 25, 3, quoted in Snodgrass, op. cit., p. 121.

18. While as a rule every link is threaded through four others to make the fabric of the armor, the most painstaking work would involve making the individual rings, punching the ends for the rivets, and then riveting them closed. It appears that much of this work was done with a set of special tongs each with a die at the end. A piece of wire or narrow strip of metal was closed in the first set to form the ring. The ring was then introduced into the second set of tongs which were closed on it to flatten the ends of the ring and at the same time punch a hole in each end; and finally, after interlacing the ring with four others,

a third set of tongs holding a small wedge of metal was squeezed over the ring, forcing the wedge into the holes and flattening and riveting them closed.

19. Cassius Dio Cocceianus, *Roman History*, trans. Ernest Cary, New York, G.P. Putnam's, 1927, pp. 23–25.

20. Sulimirski, pp. 175–76.

21. Denis van Berchem, *L'Armée de Dioclétien et la Réforme Constantinienne*, Paris, Institut Français d'Archéologie de Beyrouth, Imprimerie Nationale, 1952, p. 64.

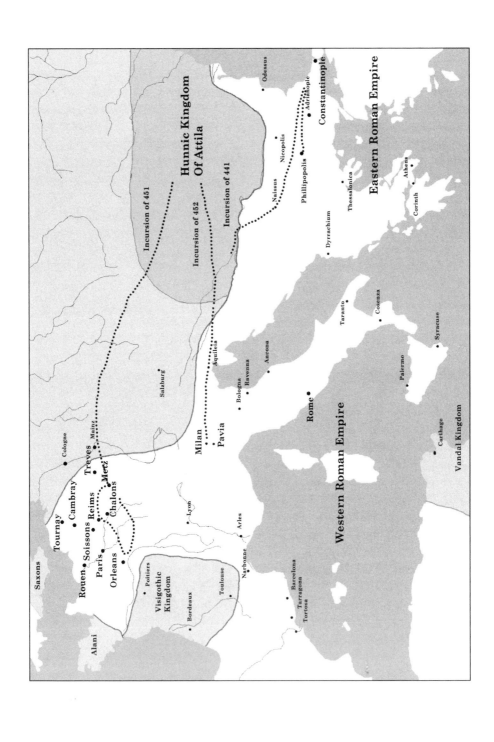

4

The Huns

No steppe people, save perhaps the Mongols, have been so feared in the West as the Huns. The Romans debated whether they were quite human—their appearance was so different from that of the Europeans, Middle Easterners and North Africans who made up the Empire. The historian and retired soldier Ammianus Marcellinus expressed a common view:

> The people of the Huns who are mentioned only cursorily in ancient writers and who dwell beyond the Sea of Azov [Palus Maeotis] near the frozen ocean, are quite abnormally savage. From the moment of birth they make deep gashes in their children's cheeks, so that when in due course hair appears its growth is checked by the wrinkled scars; as they grow older this gives them the unlovely appearance of beardless eunuchs. They have squat bodies, strong limbs, and thick necks, and are so prodigiously ugly and bent that they might be two-legged animals, or the figures crudely carved from stumps which are seen on the parapets of bridges.[1]

For the first time we have a description of an Asiatic steppe warrior from Western eyes. Marcellinus goes on to say this of their warfare:

> They sometimes fight by challenging their foes to single combat, but when they join battle they advance in packs, uttering their various war-cries. Being lightly equipped and

very sudden in their movements they can deliberately scat-
ter and gallop about at random, inflicting termendous
slaughter . . .[2]

We have now returned to the classic steppe warrior: the mounted archer, first exemplified, in the western steppe, by the Scythian.
This type would preponderate from the appearance of the Hun
onwards until the last of the steppe warriors, such as the seventeenth
century Crimean Tatars with whom they naturally shared a great
number of traits: nomadism, predation, even a taste for raw meat
which "they warm a little by placing it between their thighs and the
backs of their horses." Marcellinus adds:

> They have no fixed abode, no home or law or settled man-
> ner of life, but wander like refugees in the wagons in which
> they live. In these their wives weave their filthy clothing,
> mate with their husbands, give birth to their children and
> rear them to the age of puberty. No one if asked can tell
> where he comes from, having been conceived in one place,
> born somewhere else, and reared even further off. You can-
> not make a truce with them, because they are quite unreli-
> able and easily swayed by any breath of rumour which
> promises advantage . . .[3]

Ammianus' description of the Huns is harsh, but in time the
Romans must have softened their view. The emperor Theodosius the
Great (reigned 378–395) found the Huns useful as *numeri*, or allied
soldiers, and Flavius Stilicho did as well, when he served as regent
for Theodosius' minor children and in his capacity as Magister
Utriusque Militiae,[4] or supreme commander in the west. Stilicho had
a Hun bodyguard and the practice of using Hun bodyguards persisted even after the fall of the western half of the Roman Empire;
Belisarius, the great sixth-century Byzantine commander employed
Huns among his own household troops more than a hundred years
later, and used them to fight in Italy, North Africa and against the
Persians. The philosopher Synesius of Cyrene produced an essay in
398 directed to Arcadius, Emperor of the East, in which he rec-
ommended, among many other things, that he discontinue using

non-Roman mounted archers in his army—probably a reference to Huns.[5]

This picture of the Huns is often discounted; certainly the popular view of them ignores it completely. What the West recalls, and with some reason, is the tumultuous reign of Attila (443 or 444–453), who united the Huns for the first and only time into a single nation. Having done so he raided both halves of the Roman Empire and invaded Gaul and Italy. But in fact the Huns could be ally or enemy; they were opportunists who could often be profitably employed by the Romans, but who might turn on them as well. There was nothing unusual in this: the Huns merely displayed the predatory and main-chance characteristics common to all steppe people.

Historians in the last century confidently identified the Huns with the Hsiung-nu recorded in Chinese documents of the second century B.C. The name seems to mean "common slave" or "barbarian" and tells more about the Chinese attitude to them than anything else. The Hsiung-nu had posed a serious threat to the Chinese, who finally defeated them and drove them west into the steppe where they disappeared from history unless, perhaps, they reappeared as the Huns. Contemporary historians are less sure that the Huns were in fact the Hsiung-nu, but their ultimate origins are not of great importance from a military standpoint. They seem to have been Turkic-speaking, though as an illiterate people they have left nothing to confirm this and such speculations stem from their names as found in Roman records. The Huns have made even this area of study uncertain by their habit of sometimes taking Alani and German names from their subjects.

The Romans first became aware of them in the fourth century, as suggested by Ammianus, above, when he states that the Huns were "but little known from the ancient records." In fact, Huns were never mentioned in the ancient records, and when the civilized world first heard of them it was only vaguely as a ferocious people who were driving the Sarmatians and Goths into the Hungarian plain and south against the Danubian frontier. A few Huns had crossed the river to join the Goths in the revolt of 376 that had culminated in the disastrous Roman defeat of Adrianople, and some were probably present at it. The Huns had doubtless sensed an opportunity for freebooting inside the Empire while it was distracted by the Goths, and these Huns were probably the first that the Romans encountered directly. Ammianus Marcellinus, an historian of the Gothic revolt and the Battle of Adrianople, mentions them only in passing as joining the Goths, as did some Alani, and he never specifies them again, though he does mention the Alani, and so we can assume that they were not numerous.

What were these people like? Nomadic and broken into different groups or tribes, the Huns had followed their flocks west into the Ukraine. One of their own myths told how a party of Huns followed a magic stag which had led them through marshes they had thought impassable, thus discovering the Hungarian steppe. Whatever the specifics of their arrival, they lived in tents that they took with them from place to place, some mounted on wheels to be pulled by oxen. The archaeological record of their graves shows that they were primarily a people of oriental extraction, though measurement of the facial planes of skulls suggests that some were of mixed blood, having intermarried with Caucasians. The Huns also practiced the head-binding of children so that their skulls grew long and narrow, giving them a grotesque apprearance. (This practice was passed on to some of the Germans subject to them, such as the Gepids.) They shared the predatory nature common to steppe dwellers which, once they came into contact with the Roman Empire, came to the fore time and again.

The Empire was already a beleaguered polity when the Huns made themselves known. It was not only troubled, but quite different from the state of a hundred or two hundred years before that had faced barbarians on one front at a time, and relatively primitive ones at that. During the first century Rome's most dangerous frontier had been the Rhine, and six legions were posted there against the incursions of Germans into Gaul. As time passed, however, more pressure was exerted along the frontier marked by the Danube.

This pressure was exerted by Dacians (until their territory was annexed), Sarmatians (particularly the Iazyges and Roxolani), and by strong German tribes such as the Marcomanni and Quadi. The Emperor Marcus Aurelius spent most of his reign along the Danube fighting these last two people as well as Sarmatians. These people were not as primitive as the Germans whom the Romans had faced in earlier centuries along the border between Germania and Gaul; fighting them required great resources as they repeatedly attempted to break into the Roman provinces in the Balkans, northern Italy and the areas of modern Hungary and Greece. The Danube became heavily strengthened with forts, military camps, walled cities and fortified bridges to allow the Roman army to cross into the Barbaricum for punitive expeditions. Legions were moved from the Rhine to the Danube. Still, the pressure increased.

By the third century the Romans faced Goths of the Tervingi[6] tribe across the Danube. Constantine the Great fought them successfully in the early fourth century and took great pride in this, since most of his significant military victories had been against other Romans. He even fictitiously claimed descent from the earlier emperor Claudius II, nicknamed Gothicus, to whom were attributed great victories against the Goths along the Danube in a campaign between 266 and 268. Constantine defeated Sarmatians as well and had himself acclaimed "Sarmaticus" four times.

However, in spite of victories over the barbarians, the menace persisted together with the constant problem of usurpations. There was no constitutionally established procedure to ensure an orderly succession, and the Roman army had long since learned that it was the real power behind the throne. As a result, armies proclaimed new emperors, or were provoked to do so, with astonishing frequency. Civil war had become a regular feature of late-Roman life, and the solution generally adopted from the late third century onward was to divide the empire into an eastern and western half with an emperor over each. This ensured that there was an emperor near enough to any frontier to face barbarians or Persians, and close enough to respond to any usurper who might try to establish his legitimacy through war. By the time the Huns came into contact with the Roman Empire, it was soon to be permanently divided into halves with capitals at Constantinople in the east and Milan (later Ravenna) in the west.

The Huns too were divided at this time, and even under Attila there is evidence of Huns who were not under his sway.[7] Still, they were powerful enough to drive the Tervingi and many of the Gothic Greuthungi to the banks of the Danube, where they sought refuge in the Empire, leading to the Roman disaster of Adrianople. The Huns also amalgamated into their horde most of the Greuthungi, as well as the Gepids. They had earlier incorporated many Alani as well, although these people later managed to break free and head west toward the Empire before the mid-fifth century. Many settled in the Balkan provinces or northern Italy and Gaul, where they served Rome as auxiliary soldiers. As the Alani commonly fought in complete scale or chainmail armor, armed with lance and broadsword and mounted upon armored horses, their influence on the Romans (who fielded cavalry so armed: the *cataphracti* or *clibanarii*) is obvious, and the idea of the fully armored cavalryman which culminated in the medieval knight continued to spread.

Despite their alarming or alien aspects, the Huns soon came increasingly into contact with the Romans and eventually became involved in that prominent aspect of internal Roman politics: civil war. In 383 Maximus had proclaimed himself emperor in Gaul and stood against the legitimate ruler of the west, the young Valentinian II. This emperor was under the tutelage of the Frank Bauto,[8] his master of soldiers. Valentinian had few troops, and his Catholic mother, Justina, had spent some time in religious persecutions against her Orthodox Christian subjects, who, as a result, might not have been too inclined to resist Maximus as he advanced upon Italy. Valentinian's real support was Theodosius, Emperor of the East, who was much more powerful and could be expected to support Valentinian if Maximus attacked Italy. In the event, Maximus did not do so, or at least not directly. Instead, he engineered attacks by barbarian Juthungi on the province of Raetia (today most of the Tyrol).

It was Maximus' hope that the Juthungi would continue to advance and breach the passes in the Alps and descend into Italy. Bauto would then fall and Maximus could intervene and drive the Juthungi out, rescue Italy and validate his position as emperor in the west. Bauto countered by hiring a force of Huns and Alani who, in 384, utterly defeated the Juthungi. Not satisfied with what they had done, they continued toward Gaul, apparently to attack Maximus' territory.

The political situation was delicate: Theodosius was prepared to defend Italy, but not to engage in open civil war with Maximus, which would certainly result from a Hun–Alani attack on his domain. Bauto did manage to call off the Huns and their subject Alani, though he had to pay them for their forbearance. There is no record detailing the battles fought, let alone describing them, but from what is known of the Huns we can suppose that they consisted of sweeping and encircling maneuvers of bodies of men shooting from the saddle and rarely closing, at least until the fight was nearly done. Their Alani subjects were more heavily equipped, as described above, and could have supported the Huns and fought at close quarters with their heavy lances and long swords. It would have been a handy combination of heavy and light cavalry such as the Parthians had used and which would not be generally seen again until the rise of the Mongols in the late twelfth century.

Three years later the Romans hired them again. Maximus had finally succeeded in his efforts to take the entire Western Empire and he drove Valentinian and his mother from Italy. Mother and son sought refuge at the court of Constantinople and Theodosius resolved to put Maximus down. However, Theodosius was faced with a problem: it had been only nine years since the disastrous battle of Adrianople at which the Eastern Roman field army was largely destroyed. In time, Theodosius would rebuild by conscripting large numbers of barbarians, principally Germans, and integrating them into units of the regular army as had been done for generations. The Germanic component of the army would become even more marked than it already was. But he took a further step: he accepted whole troops of barbarians to fight in their native way under their own leaders for a particular campaign. The contract was called a *foedus* and these *foederati* included troops of Huns.

The campaign against Maximus in 387–388 was a complete success. Theodosius' largely barbarian army of Huns, Alani and Goths advanced through the Balkan provinces defeating Maximus at Siscia (now Sisak) and also near Poetovio (now Ptuj), both in present-day Yugoslavia.

Loyal though they may have been on many occasions, the Huns were equally prepared to devastate Roman soil; in 392, bands of Huns joined Visigothic bandits who had deserted from the army, and they ravaged the Balkan provinces. Theodosius put down the revolt, but in 394 had to contend with Eugenius, another western usurper. Once again Theodosius assembled a largely barbarian army of *foederati*. This force consisted of Armenians, Arabs, soldiers from the Caucasus Mountains, Visigoths and of course Huns and Alani. While this army was victorious as the last had been, reliance upon these troops was a dangerous step and marked the beginning of the end of the regular Roman army in the west. From now on it would sink in importance and virtually disappear as the Western Empire came to rely more and more upon federate troops for its field army.

The following year Huns invaded Persia and advanced as far as Osroene in Mesopotamia. Their expedition was less than successful, for the Persians attacked them when they were lumbered with spoils and recovered most of them. Still, this shows how swiftly the Huns could move and how little the frontiers meant to them. They crossed the Danube, passing through Roman territory into Persia, and rode into the heart of that country. According to Claudian, a poet in the service of the Roman general Stilicho, the Huns passed the Caucasus Mountains through the Daryal Pass, advancing to Antioch and Edessa and into Mesopotamia before they were driven out. The campaign shows the great distances the Huns could cover in a single campaign—a characteristic of steppe people. Ironically, two years later the Romans had some reason to fear a Persian war in which the Huns might act as Persian allies, although as it turned out, the conflict did not develop.

What kind of equipment did these Huns use? The composite bow, of course, as well as the lance. Specimens of lance heads survive in graves, though the length of the weapon itself would be a matter of speculation. The heavy Sarmatian *kontoi* seem to have been about ten feet long and the Hunnic lance was probably somewhere in this neighborhood, though it was likely much lighter.[9] Some of the Huns would have carried swords as well; long, straight, slashing swords of the type favored by the Sarmatians and Goths, similar to that called the *spatha* by the Romans and used by their cavalry. As did many steppe people, the Huns used the lasso in battle as a weapon.

The Huns carried shields, and the literary evidence indicates that the nobles and the wealthy wore armor. As scale armor is the earliest found on the steppe and was widely used by both Scythians and Sarmatians, it is probable that this kind of armor was used by the Huns as well, although prolonged contact with Romans would probably have eventually resulted in the introduction of chainmail, either through trade or by looting after battles with the Romans. The Huns also wore helmets, most likely on the late Roman pattern now called a *spangenhelm* by archaeologists. This is a conical helmet of four or six sections joined together and reinforced by bands over the joins. It generally had large cheek pieces, a neck guard and a nose piece. The helmet may be of Sassanian–Persian origin and it became common in the Roman army in the late third or early fourth century. It was often used by barbarians and was the pattern for such armor as the famous Sutton Hoo Anglo-Saxon helmet, which is a spangenhelm with a decorated face-mask added.

Thus, a well armored Hun noble would have had a mail jacket, helmet and shield, and would have carried a lance as well as his bow. His skill with these weapons and with his horse made him formidable—though even the common Huns who were wholly, or incompletely, armored would have posed a grave threat. This threat, however, increased in direct proportion to their organization, and gradually the Huns were becoming more unified. By 400 some of them were subject to a powerful king, Uldin. Although the extent of his kingdom is uncertain, it clearly included that part of Romania east of the Olt (Aluta) River and west into Hungary to the Danube.

There were other kings as well, such as Octar, Mundzik and a certain Ruas or Rugilas, apparently the uncle of the brothers Bleda and Attila. It was during Ruas' reign that Flavius Aëtius, a young Roman noble, had been sent to live among the Huns as a hostage. He had already lived among the Visigoths as a hostage of the Gothic king Alaric, who would sack Rome in 410. During his stay, Aëtius came to understand the Huns, to learn archery and horsemanship, and no doubt the Hunnish language as well. He became a friend of Ruas and probably was acquainted with Attila. All of this would stand him in good stead during both his political and military careers.

In time Ruas' nephews assumed the status of kings, but did not rule together; Attila apparently ruled the Huns along the border of the Western Empire while his brother ruled those bordering the Eastern. By 443 or 444 Attila had killed Bleda and assumed sole power over most of the Huns. The heart of his kingdom was the Hungarian plain and extended east into the steppe north of the Black Sea. This meant that the Huns could and did menace both halves of the Empire. Tribute paid to them increased over time by a factor of ten.

In spite of their new unity and the threat it presented, the Romans still found the Huns useful. When Aëtius held the position of Praetorian Prefect at the Western court he supported the usurper John against the imperial candidate supported by the Eastern Roman Emperor, Valentinian II. Aëtius' task was to procure military support and he did this by traveling to the Huns and recruiting an army of them. Unfortunately for John, the Huns arrived a few days after his fall and execution, but all the same their presence assured Aëtius' survival in spite of the intense hatred of Galla Placidia, the mother of the legitimate Emperor of the West, the minor Valentinian III.

The Huns continued to be Aëtius' support and he was able to achieve the position of Magister Utriusque Militiae, or Master of Both Services, the supreme military commander in the West and to have himself made the regent for the boy emperor Valentinian in spite of Galla Placidia's opposition. Supported by the Huns, Aëtius was the de facto ruler of the Western Empire during Valentinian's minority.

More than a political support, however, the Huns were a valuable military tool. Of paramount importance to Aëtius as Master of Both Services was the containment of Burgundian, Frankish and Visigothic power in Gaul, where each of these Germanic peoples had set up independent kingdoms by treaty with Rome. Not satisfied with their territories, they sought constantly to enlarge them at Roman expense. Time and again Aëtius' Huns, either under his command or that of his lieutenant Litorius, drubbed these Germans and slowed their inexorable expansion. Only the Visigoths were able to face the Huns effectively from time to time; the Burgundian kingdom, on the other hand, was completely destroyed and its people resettled to what is now Savoy. When Aëtius fell out of favor in 433, it was to the Huns that he went for protection. In spite of their support for Aëtius, however, he would in the end become the bulwark of the West against his familiar Huns.

Meanwhile, however, Aëtius' good relations with the Huns meant that, for the most part, their depredations against Rome were limited to incursions into the Balkan provinces of the Eastern Empire. In 441, while the Eastern Emperor Theodosius II was busied with the Vandals and Persians, Attila attacked, claiming that Rome had been desultory in paying the tribute by which it bought peace, and that certain Hunnish deserters had not been restored. Theodosius refused to consider his complaints, and Attila took and plundered Ratiaria, a Roman city on the Danube. The Huns then followed the Danube, taking other Roman towns: Viminacium, Singidunum and Margus. Going up the Margus valley they took Naissus and then advanced on Constantinople itself, though they did not dare attack it; instead they took Philippopolis (today Plovdiv), Arcadiopolis and the fortress of Athyras. The fortress of Asemus, however, put up a brave and successful defense.

Meanwhile the Eastern army had returned from Persia and Sicily and took the field against Attila in Thrace. The Romans were defeated, however, and peace was made at a heavy cost: Theodosius agreed to triple the annual tribute of seven hundred pounds of gold and to pay an additional six thousand pounds as well. Any Romans rescued during the campaign had to be ransomed for ten pieces of gold each or returned to the Huns. This was agreed to in 443, the year in which, or the year before, Attila murdered his brother to become sole king of the Huns.

In 448 the Eastern Roman diplomat Priscus visited Attila's court and attended a banquet there which he described vividly, referring to the Huns in late-Roman fashion as "Scythians":

> When this ceremony was over the cup-bearers retired, and tables, large enough for three or four, or even more, to sit at, were placed next to the table of Attila, so that each could take of the food on the dishes without leaving his seat. The attendant of Attila first entered with a dish full of meat, and behind him came the other attendants with bread and viands, which they laid on the tables. A luxurious meal, served on silver plate, had been made ready for us and the barbarian guests, but Attila ate nothing but meat on a wooden trencher. In everything else, too, he showed himself temperate; his cup was of wood, while to the guests were given goblets of gold and silver. His dress, too, was quite simple, affecting only to be clean. The sword he carried at his side, the latchets of his Scythian shoes, the bridle of his

horse were not adorned, like those of the other Scythians, with gold or gems or anything costly.[10]

Eight hundred years later, Chinggis Khan's modesty of manner and dress would recall that of Attila. And, as Chinggis Khan would do later, the Hun king knew how to use superstition to futher his aims: when a Hunnish herdsman discovered that a limping heifer had stepped upon an ancient, rusty sword, Attila proclaimed it a divine omen. The sword was "The Sword of Mars" and a sign of his greatness as a conqueror, and recalled the swords worshipped by the Huns' Scythian and Sarmatian forerunners.

It was in the year of Priscus' embassy that Hun armies descended once more into the Thracian and Illyrian provinces, one group reaching, it is said, Thermopylae. Once more the Huns approached Constantinople and, while they did not attack the city, they caused devastation in its neighborhood. Again a peace was concluded, but this time Attila demanded that the Romans abandon the right bank of the Danube from Singidunum to Novae to a width of five days' travel, thus creating a no-man's-land between Roman and Hun territory. The purpose was probably to prevent the Romans from mounting attacks against him without notice and to prevent Huns or other subjects from fleeing to the Empire. As a practical matter the Romans were unable to depopulate the march, for the peasants were obstinate and would sneak back. Still, this was unimportant because, upon Theodosius II's death in 450, his successor, Marcian, refused to pay the tribute any longer, surely a more pressing excuse for war.

The following year Attila attacked the Roman Empire, though not the eastern half. Most probably he thought the Thracian and Illyrian provinces were too stripped from earlier raids to be worth ravaging. Instead he headed west toward Gaul. His army consisted of Huns and allied subject peoples: Ostrogoths, Rugi, Heruli and Gepids. The Gepid king Ardaric was in fact Attila's closest advisor.

Upon reaching the Rhine, Attila attached to himself a force of Franks as well, for he had earlier resolved a dispute over a kingship in favor of the current ruler. The loser had fled with a smaller number of Franks into the Empire. On April 7 Attila took the city of Metz and wasted the neighborhood, taking many other towns.

It was left to Aëtius to confront the Huns. At the time of their advance he was in Italy and he assembled the forces he could, a small army mostly of barbarian troops: Salian Franks, some Ripuarian Franks, Burgundians and Armorican (western) Celts. Still, the army was too small to contend with the Huns, who by then were advancing on what is today Orléans. A group of Alani had been settled in the neighborhood of that city and their king, Sangibanus, had communicated his willingness to betray the town to Attila, notwithstanding his nominal allegiance to Rome. Aëtius needed the support of the Visigoths, whose kingdom was centered around Tolosa (Toulouse), but he had been at war with them for twenty years and their king, Theodoric, son of Alaric, was his bitter enemy. While it was evident that the Visigoths would fight the Huns to protect their own kingdom, Aëtius needed them to advance east and fight with him to prevent further depredation of Roman territory.

Aëtius relied upon a certain Avitus as intermediary and he prevailed upon Theodoric to join the Romans against the common threat. Theodoric no doubt saw the wisdom of joining his enemy against the Huns instead of risking defeat by allowing Attila to face his opponents piecemeal. By then, too, horrific reports were no doubt flooding in from survivors of towns that had lain in the path of Attila's advance. The Romans and Visigoths would temporarily suspend their hostilities and unite against the menace from the east.

The allied army reached Orléans before the Huns and prevented its capture on June 14. King Sangibanus' Alani were pressed into the Roman forces. The Huns pulled away and advanced toward Tricasses (Troyes), preparing to face the Roman-Visigoth army in a place called Locus Mauriacus.[11] The exact site is disputed but may have been somewhere between Méry-sur-Seine and Troyes. Likewise the precise date of the battle is unknown, though some historians estimate it must have taken place about June 20, 451.[12]

The first engagement began the night before between the Burgundian vanguard of the Roman-Visigoth army and the rear of the Hun forces; however, the real struggle took place the next day. Aëtius drew up his mixed force on the left wing while Theodoric and the Visigoths were on the right. In the center were the untrustworthy Alani; Aëtius judged correctly that they would fight for him—if they had no choice. Attila was in the center of his army opposite, facing the Alani.

The battle site had a hill that both sides wished to occupy, and soldiers from each army took portions of it, although the crest remained free. As the fighting began the Huns were driven from the hill and the fighting became general. There is no detailed description of the battle, but the fighting was described as ferocious. The Visigothic king, Theodoric, fell and the fighting went on into the darkness. Apparently the slaughter on both sides was heavy, although the historian Jordanes' statement that 165,000 died cannot be taken seriously. It is doubtful that either side fielded forces larger than twenty-five or thirty thousand men. Nevertheless, even these numbers would constitute large armies so late in the history of the Empire.

The battle itself was something of a draw, although the fact that the Romans and their allies had stopped the Huns at all was a major accomplishment. Moreover, when the fighting was over Attila was in a bad position. He retreated to his wagons, drawn up as a protective enclosure, and prepared to withstand a renewed assault. He is said to have piled saddles to be set alight as a funeral pyre into which he intended to throw himself if the Goths and Romans broke into the enclosure. However, this second attack never came. Instead late-Roman imperial politics came into play.

Aëtius was a realist. In the west Rome now depended almost completely on federate and allied barbarian troops to do its fighting. Even the army that had stopped the Huns must have contained relatively few Roman troops, and certainly not enough to have stood against Attila alone. Federate troops were an utter necessity to the Romans and the Huns might in the future be as good a source of them as they had in the past.

And then there was the Visigothic Kingdom. Aëtius could not forget that he had fought it for twenty years to maintain the integrity of Gaul as a Roman territory. With the Huns destroyed, there would be one less power to balance against it. King Sangibanus, the Alani, had recently proved less than reliable. Aëtius was in the unenviable position of a juggler tossing knives. He made a decision: he would let the Huns escape.

Thorismund, Theodoric's son, was intent on revenging his father's death by an attack on the Hun laager. Aëtius dissuaded him by suggesting that with his father's death it would be in his interest to return to Tolosa to ensure an orderly succession and his installation as king. Aëtius apparently made some similar political argument to the Frankish king, who departed immediately too.

Attila pulled out of Gaul to his territories in Hungary, severely damaged in prestige, but not humbled. If Aëtius thought Attila suitably chastened, he was mistaken. The following year Attila decided to invade Italy itself.

In the summer of 452 Attila led an army, as large as the one of the year before, into the Pannonian provinces (in what are now Hungary and northern Yugoslavia) and through the Alps into Italy. Aëtius was apparently taken by surprise because he did not block the passes in the Alps which would have made the Hun invasion far more difficult. The nomad horsemen could not have fought effectively in the mountains—something pointed out by at least one contemporary. The reason Aëtius failed to anticipate Attila may have been simply that he gauged Attila to have been weakened politically: he had lost many men to no good purpose and had been forced to retreat without spoils.

Aëtius may have considered Attila unable to mount a second war without taking time to reconsolidate his position, but while he was doubtless correct in his estimation of Attila's precarious status, the Hun may have decided upon another campaign precisely to consolidate his position, damaged after the Battle of the Mauriac Plains. He may have been indirectly driven by his nobles to campaign soon, and this theory is supported by the fact that the new campaign was conducted in summer, not a favorite campaign season for nomads, who generally prefer to march in the winter when the horses have grazed all summer and rivers are more apt to be frozen and easy to cross.

Having determined to campaign, however, Attila likely counted upon the advantage of surprise and mobilized so quickly that he was on the march before the Romans realized it. There is a more modern example of this natural advantage of a steppe army: the Tatars of the Crimea in the sixteenth and seventeenth century. These nomadic Mongol successors could field armies to fight the Poles and Russians in two to four weeks, much less time than a sedentary state needs to marshal its forces.[13] The Huns could doubtless do the same and be crossing the Alps before the Romans learned of the need to defend the passes.

The Huns swept into northern Italy and took the city of Aquileia (near modern Venice), destroying it utterly. A hundred years later there was barely a trace of it. They failed to take Verona and Vicentia (Vicenza), but did exact tribute from Ticinum (Pavia) and Mediolanum (Milan). There was nothing to stop Attila from marching south, crossing the Po and even taking Rome. Aëtius did not have the forces in Italy necessary to prevent the Huns' advance and at first counseled the Emperor Valentinian to flee Italy. Aëtius changed his mind however, and the Emperor took shelter in the imperial capital of Ravenna, protected by massive walls and surrounded by swamps.

Instead, an embassy was sent to Attila which included Leo, Bishop of Rome, and two senators, Avienus and Trygetius. Folk tales claimed that Saints Peter and Paul accompanied Leo and terrified Attila into foregoing an advance on Rome. There was a famine in Italy, in addition, and plague had broken out among the Huns. Meanwhile, during the negotiations Marcian, Emperor of the East, managed to land troops in support of the Western Empire. These are the factors that likely convinced Attila to withdraw from Italy. As J.B. Bury so aptly said: "It is unreasonable to suppose that this heathen king would have cared for the thunders or persuasions of the Church."[14]

Attila did not long survive the Italian campaign. He decided to marry again and died in 453 during his wedding night to a German woman, Ildiko. The cause may have been drunkenness or the rupture of an artery, although there is some suggestion that Ildiko murdered him. Whatever the cause, upon his death the Huns dissolved as a polity in true steppe fashion. His sons tried to divide up the kingdom among themselves and parcel out the various subject peoples, but the tribes revolted. The Germans, under the leadership of Ardaric, the Gepid king and former advisor to Attila, defeated the Huns at the Battle of the Nedao in 454 by a river of that name somewhere in Pannonia.

The Huns were broken as a cohesive state and, while they did not quite disappear from history, they fell into the background, serving to supply soldiers for the Eastern Empire until they vanished, no doubt through assimilation with other more numerous peoples, by about the seventh century. As far as the army of the Eastern Roman

Empire was concerned, however, they left something more than their memory; they left a military technique: mounted archery. The sixth-century historian, Procopius, described the army of his day:

> But the bowmen of the present time go into battle wearing corselets and fitted out with greaves which extend up to the knee. From the right side hang their arrows, from the other the sword. And there are some who have a spear attached to them and, at the shoulders, a sort of small shield with a grip, such as to cover the region of the face and neck. They are expert horsemen, and are able without difficulty to direct their bows to either side while riding at full speed, and to shoot an opponent whether in pursuit or in flight. They draw the bowstring along by the forehead about opposite the right ear, thereby charging the arrow with such an impetus as to kill whoever stands in the way, shield and corselet alike having no power to check its force.[15]

The Byzantine army had paid the Huns the compliment of equipping themselves in much the same way as the better-armed Huns. It was with small armies of such soldiers (and with federate Huns) that the Byzantine general Belisarius stood the Persians off and destroyed the Vandal Kingdom, thus returning North Africa to the Empire after a loss of a hundred years, before going on to reconquer much of Italy lost to the Goths. The Byzantines had learned from steppe people to fight as horse archers, and through the cultivation of this skill withstood their enemies for generations.

NOTES
1. *Ammianus Marcellinus*, Book 31, trans. Walter Hamilton, Hammondsworth, UK, Penguin, 1986.
2. Ibid.
3. Ibid.
4. "Master of both Services," that is, cavalry and infantry. This was the highest military rank attainable in the late Roman Empire.
5. Thomas S. Burns, *Barbarians Within the Gates of Rome*, Bloomington and Indianapolis, Indiana University Press, 1994, p. 163.
6. Scholars generally equate the Tervingi with the Visigoths, and their eastern

Gothic neighbors, the Greuthungi, with the Ostrogoths—though these terms were not used at this time. Peter Heather, in *Goths and Romans*, New York, Oxford University Press, 1994, makes a good argument that these groups were not identical, but coalesced and reformed in the later fourth century into Visigoths and Ostrogoths.

7. Otto Maenchen-Helfen, *World of the Huns*, Berkeley, University of California Press, Berkeley, 1973.

8. That Valentinian's Master of Soldiers was a German shows the dominance that Germans had achieved in the Roman army by this time.

9. European cavalry lances from the nineteenth century were roughly of this length. See Hans Delbrück.

10. Translated by J.B. Bury in *History of the Later Roman Empire*, Vol. I, New York, Dover, 1958.

11. This battle is sometimes referred to as the Battle of the Catalaunian Plains or the Battle of Chalons-sur-Marne. According to Bury, the Catalaunian Plains would have encompassed the whole of Champagne and it is generally agreed that the battle actually took place near Troyes. Bury, p. 293, fn. 1.

12. E.A. Thompson, *A History of Attila and the Huns*, New York, Oxford, University Press, 1948, p. 141, citing Bury, op cit.

13. L.J.D. Collins, "The Military Organization and Tactics of the Crimean Tartars During the Sixteenth and Seventeenth Centuries," in *War, Technology and Society in the Middle East*, ed. V.J. Parry and M.E. Yapp, London, Oxford University Press, 1975, p. 259.

14. Bury, p. 295.

15. Procopius, *History of the Wars*, trans. H.B. Dewing, Cambridge, MA, and London, Harvard University Press, 1953, pp. 9–15.

5

Avars, Bulgars and Magyars

With the dissolution of the Huns as a power in the West, their place was taken, predictably enough perhaps, by a series of other nomadic peoples moving in from the Eurasian steppe. Central Europe, and in particular the Hungarian plain, has always been a magnet for nomads from the east, and the first to follow the Huns were the Avars. These people appear to have been an amalgamation of two hordes: the Var and the Hunni. The latter were probably Hunnic, although the Avars are generally regarded as a Mongol people.

The Byzantines thought they were much like Huns: they were nomadic horse archers from the steppe and shamanistic in religion. They wore their hair differently than Huns—two braids down the back—but in most respects were so like them that the Byzantines and Franks often called them Huns. The Byzantine Emperor Maurice (reigned 582–602) had served in the army before his accession and was more precise in his military treatise, the *Strategikon*, in which he noted that the Avars and other nomads lived in a way like that of the Huns and were really "one nation."[1]

When the Byzantines first became aware of them the Avars were still on the steppe, having not yet moved west into the former Roman province of Pannonia, which corresponds to Hungary. In 557, near the end of the reign of Justinian I, the Avars sent their envoy Kandikh to Constantinople to demand tribute and land of the Empire. Justinian convinced the Avars to attack two tribes of Huns—the Kutrigurs and Uturgurs—who lived northwest of the Sea of Azov. The Avars obligingly did this and absorbed them into the horde in Turco-Mongol steppe tradition.

The Avars then moved west into Europe, pushing groups of Huns ahead of them and campaigning to the north against the Slavs. After defeating these people the Avars turned their attention to Germany, until they were halted in 561 by King Sigebert of Austrasia. Shortly thereafter, in 565, Bayan ascended the Avar throne as kaghan or great khan. The Avars were the first to use this term, which would persist thereafter among steppe peoples. Bayan was the greatest of their leaders and he allied his horde with the Lombards, thus working to destroy the Gepids. The Avars then settled in Pannonia, an area already inhabited by Bulgars, who may have been of Kutrigur Hun origin. These were driven into Bessarabia (today's Moldova) and Wallachia (to the south) from which they would be driven again a hundred years later by the Magyars, to settle finally in the former Roman province of Moesia, where they would establish the state of Bulgaria.

The Avars established their headquarters near Attila's old capital of a hundred years before and fortified it. It was known as the Ring. Now well established in Pannonia, Bayan fought the Franks of Sigebert again and defeated them in 570. A dozen years later Bayan attacked Byzantine territory and seized the city of Sirmium on the Sava River. He followed this with further campaigns against the Byzantines, the Avars taking Singidunum (Belgrade) and ravaging Moesia until they were finally defeated near Adrianople in 587. To the Byzantines it must have seemed like a reprise of the Hunnic aggression of the fifth century.

And still the Avars attacked. They took Anchialus and wasted Thrace until finally stopped by the Byzantine general Priscus, who then carried the war to the Avars. The Byzantine army was well prepared to do this. As a legacy of fighting the Huns and employing them during the fourth and fifth centuries, the Byzantine cavalry had come to resemble them, though they were doubtless better equipped because only the nobility among barbarians would have had much armor. Each trooper wore a chainmail or scale-mail jacket, although lamellar armor was also used, another legacy from the steppe. He wore an iron helmet and carried a shield; if he were an officer or a soldier of the front rank his horse wore a frontlet and a poitrel to protect its head and chest. With this heavy equipment he was well suited to shock-action and could fight with lance and broadsword.

However, he was also armed with a recurved composite bow which, like a steppe warrior, he was trained to use from the saddle. This ability to engage in either shock or missile combat made the Byzantine horseman the preeminent cavalryman of the age. The East Roman state had both the advantage of experience with nomad warriors and an institutional approach to battle codified in military manuals such as the *Strategikon* of Maurice, in which he wrote:

> The Scythian nations are one, so to speak, in their mode of life and in their organization, which is primitive and includes many peoples. Of these people only the Turks and the Avars concern themselves with military organization, and this makes them stronger than the other Scythian nations when it comes to pitched battles. The nation of the Turks is very numerous and independent. . . . The Avars, for their part, are scoundrels, devious, and very experienced in military matters.[2]

Maurice could see that all steppe nomads, whatever their peculiar tribe or origin, were cut from the same cloth and would exhibit the same military characteristics. For the benefit of his officers he described them in terms which recall those of Ammianus recounting Hun tactics:

> In combat they do not, as do the Romans and Persians, form their battle line in three parts, but in several units of irregular size, all joined closely together to give the appearance of one long battle line. Separate from their main formation, they have additional force which they can send out and ambush a careless adversary or hold in close behind their main line, and their baggage train to the right or left of the line about a mile or two away under a moderately sized guard. Frequently they tie the extra horses together to the rear of their battle line as a form of protection. They make the depth of their files indefinite depending on the circumstances, being inclined to make them deeper, and they make their front even and dense.
> They prefer battles fought at long range, ambushes, en-

circling their adversaries, simulated retreats and sudden
returns, and wedge-shaped formations, that is, in scattered
groups. When they make their enemies take to flight, they
put everything else aside, and are not content, as the
Persians, the Romans, and other peoples, with pursuing
them a reasonable distance and plundering their goods, but
they do not let up at all until they have achieved the complete destruction of their enemies, and they employ every
means to this end.[3]

He remarked also that, because they were nomads, they easily
suffered privation and harsh conditions, a most useful quality in soldiers. They were also superstitious, untrustworthy and greedy, he
opined, and, "They prefer to prevail over their enemies not so much
by force as by deceit, surprise, and cutting off supplies."[4] This theme
would be sounded again and again across the centuries when sedentary people encountered nomads.

As for the Avars' equipment, they wore mail and fought with the
lance as well as the bow. They gave particular attention, Maurice
says, to archery practice. Further, the Avars did have one peculiar
device they seem to have imparted to the West: the stirrup. It was not
long after contact with these nomads that the Byzantine army took
them up, followed by the Franks and the rest of Europe.

There has always been a great deal of discussion concerning the
value of the stirrup. Some suggest that it was one of the most important developments of the Middle Ages, while others argue that while
it was significant, it did not fundamentally alter the balance of power
in favor of the horseman and, on balance, this seems the better view.

The stirrup did confer the signal advantage of great stability to
the rider, particularly if he were encumbered by heavy armor.
However, any good rider is quick to point out that a horseman can
ride well enough without stirrups because of both skill and the development of leg muscles that allow him to grip the horse. Furthermore,
the Sarmatians and some of the Parthians rode in full armor and
fought with heavy lances without the use of stirrups, so the empirical evidence shows that it is possible to do this, even though the stirrup improves stability. It seems likely that the Sarmatians and
Parthians used a heavy lance because its mass would help absorb

some of the shock of striking an opponent, and it was probably held fairly loosely in one or both hands for this reason; the less shock transmitted to the rider, the less likely he was to be toppled by his own blow.

The stirrup, of course, solved much of this problem and led in time to using the lance in the couched position. In this way the weapon is held in the rider's right hand and at the same time is braced under the folded arm—kept in the armpit really. Thus, holding the lance at two points meant that the weapon was held rigidly and this, along with stirrups, allowed the rider to attack his opponent not merely with the strength of his arm, but instead with the full force of the charging horse that he rode. Upon contact the stirrups helped him keep his seat instead of being driven back over the crupper. In this regard the stirrup was of great significance, notably in knightly warfare, where the charge with the couched lance was of prime importance.

Still, there is evidence that after the introduction of stirrups knights did not adopt the couched lance position, at least not exclusively, for some time. The Bayeux Tapestry, which was embroidered by Norman ladies a few years after the Norman invasion of England in 1066, shows knights still using their lances either by striking downward with them while held in one hand, or held out from the side in one hand. Since these practices obviously continued for centuries after the introduction of the stirrup, and because armored horsemen had fought without the device for generations, it may be that the stirrup, while unquestionably important, was not quite as critical an innovation as is sometimes claimed. For the horse archer the stirrup was important too, though somewhat less so; since he depended upon the bow, he was naturally more able to sit his horse safely than a lancer, and he wore his stirrup leathers short anyway, to ease his weight on the horse.

Other Avar influences on the Byzantine cavalry consisted of the issuing of full-cut Avar-style tunics to the horsemen, and the use of Avar-style lances. There is no explanation of how such a lance differed from those in use before (if much at all) except that it was fitted with a pennant behind the head and a wrist thong along the shaft for a secure grip. It may be that this lance was somewhat lighter than the *kontos*, as suggested by the wrist thong, and suited to a more delicate use. In any case, the steppe influence apparent in the army of the Emperor Justinian continued into the reign of his successors, though with an Avar tinge to it.

Strongly influenced as it was by the nomads, the Byzantine cavalry could shoot arrows within the framework of mobile tactics and then, if the opportunity presented itself, charge and ride the enemy down with their more generally issued heavier equipment. Against infantry or heavy horsemen such as Goths or Franks they simply fought with the bow, keeping out of contact with their opponents' lances and swords.

Although there are no tactical details of Priscus' campaign against the Avars, it was likely one of skirmishes, ambushes and chases until the Byzantines could trap them against an obstacle and bring superior weight to bear. In the end Priscus engaged and badly beat the Avars on the Tissus (Tisza) River in 601 at a battle in which four of Bayan's sons were killed. He himself died a year later. The Avars' activities continued, though for now only against Italy: in 610 they sacked Friuli.

Within a few years, however, they were once again engaged against the Byzantine Empire, going so far, in 619, to personally attack the Emperor Heraclius at a parley in Thrace. He escaped and the Avars then attacked Constantinople, but without success. A few years later, though, they had a second chance when in 626 the Persian King Chosroes II cooperated with them to besiege the city. The Avars camped on the European side while the Persians established themselves across the Bosphorus. Constantinople was not an easy prize, however, no matter how strong the besieger.

This "New Rome" had been established with a view to defense by Constantine in the fourth century. He built his capital at the small city of Byzantium on the Golden Horn, a bend in the Bosphorus, the strait between Europe and Asia. Because the city was built in this bend the only practical approach to it was from the west on the neck of land extending into the Bosphorus. However, Constantinople was protected on the land side by a system of three walls, each higher than the last to allow the defenders, if they needed, to pull back to a second line of defense from which they could shoot at the wall ahead and below. This elaborate system was unmatched anywhere and was clearly beyond the power of barbarians without knowledge of siege-craft to take. In fact, these walls did not fall until they were battered apart by huge Ottoman cannon in 1453. There were walls along the seaward sides too, so that attacking from boats was also difficult and the harbor contained a great chain to prevent the passage of ships. The Byzantine fleet operated freely in the Bosphorus during the siege, preventing effective cooperation between the Avars and Persians on either side.

For five days between July 31 and August 4, 626, the Avars launched assaults against the city which were bloodily repulsed. Then, reckoning that he had lost too many men, their khan ordered the encampment struck and the Avars headed home.

During this period of Avar ascendance they had subjected the neighboring Bulgars. After 634, however, they were no longer able to control these people, who began to go their own way. The Avars were therefore no longer so powerful, albeit they were still formidable. The Franks judged their struggle against them as the most important after that with the Saxons.

In Charlemagne's reign, there were numerous Avar raids into the Frankish kingdom. In 788 three battles were fought with them in Italy, and in that year Charlemagne oversaw the organization of his Bavarian borders to be sure that the Avars could be repulsed. In 790 the Avars sent ambassadors to Charlemagne's court in Aachen to cavil over their border along the River Enns (today in central Austria). By the following year this dispute had erupted into war.

Charlemagne's army was not built upon the "Hunnish" model. Still, it showed steppe influence: its great strength was in the knight, the heavily armored horseman who fought with lance and sword, and who recalled the Goth and the Sarmatian. In response to Viking raids in the west and Avar raids from the east, the Franks had come to rely more and more upon horsemen because the traditional Frankish infantry could not move fast enough to deal with either of these raiders. On balance, the light horseman would still have had the advantage over the heavy one in maneuverability and speed, yet in hilly or forested areas where there was less chance to use these advantages, the heavy knight might have been adequate to the task of dealing with the light one, at least if he were present in sufficient numbers.

Charlemagne gathered an army of Franks, Saxons and Frisian subjects and marched along both sides of the River Enns with boats between them until they reached the confluence of the Enns and Kamp. It was here that the Avars had built a fort, the Cumeoberg. The Royal Frankish Chronicle records a bloodless victory, stating that the Avars were taken by fear upon seeing the Frankish army, and that they fled, abandoning their fort. If true, it would appear that in this instance the Avars had entertained a Western approach to fighting, but in the end did not wish to engage in hand-to-hand combat from a fixed position. Perhaps it was too unfamiliar to them.

The war between the Franks and Avars lasted eight years and was brought to an end by two expeditions into the Avar country itself. It was an opportune time for such forays because the Avar khan had been fighting with his own nobility and was not able to resist effectively. The internal instability common to steppe peoples was indeed evident.

Duke Eric of Friuli, one of Charlemagne's vassals, sent a Lombard army under the command of a Slav named Wonimir against the barbarians. Wonimir attacked and partly sacked the Ring. The treasure was sent to Charlemagne, who sent much of it to Rome. The Avars apparently made some pledge of submission, although shortly thereafter, in 796, Charlemagne marshaled his army against them again because they had not honored this pledge. The king himself marched through Saxony while his son Pepin went straight into Pannonia. Charlemagne was still on the march when he learned that Pepin had taken the Ring. The treasure taken this time was enormous, part of a hoard gathered from over two hundred years' raiding. The Avars were brought to heel and declared themselves Charlemagne's subjects. Their two-centuries-long reign of plundering was over.

With the decline of the Avars the Bulgars rose to some prominence. In 824 the Frankish king Louis the Pius received the first embassy from them. Part of these people had remained on the steppe to establish the state of "Great," or "Black," Bulgaria, which prospered until it was destroyed by the Mongols in the thirteenth century. Other Bulgars moved west where they were subject to the Avars until 634, at which time they achieved freedom under their leader Cubrat.

Eventually these Bulgars crossed the Danube in the late seventh century under Khan Asparukh and settled in the old Roman province of Moesia, establishing the Bulgarian kingdom of "White," or "Little," Bulgaria, the precursor of the modern Bulgarian nation. These people had crossed the Danube in 679 at a time when the Byzantine Emperor Justinian II was busied with a civil war, so he bought peace by acquiescing in their territorial acquisition.

Kept from expanding east by the Magyars (another steppe people who would soon press west) and from the west by the Frankish Kingdom, the Bulgars turned their attention toward Byzantium. In 762 they marched against Constantinople as the Avars had done before them, but were defeated by Constantine V on June 30. Fifty years later a second Byzantine emperor was not as successful.

In 811 Nicephorus I marched against them, advancing into Bulgaria itself where he burned the capital, which was probably no more than a permanent encampment of timbers. The army looted it nonetheless for two days. It was perhaps the distraction of plunder that allowed the Bulgars, who had recovered from the shock of their initial defeat, to storm the Byzantine camp, where they killed Nicephorus and a number of his officials. The emperor's skull was made into a goblet in the ancient Scythian fashion, and was gilded. The Bulgars followed this success in 813 with an assault on Constantinople under Khan Krum, though they were no more successful against its massive walls than anyone before them.

The Bulgars were finally broken as a military threat by Basil II who, after he had defeated them, took the prisoners and blinded all but every hundredth man. These he deprived of one eye and they were obliged to lead their blind fellows back to Bulgaria. It is said that upon seeing this grisly spectacle their khan sickened and died.

Khan Omertag made peace and, subject to increasing Slavic influences, the Bulgars became Christians under their king Boris. They not only adopted Christianity, but from their numerous Slavic subjects they took their language. As always with steppe people, cultural assimilation removed much of their threat.

The Bulgars were followed by worse, however. The Bulgar incursions had been damaging but were fortunately of a rather narrow scope. This was not to be the case with the Magyars—or Hungarians—the last steppe people to settle in the Hungarian plain. They were distinguished from the majority of steppe peoples in that they did not speak a Turkic or Mongol language. Instead, their speech belongs to the Finno-Ugric language group and is related to Finnish. It does however have certain affinities with Turkish, which leads many to think that they were at one time a Finnic group ruled by a Turkic aristocracy. Certain of their goods seemed Turkish and certainly their method of warfare—mounted archery—is consistent with this. Furthermore, Byzantine court etiquette required that Magyar chiefs be referred to as "Turkish princes."

The Magyars were clients of the Khazars, a powerful Turkic people who remained on the steppe. All the same, they were subject to pressure from the Petchenegs, yet another Turkic people who ruled the Russian steppe at that time, and they were forced to leave it, heading, as so many others before them, to the west. It was the Khazars, however, who had assigned a chief to the Magyars: Arpad of the Turkic Khabar tribe. The Arpads became the royal family of Hungary.

As had happened frequently with nomads in the past, they were engaged by a settled people to fight for them. In this case the Byzantine emperor Leo VI was at war with the Bulgars and asked the Magyars to join him. They obliged by ravaging Bulgaria. The Bulgars in turn asked for help from the Petchenegs, who attacked the Magyars from the east; the Magyars fled to the Transylvanian mountains where they were called upon once again to fight. In this case the German King Arnulf was at war with Sviatopolk, King of Great Moravia, whose territories included what is now western Hungary. The Magyars were willing to oblige and utterly destroyed Sviatopolk in 895. In 899 they settled down in this territory and used it as a base for raiding much of Europe for the next half-century.

That very year the Magyars made a major raid into northern Italy, sweeping as far south as Pavia. The raid and the Italian response illustrate steppe strategy quite well. Learning of the raid, the Italian king, Berenger I, called out the feudal levy. The numbers given for his forces are confused, but they suggest that the Italians outnumbered the Magyars, though to what degree is uncertain. Certainly Berenger's force was not large, nor could it have been. Feudal armies of the period relied almost entirely on land tenure for mounted soldiers and this does not turn out large numbers of men.

Even Charlemagne, whose kingdom was vast, probably never fielded an army of more than ten thousand. Berenger's must have been
much smaller, and of that force only the mounted men could have
engaged in the pursuit of the Magyars, for that is what they did; they
chased the barbarians for one hundred forty miles—with disastrous
results.

The Italians first pursued the Magyars to the Adda (north of the
Po) which they crossed, apparently losing a number of men to
drowning. The Magyars then sought a parley and offered to give up
their loot if they were permitted to return home. The Italians were
confident and refused the offer. Flight and pursuit began once more
until, in the neighborhood of Verona, the Italian advance guard and
the Magyar rear engaged each other. The Magyars appeared to have
the upper hand, but broke off the fight when the Italian king and his
company appeared.

The flight and pursuit now resumed for another thirty-five miles
to the Brenta, which the Magyars crossed. They parleyed with the
Italians again, but their offers were declined. It is unlikely that this
disconcerted the Magyars for they probably had never negotiated in
good faith—they were playing with the Italians. Whereas Berenger
and his men were confident, they had been drawn a great distance
from home, lulled by talks that led them to think their enemies were
desperate. Meanwhile, the Magyars had been able to rest their horses during the parleys.

The Italians were camped on the west bank of the Brenta when,
on September 24, the Magyars crossed the river in a rush and
attacked the unprepared Italian battle line. The Italians were routed
and chased some distance while the Magyars ran them down. What
the Italians had thought was a Magyar defeat was really a long-
drawn battle which they had lost. Steppe tactics were utterly
unknown to these early Italians and they suffered badly for it.

Things continued apace for the Magyars. In 910 they defeated
the army of the German Ludwig the Child, whose divisions were
beaten in detail before they could join one another. The king's own
division suffered from the steppe ruse of the feigned retreat: the
Magyars met the Germans and then fled as if defeated after the initial engagement. A number of Magyars, however, were hidden in
ambush, and when the enemy had become disordered in pursuit

these attacked the knights' flanks and rear while their fellows who were leading the chase turned about and faced them in front, thus defeating them.

In 919 the Magyars struck west into the Lorraine. Then in 924 they returned to Italy and burned Pavia. They also attacked the Frankish kingdoms of Burgundy and Provence. In 926 they returned to France and struck Champagne. This was followed by another raid on France in 937, during which they attacked and looted the neighborhoods of Rheims, Sens and Berry. They raided again in 954: the Lorraine, Champagne and Burgundy. Indeed, they must have seemed worse than Huns.

As though Magyar raids from the east were not horrific enough to the young nation of France, it was plagued as well by Viking incursions along the coasts and up the rivers into its countryside. These pressures from both sea raiders and steppe raiders such as the Magyars hastened the development of that most characteristic feature of European society: feudalism. The decline and final disappearance of Roman power in the West led not only to a lack of security and the disintegration of the continent into a number of states, but to the disappearance of money as well, and this exacerbated the weakness of the medieval economies, which then had to operate through barter and taxation in kind. Soldiers were, as always, an expensive proposition, but the lack of a money economy made it difficult both to raise taxes and to build up capital from which armies could be paid. The solution taken was reasonable, if subject to certain drawbacks: land was given to soldiers instead of money.

The sovereign would keep knights in his household whom he supported, but he would distribute large tracts of land to his nobles, who in consequence were obliged, when called, to come to war in aid of their king. The nobles themselves retained knights in their households, or doled out land to individual knights in grants called "fees." The fee was sufficient to feed, house and equip the knight and his horse and he would have any necessary tenants to work the land for him while he, in theory, was to keep himself prepared for war, practicing mounted combat. Church lands were subject to the same obligations; in time of war a bishop or an abbot, just like a lay noble, was obliged to furnish his king with an agreed number of knights.

Under this system the king could call upon his knights for service, and he could call upon his nobles and the churchmen to turn out with their knights for a specified amount of service at their own expense each year, often no more than forty days. The king might be able to oblige them to serve longer but he would then have to pay them. The grants, or fees, were generally hereditary, a military obligation passing from father to son. As might be expected, in time the knights became a form of minor nobility.

The advantages to the king were clear: he could raise an army of mounted men who were possessed of some training and who were adequately equipped for their tasks—and all without any cash outlay. As mounted men they were more effective in dealing with raiders such as Magyars or Vikings than were foot soldiers, who could not catch them before they disappeared on horseback or aboard their longships.

The disadvantages, however, are equally clear: the nobles and knights (except for those of the king's own household) could not be compelled to serve very long. Any army collected from such disparate elements was not used to operating together and so could only exhibit the most rudimentary tactics. Furthermore, the nobles each had followings of knights beholden to them, so they could easily dispute and contend with the king, giving rise to serious internal problems or complicating the conduct of a war. The arrangement was not efficient from the standpoint of numbers either: while a feudal monarch could raise a number of mounted soldiers for a campaign, he could not raise many of them. Distributing land to support soldiers meant that large tracts of territory supported relatively small numbers of men. All of this naturally encouraged kings to hire mercenaries when they could afford it, though it was not until much later—when trade had recovered and money was to be had—that this could be done on any regular basis. Still, it was a solution of sorts and its offspring, the mounted knight, really came into his own against the Magyar horse archer and the Norse raider.

Another direct result of Magyar raids was the castellation of the eastern German frontiers with Hungary. Over time, castles began to dot the borders and command those areas over which the steppe warriors had been accustomed to sweep. Without any siegecraft they could not reduce the strong places, but leaving them intact meant that forces of knights could pursue them or wait to fall upon them during the raiders' retreats when they were burdened with loot. The Germans were steadily closing off their borders to Magyar raids, and these horse warriors knew it. Accordingly, they seem to have decided upon one last great raid—to be carried out in 955.

In the summer of that year the Magyars invaded the kingdom of Germania and its sovereign, Otto I, hurriedly mustered what forces he could to march against them. In this instance the Magyars would do something atypical, something they were not suited to: they would lay siege to a city, Augsburg, built in a corner formed by the confluence of the Lech and Wertach rivers. This novel activity probably reflects the Magyars' understanding that, as the country had become more fortified, they would have to deal with city walls, even if they were not really skilled at it.

The siege did not last long before the arrival of the king and his army; it was perhaps as short as two days.[5] This would imply that King Otto was gathering his forces before the Magyars had settled around the town. During this time the defense of Augsburg was in the hands of its bishop, Ulrich, who bravely led sallies out against the enemy.

Otto's army was said to number eight thousand, which is quite possible, and it consisted mostly of Bavarians, Swabians, Saxons, Thuringians, Franconians, Bohemians and the king's retinue, all equally divided into eight divisions. Otto cleverly made an indirect march on Augsburg from the north or northwest with a view to keeping his army between the Magyars and the roads leading to Hungary, thereby impeding any flight. This was of great importance because the heavy German knights in chainmail coats and iron helmets, carrying large shields and heavy lances, rode weighty horses and could not hope to catch the Magyar horse archers if they had a clear field to run. Thus Otto's army probably marched to the north of Augsburg and down the east bank of the Lech to block the Magyar retreat.

The Magyars did not trouble Otto as he established a camp across the river. However, when they realized he was there they left off the siege and crossed the Lech in a rush to engage the Germans. The German army was arranged in one line; from the left were the two Swabian divisions and then Otto's own, and the Thuringians and Saxons. These were followed by three Bavarian divisions and a division of Franconians under the command of Duke Konrad. The Bohemians were left to guard the baggage.

The Magyars crossed the river more quickly than expected and headed straight for the German line. This attack, however, was merely intended to hold Otto's army fast while a second Magyar force swept around and attacked the Bohemians at the baggage train, which must have been near the German left wing because it became disordered as a consequence. King Otto ordered Duke Konrad to lead the Franconians from their postion on the extreme right and pass behind the German line to help the Swabians on the left. The Duke carried out the maneuver and crushed the Magyars at the baggage train; they fled to their main body, which became disheartened at the failure of their sweep. Otto then commanded a general advance.

The Magyars did not wish to close with the heavily equipped Germans and so pulled back with the knights in pursuit. Some Magyars tried to cross back across the Lech, but found it difficult as the west bank was high, and many drowned. Others raced along the Lech with the knights after them, searching for other places to cross. Again, many were killed by the knights or were driven fatally into the river by the press of their fellows. Finally, because of Otto's position, the defeated Magyars could not take a direct route home and many were killed by peasants in the countryside as they attempted to get back to Hungary.

The Battle on the Lechfeld stopped Magyar raiding and it was followed soon enough by the conversion of the Magyars, or Hungarians as they came to be known, to Christianity. As with the Bulgars before them, their entry into the mainstream of European culture did as much as anything to curb their predatory tendencies. However, three hundred years later, as a settled European nation, the Hungarians would bear the brunt of the last and most dangerous incursion from the steppes.

NOTES
1. Byzantine Emperor Maurice, *Strategikon: A Handbook of Byzantine Military Strategy*, trans. G.T. Dennis, Philadelphia, University of Pennsylvania Press, 1984, p. 116.

2. Ibid.
3. Ibid., p. 117.
4. Ibid., p. 116.
5. Hans Delbrück, *Medieval Warfare*, 3 vols., trans. W.J. Renfroe, Jr., Lincoln and London, University of Nebraska Press, 1990, Vol. II, chapter. 2.

6

The Seljuks

The next contact between Western knights and steppe warriors took place not on the edges of the steppe, or in Central Europe against steppe warrior-settlers like the Magyars, but on the plains and valleys of the Holy Land, amid its ancient cities. It was there that Western invaders—the Crusaders—encountered the Turkish horse archers of the Seljuk Emirs of Syria, themselves fairly recent conquerors of the area. It was here that that Western fighters met and against all odds established themselves for a hundred years, and it was here that Europeans fought to take land in the possession of nomadic conquerors—a reversal from Europe's previous experience as victim of invasion.

Furthermore, the European knights did better than anyone could reasonably have hoped against nomadic tactics, and better than any Western power was to do again for three hundred years despite every obstacle: small numbers, a complete initial ignorance of the geography, heavy armor and equipment, and tactics designed for fighting similarly fitted Europeans. Like the Sarmatians centuries before, Western knights and mounted men-at-arms (or sergeants) wore complete armor and fought with lance and sword against those they could catch or trap against an obstacle. They were protected with chainmail coats, or hauberks which covered their arms below the elbow and hung down to the knee. Hauberks were often fitted with hoods as well as with a metal cap underneath, or a conical helmet with a nasal worn over the top. Such a helmet was the descendant of the late Roman cavalry helmet, but without cheek plates or neck guard. The knight wore a padded coat called a gambeson to absorb the shock of blows and to prevent the rings of the chainmail from being driven into his flesh by a weapon stroke. His armor was completed with a kite-shaped shield whose tapering shape covered the left leg as he rode. He was very well protected and because stirrups had been in use for several hundred years he now usually charged with the lance couched beneath his arm to transmit the weight of the rider and the force of his mount against his target.

Furthermore, the anarchy in which much of Europe found itself had resulted in greater militarization than was the case in the Muslim world or in the Far East, and this showed itself both in a great deal of castellation not only along the borders of European states, but also in their interiors. And this militarized society produced a large number of skilled fighters, particularly knights and sergeants who were willing to go abroad.[1]

Still, the Western knightly armies were not well suited to the task of grappling with the Turkic armies they encountered in the Near East: the knights were slower, less agile, unused to fighting as an army and often unable to come to grips with the enemy. After initial successes, the Crusaders found it better to hold the land they won, as they did in Europe, by castles and strong places rather than through pitched battles.

This is not a detailed or even cursory discussion of the Crusades, their aims or their effect. Instead this chapter focuses only on their military aspects, as shown by a handful of representative battles and the nomadic tactics of the Turkish response—such battles as Dorylaeum, Antioch, Arsuf and Hattin.

The Turks who faced the crusaders were Seljuks, a tribe related to the Oghuz or Ghuz. These Turks were also related to the Kipchaks who were settling southern Russia, displacing the Petchenegs. As was often the case with steppe nomads, the Turks took their name from a chief, one Seljuk, who separated them from the Oghuz. The Oghuz themselves became known as Turkmen or Turcoman; they were another example of the fluid nature of nomad states which easily dissolved and reformed into new tribes not much different from their predecessors.

The Seljuks began their rise to prominence after the collapse of the ruling Samanid dynasty of Transoxiana. The Samanids had asked for Seljuk assistance against the Karakhanid Turks of Issykkul and Kashgaria and paid the common price for inviting nomadic military support: the Seljuks swept across their territory. The Seljuks under Toghrul-beg next defeated the Ghaznavid rulers of eastern Persia at Dandanaqan on May 22, 1040. Seljuk conquests were slowed, however, by the usual nomad ineptitude at taking cities; still, Toghrul-beg went on to take the rest of Persia and, in 1055, the city of Baghdad, where the Caliph bestowed upon him the title of "King of East and West." The Seljuks now controlled Transoxiana and all of Persia. They were to do even better under Toghrul-beg's nephew, Alp Arslan ibn Chagri-beg (1063-1072), who would deal the Byzantine Empire a blow from which it would never recover.

The Byzantine Empire had lost much of its territory to the Arabs and their Muslim coreligionists during the course of the seventh and eighth centuries; all of North Africa and Egypt were lost as well as Syria. The Muslims controlled Sicily, and Spain was riddled with Islamic kingdoms. Byzantium stood as the easternmost bastion of Christianity against the Muslim world, though its sway on the Asiatic side of the Hellespont was limited to Anatolia (modern Turkey) and Armenia. Still, these were extremely important territories and the source of many recruits for the East Roman army. The Seljuks, now Muslim, raided the eastern provinces (divided into military districts called themes) and had become a cause of concern to the Byzantines.

In 1071, Romanus Diogenes had risen to the throne through marriage to Eudocia, widow of Emperor Constantine XI. He was not well liked (as he was aware), and was impetuous, although he had had some military success. It seemed to Romanus that the way to stabilize his throne was to deal the Seljuks a hard blow, and he had in fact defeated Alp Arslan earlier. So in the spring of 1071 he mustered a very large army, said to have numbered sixty thousand (though probably not half of that), and set out to meet the Seljuks on the eastern frontier. His excuse was the Turkish seizure of a pair of fortresses in Armenia: Akhlat and Manzikert. Romanus retook Manzikert and laid siege to Akhlat when he learned that a large Seljuk army was approaching. It has been claimed that the Seljuks numbered one hundred thousand, but again this must be an exaggeration. Still, they were a significant force, which probably numbered twenty to thirty thousand like the Byzantines themselves.

Contact began, predictably enough, with trickery. When a party of Turkish scouts was seen reconnoitering the Byzantines, Basilakes, commander of the Theodosipolitan theme, or military commandery, charged and hotly pursued the handful of Turks until his troop was ambushed, then killed or taken prisoner. Romanus sent a column in support, but they only found corpses. He prepared for a battle.

Romanus drew up his army in two lines. The front was of cavalry from the various themes. He himself rode in the middle with his guards and metropolitan provincial troops. The second line consisted of foreign mercenary cavalry such as Germans, Normans from Italy and troops from the eastern borders belonging to the marcher lords whose territories lay along the frontier. The horsemen were probably largely armored as the Byzantine cavalry had been from the fifth century onward, and they were equipped with lances and broadswords. It seems, however, that fewer of them carried bows or fought as mounted archers than had been previously the case; because of internal political wrangling at Constantinople the army had declined in quality and the bow appears to have fallen out of favor as a horseman's weapon.

The mercenary horsemen fought, of course, as conventional Western armored knights. This second line, meant to function as a reserve, was under the command of Andronicus Ducas, a relation of Romanus's predecessor, Constantine XI. Unknown to the new emperor, Ducas was his enemy.

Alp Arslan offered to withdraw instead of fight, but the emperor refused the offer, which he probably did not regard as legitimate; and he may have been right to doubt the offer. Negotiations for the purpose of delay or confusion were a common steppe device: the Magyars had gulled the Italians two hundred years before with such offers, only to attack them when they were unprepared.

The Battle of Manzikert began as numbers of Turks rode about the Byzantine line shooting arrows but never closing. After some time Romanus ordered an advance along the line with the reserves in the second line following. The Turks fell back before the advance and declined to come to grips with the Byzantines, so that the advance went on for several hours without much harm to the Turks. As the evening came on, Romanus commanded his tired army to turn about and return to camp. The army's center obeyed, but the wings did not receive the order timely and, when they did, failed to keep formation. Breaks appeared in the line. The Turks closed back in and began to harass the retreating Byzantines, so much so that Romanus ordered the line to turn about, threaten the Turks and drive them away. Andronicus Ducas, in charge of the second line, now saw his chance at betrayal. Instead of stopping and facing the enemy as ordered, he led the second line back to the camp, abandoning the emperor and half of the army to its fate.

The Turks took full advantage of the reserve's disappearance to surround those who remained. Enveloped by the Seljuk horse archers, the emperor's right wing tried to face both ways, fell apart— and then ran. The Turks then concentrated on the center, where the emperor fought hard but was finally captured. The left wing was chased off the battlefield.

With this one battle a great army was destroyed and all of Anatolia lost forever. Byzantium was weakened, and, while it would last another four centuries, it would never recover its earlier strength.

Alp Arslan was killed in 1072 fighting to seize Transoxiana and was succeeded by his nephew Malikshah, who ruled for twenty years. Despite this territorial acquisition, however, the Seljuk Empire was already dissolving into smaller states. Malikshah ruled Persia proper, but controlled no other areas, and upon his death in 1092 the Seljuk realm broke up further. It was this fragmentation that would allow the Europeans to establish themselves in Syria and southern Anatolia. Furthermore, these antagonistic states were ruled by Turks with a problem new to the steppe warrior: how to hold cities and territory. In other words, the Seljuks, though they might continue to use steppe tactics, could no longer use steppe strategy. They could not, for instance, simply retreat before an enemy until he was exhausted. They could not indefinitely avoid a fight until it suited them, and this, along with their internal divisions and the geography of the Middle East, gave the Crusaders enough of an advantage against them to be able for a time to achieve something.

Although accompanied by pilgrims who might fight, the strength of the armies of the First Crusade, in 1096, lay almost wholly in the knights, the sergeants, both mounted and foot, and the infantry. The mounted sergeants as already noted, were those men who, while not knights, were equipped like knights and fought like them. Their equipment might be somewhat lighter or less complete, but they were expected to fight hand-to-hand with lance and sword. The foot sergeants were simply professional foot soldiers. Most of the infantry was armed with the spear, though many were crossbowmen, and these would prove the most important of the footsoldiers. From a larger perspective, however, Crusader armies were not very promising. As British military historian Charles Oman remarked: "The first crusading armies displayed all the faults of the feudal host in their highest development."[2] He elaborated, noting that they were led by no king or emperor who might exact obedience; on the contrary, the dukes and counts who led their troops from Europe were all free agents, hardly a status conducive to cooperation and discipline—and they were completely ignorant of the military methods of their opponents. It was only by chance that their first encounters with the Turks went well.

The Crusaders gathered outside of Constantinople in 1096 and in May 1097 were ferried across to the Asian bank of the Hellespont by Alexius Comnenus, the Byzantine emperor. The predominantly French army was led by Hugh, Count of Vermandois (and brother of the French king), Count Raymond IV of Toulouse, Duke Godfrey of Bouillon, the Sicilian-Norman lords Bohemund and Tancred, Duke Robert II of Normandy, Count Robert of Flanders and Count Stephen of Blois. These men had managed to take the city of Nicaea and prevent Turkish efforts at its relief. The Crusaders' next move was to march directly into the Seljuk kingdom of Iconium, or central Anatolia, on an out-of-the-way march to Antioch in Syria. The march began on June 27, along a Roman road that led eventually to Tarsus (Saint Paul's birthplace) in Cilicia. For some reason, possibly a lack of forage or possibly recklessness, the Crusader army broke into two divisions marching parallel to each other about seven miles apart. Bad as this was, they compounded their folly by not taking the elementary precaution of keeping in communication. One division comprised Godfrey, Raymond and Hugh with their men, while the second was made up of Bohemund and Tancred, the two Roberts and Stephen with their troops. These divisions probably comprised similar troops and were likely of about the same size, though precise figures are difficult to assess.

The columns marched through a wasteland, passed through forested mountains in Bithynia and came out onto a plain across which they proceeded. The division under Bohemund and his fellows seems to have come out of the mountains first and they began to find themselves harried by Turkish horse archers. On June 30 Bohemund's column camped near the ruined town of Dorylaeum in central Anatolia, then resumed its advance the following day. After marching a short distance the Crusaders' scouts reported a large Turkish army advancing on them. Bohemund sent messengers to find Godfrey, Raymond and the other column. He then ordered the baggage to be taken down and the foot soldiers to make camp since he judged them—in typical medieval fashion—to be essentially ineffective. The camp was to be placed near swampy ground that might offer some protection, but while it was being set up and as the horsemen deployed the Turks appeared, encircling the Crusaders and shooting at them. The writer of the *Gesta Francorum*, who was present, said: "After we had set ourselves in order the Turks came upon us from all sides, skirmishing, throwing darts and javelins and shooting arrows from an astonishing range."[3] This Turkish army was commanded by Sultan Kilij-Arslan Ibn Suleiman himself. The effect of this novel (to the Crusaders) form of warfare, drove the knights back upon the foot soldiers. The French priest Fulcher (Foucher), later chaplain of Baldwin, King of Jerusalem, and also an eyewitness, said:

> Meanwhile the Turks were howling like wolves and furiously shooting a cloud of arrows. We were stunned by this. Since we faced death and since many of us were wounded we soon took to flight. Nor is this remarkable because to all of us such warfare was unknown.[4]

The Crusaders, both knights and footmen, were thus pressed into a mass into which the Turks shot as they hemmed the Europeans in on all sides. The knights' armor was fortunately effective against the Turkish arrows, for they suffered showers of arrows for five or six hours. Their horses were not armored, however, and more of these were killed than men. Still, the Crusaders would only have grown more and more demoralized at taking such punishment passively, and they would surely have broken had it continued much longer; thereupon a rout and slaughter would have followed as the Turks closed. But Bohemund was lucky.

The messengers he had sent out hours before had finally managed to find the other division of Crusaders, encamped six or seven miles away. The horsemen of the column, under Godfrey of Bouillon, raced off to the rescue of Bohemund's division and met no opposition for, amazingly, the Sultan had either failed to discover them or had reckoned they were not a threat. Godfrey and his followers topped a rise and found themselves looking down on the Turkish left flank and rear. They charged the enemy's flank and surprised the Turks, who dashed off, leaving Godfrey and his men an opportunity to attack the rear of the Turkish center. Other bands of knights topped the rise and followed, charging the disordered Turks, who fled without fighting. It was, against all rights, a Crusader victory; the Crusaders had won Dorylaeum by luck in spite of gross mistakes and complete ignorance of their enemy. Had the Turks reconnoitered, Godfrey could not have worked such a rescue.

Undeserved as it was, Dorylaeum shook the Turks and opened the way to Antioch which the Crusaders took, through the treachery of one of its inhabitants, after a siege of several weeks during which hunger affected the besiegers as much as the besieged. It is claimed that only seven hundred Crusader horses remained fit for service, and while this is another exaggeration, many of the knights did lose their mounts. During the siege the Crusaders repulsed two Seljuk efforts to relieve Antioch. The Turkish failures were due, in part, to the unsuitability of the terrain. During their first attempt the Turks allowed themselves to be caught in a defile from which they could not evade the heavy Crusader knights, while their second found them caught against the Orontes, which flowed along Antioch's north wall. With the Seljuks trapped against the river, the Crusaders forced them to receive a devastating charge.

The Crusaders had done well, but their successes were less a tribute to their tactics than an indictment of Turkish carelessness in throwing away one of their greatest assets: mobility. The Turks would eventually learn that the Crusader knights were suited to a single tactic: the charge. Furthermore, it was a charge from which the knights could not recover; unlike modern cavalry, which is trained to regroup afterward (as steppe warriors did naturally), a knightly charge would disintegrate after contact with the enemy, and the horsemen, while they might engage in individual combats, could not function further as a unit. In short, knights were not true cavalry in spite of superficial resemblances. Turkish horsemen soon learned to await the crusader charge, to disperse before it, and then regroup after the knights had lost their cohesion and impetus. But they had not learned this yet.

Antioch fell on June 3, 1098, and the Crusaders installed themselves in the city. However, their situation was not greatly improved because the city had few supplies left after the long siege, and hunger continued to be a factor. Furthermore, the Turkish commander Karbuqa was advancing upon them at the head of a large army. After three weeks in the city, the Europeans decided to sally out upon Karbuqa since delay meant only the loss of more horses. In spite of the chroniclers' statements, the Crusaders probably still had twenty-five hundred to three thousand fit horses while, of equal value to the Crusaders though they did not know it, was Turkish dissension—which would soon cause them severe problems. The Crusaders, of course, were unified in their danger and were further encouraged by their discovery of what they believed was the actual lance that had pierced Christ's side on the cross. They prepared to use the holy lance as a standard.

The Orontes flowed along the northern edge of Antioch and a gate opened from the northern city wall onto a bridge across the river. The Crusaders mustered their forces in the street just inside the gate and prepared to march out. The men were divided into a number of bodies of horse and foot together. The number of these "brigades" is uncertain; there may have been about a dozen and they were commanded by Bishop Adhemar, Count Hugh, Bohemund and Godfrey of Bouillon—who, after the fall of Jerusalem in 1099, would be elected "Baron and Defender of the Holy Sepulcher."

Antioch was the first considered use, in a medieval European army, of horse and foot to support each other in something of a combined-arms approach. The decision was the product of necessity: many knights had lost their horses and by far the greater part of the army were foot soldiers. Nevertheless, it would soon become something of a standard approach in meeting the Turks; the dismounted knights, as seasoned fighters, could steady the foot soldiers. Despite this, the most important among the Crusaders were the crossbow-men and archers because their weapons could shoot further than a horse archer's bow. In particular the crossbow—spanned with both arms and shooting a heavier and more aerodynamic projectile—was dangerous to such a large target as a mounted man.

The Crusaders marched out of the city a brigade at a time, the infantry marching first and the cavalry following. The first brigade advanced over the Orontes bridge and, once across the river, faced right, toward the east where the Turks were arrayed. The second brigade followed, crossing behind the first, and then, once past, it too faced east. The remainder of the brigades were to follow suit save for a reserve under Bohemund, which kept back from the bat-tle line.

Karbuqa allowed all of the Crusader army to leave the city unhindered. It is unclear why he did not attack the Christians as they came off the bridge, or why he did not attack after only a portion of the troops had sallied out. Had he done so he would have outnum-bered them greatly and driven them against the river and upon the bridge, where they would have fallen into disorder and been cut down. That part of the Crusader army remaining within the city walls would have been sufficiently reduced in number to cease being a threat and would soon have succumbed to starvation if not assault. Possibly Karbuqa did not realize how many Crusaders there were. He is supposed to have claimed he wanted all of the Crusaders out on the plain so that he might destroy the entire invading force at once. However that may be, he was dismayed when he grasped their numbers.

Dismayed or not, Karbuqa sent a strong contingent around the Crusaders' left wing to threaten their rear from the southwest. These troops are said to have numbered fifteen thousand (another exag-geration), and were under Kilij-Arslan of Rum and Ridwan of Aleppo. They managed to sweep around the extreme northern end of the Crusader line, at the foot of some hills, and engaged the troops under Bishop Adhemar, who were the last troops to emerge from Antioch, and were trying to take position at the extreme left of the Crusader line. The Bishop's men did manage to fight their way into line and this effectively separated the attacking Turkish flankers from Karbuqa's main army. Bohemund then led the reserves against these Turks while the balance of the Christian army fought Karbuqa's main forces. Unhappily for Karbuqa, his Turcoman troops had been induced to betray him by Ridwan of Aleppo; they fled and disordered the line. The rest of the Turks pulled back to their camp and re-formed, but they had no room for maneuver as the Crusaders now had control of the plain. The knights attacked them again and the Turks fled. Those Turks fighting Bohemund's reserves did the same when they learned of the fate of the rest of their army.

Again, the Crusaders had won a victory that, from an objective viewpoint, seemed unlikely. In this case they did not blunder as they had done at Dorylaeum, but they had certainly profited from Karbuqa's bad judgment and the discord of the Turkish allies.

Meanwhile some of the Crusaders were learning that while it was the knight who won battles, it was the foot soldiers who furnished the support and protection they needed until that single, decisive charge. The foot soldiers, and particularly the crossbowmen, worked to keep the horse archers at sufficient distance to reduce the effect of their archery, in effect protecting the knights until they could attack. If the Turks charged in at the foot soldiers with lance and sword, then the knights could, in their turn, chase them off. However, this was not a magic formula; horse archery and dispersal before a charge were still effective, especially against any who were unwary.

The Crusaders, after their initial victories, had established themselves in a series of small states such as the Kingdom of Jerusalem, the counties of Edessa and Tripoli and the principality of Antioch. Chronically short of soldiers, the territories of these states suffered constant Muslim pressure. The Crusaders did not always charge to victory, but on the contrary suffered many defeats, settling instead for a defensive policy of holding territory through castles and garrisons rather than in the field. A single significant defeat, they knew, could harm them irreparably because there simply were not many of them. This was illustrated starkly, a hundred years after the chance victories of Dorylaeum and Antioch.

By this time the Kurd Salah-al-Din Yusuf ibn-Ayyub had came to power as successor of his uncle, Shirkuh, and ruled as Sultan of

Egypt and Syria; he is better known in the West as Saladin (1138–1193). A devout Muslim, he set himself the task of reducing the Crusader principalities and he was well situated to do so: Egypt was a wealthy state with a large army which, with the addition of Turkish forces, was now more effective than it had been earlier. Traditionally the Egyptians had fought mounted, as did the Arabs, but they were not horse archers. Centuries of conflict with Byzantium had caused them to employ a combination of mailed lancers not unlike the Byzantine heavy cavalry, with foot archers in support. The Crusaders had found that Egyptian horsemen, as a rule, could not stand up to the Western charge, however, and their archers were then easily dispersed as had happened at the Battle of Ashkelon (Ascalon) in 1099. There, Godfrey and Tancred had crushed an Egyptian army that had been intent on retaking Jerusalem.

As a result, the Crusaders had less regard for the Egyptians than for the Turks, although complete disdain for their abilities had resulted in a narrow Crusader victory at Ramleh in 1102 and a Crusader defeat, again at Ramleh, the following year. Saladin had begun his career in Syria, however, and his army contained great numbers of Turks as well as the usual lancers and infantry archers. In 1187 the crusaders made the terrible mistake of putting themselves into their enemies' hands and exposing themselves to steppe tactics.

In 1187 Saladin continued his campaigning against the Crusader states with a huge army. Again the figures given by historians are doubtless too large, but it must have been a greater army than the Crusader states could field. In June, Saladin advanced against Tiberias, the capital of the principality of Galilee, a city on the shore of the Sea of Galilee. The town surrendered quickly, but the garrison and its Countess Eschive of Tripoli retreated to the citadel and held out. Saladin, who wished to fight the Crusaders, saw to it that she was able to get a message for help out to Guy of Lusignan, the King of Jerusalem.

In response both to this call and to an earlier raid into Galilee that had gone badly for the Knights Templar, the Christians assembled in Sepphoris, a Galilean seat of learning, what was for them an unusually large army of perhaps twelve hundred knights, hundreds of turcopoles (lightly equipped cavalry recruited from among the off-spring of mixed Christian and Muslim marriages) and eighteen thousand infantry. This field army was mustered by dangerously thinning out the garrisons of cities and castles throughout the Crusader-held territories.

There was a good deal of debate about how the army should be used. Raymond of Tripoli, husband of the beleaguered Countess Eschive in Tiberias, wisely argued that it would be foolhardy to advance across the arid territory to Tiberias and then fight the Muslims. Instead, they should await Saladin, who could not, he judged, hold the city indefinitely. The advantage would then be with the Crusaders, who could meet an exhausted enemy. The Templars, by contrast, were aggressive and felt it was better to advance and meet the enemy; after all, the new army was larger than any Crusader army had been in years. King Guy ultimately decided to advance.

On July 3, the army marched out from Sepphoris and, after advancing about ten miles, was surrounded by Turkish mounted bowmen who began to harry the Crusaders with archery. The Crusaders continued their march under this harassment, the head of their column advancing to within three miles of Tiberias and the Sea of Galilee—a destination important not merely because it was held by the enemy, but because the Crusader army was marching over dry terrain and needed water. Unfortunately, even this close to their goal, they were still obliged to cross a range of hills about a thousand feet high, past which they could descend to the lakeshore. Turks were ranged along the crest of the hills to stop them. Count Raymond VI of Toulouse urged King Guy to press on, despite fatigue and danger. There were two passes, either of which would lead them to the shores of the Sea of Galilee, and if they must fight their way through, then so be it.

The Knights Templar, who, with the Hospitallers, formed the rear of the column, had become separated from the rest of the army because Turkish shooting had succeeded in slowing them down and opening a breach. The Templars were concerned that they would be left behind if the rest of the army advanced into a pass. The men were exhausted and thirsty, and there was no water to be had for a distance of three miles. Because of this, King Guy fatally ordered the army to encamp where it stood.

The men sat up throughout the night, thirsty and disheartened, unable to sleep as the Turks shot arrows into their midst and set fire to the dry grass upwind to irritate them further with smoke. When morning came, most of the men, and certainly the infantry, had lost any will to fight. King Guy took up the march again, but this time not toward Tiberias but toward Wadi el Hammam, the northern-most of the passes, and the village of Hattin, where the nearest water was. Saladin's Turks now surrounded the Crusader army and, as the knights advanced, the foot soldiers broke completely, clambering up a pair of hills called the Horns of Hattin. King Guy sent a messenger to them commanding them to descend and fight, but they replied that they could not. Meanwhile, the Templars and Hospitallers in the rear of the column send word to the king that they could no longer advance since they were already too heavily engaged. Again King Guy ordered a halt, unwilling to separate his main force from the men of the military orders, his most elite troops. But the destruction of the army was only a matter of time. Count Raymond declined to sit and wait. Instead he rallied his knights and, in a desperate charge to the hills to the north, he burst through the Turkish mounted archers and escaped.

The Turkish soldiers easily overcame King Guy's foot soldiers on the hills, dispersing them, killing some and taking the rest pris-oner. The king and his remaining knights suffered showers of arrows as they made a stand upon a hill, and they tried twice to charge down and through the Muslims, each time being driven back. After the failure of their second try, the knights dismounted and surren-dered. The King of Jerusalem himself had been taken, and a large Crusader army—such as could not be fielded again—had been destroyed. It was discovered that exhaustion and thirst had done most of the work against the knights; their armor had protected them well against the Turkish arrows.

The results of the Battle of Hattin were grave. As Charles Oman noted:

> The realm had been drained dry of men to supply the army which perished on the hillside of Hattin, and its towns and castles fell helplessly before the Moslem for sheer lack of

defenders. Places that had braved the assaults of the Infidel for eighty years opened their gates at the first summons, because there were none but clerks and women left within them. Jerusalem itself surrendered after a siege of only twelve days.[5]

Richard I of England (1157–1199), "The Lion Hearted," took part in the more international Third Crusade four years later to recapture Jerusalem from Saladin. He was not to recover the city, but perhaps with Hattin in mind he was more careful in his preparations on the march. Nowhere was this more perfectly demonstrated than during his march to Jaffa in 1191. Richard at this time held Acre and wished to retake Jerusalem. Because of the terrain he needed first to get to Jaffa and march from there. From Acre to Jaffa, however, is a march of eighty miles along the coast and the Muslims under Saladin would surely swarm about him throughout the trek. It could easily have been a disaster; instead, it was a tactical masterpiece during which Richard depended heavily upon those foot soldiers armed with the crossbow, a weapon he was partial to. He encouraged its use in the English army and, in fact, he would be killed by a crossbowman in 1199, while besieging a castle in France.

The Turks particularly liked to attack armies on the march, concentrating on the rear of the enemy column. If successful, their arrow showers would slow or halt the rear while the remainder of the column continued to advance, opening a breach which they could exploit—as had happened at the terrible Battle of Hattin.

Richard was thoughtful, however, and devised a clever order of march. As he moved along the coast he had the baggage train move in a column closest to the sea. The foot soldiers marched in a parallel column further from the sea while the knights, in bands, rode between the two columns, they and their horses protected by the foot soldiers on the right flank. The soldiers used crossbows to keep the enemy at a distance and the knights were ready to sally against the Turks if they approached too closely. These three parallel lines marched along the Mediterranean coast for nineteen days, taking the journey in easy stages and often resting while supplies were unloaded from ships offshore. Although the Turks did their best to harass the Crusaders, they were unable to shake them and remarked that the crossbowmen plodded on, methodically shooting on the march, unconcerned with the Turkish arrows that struck their padded gambesons. These thick garments protected them against Turkish archery, at least at the distance from which the Turks were willing to shoot, and the foot soldiers were often seen with a number of shafts sticking from their backs, walking and shooting.

The march began on August 22, 1191, and ended on September 10 at Jaffa. On the seventh, however, as the Crusaders approached the town of Arsuf, Saladin made a concerted attack on the column, personally joining the skirmishers and urging them closer so that they could better down the knights' horses. Meanwhile, Richard had commanded that a charge be made upon his order alone; but the Knights Hospitaller who rode, as was customary, in the most dangerous part of the line—the rear—became increasingly frustrated at the loss of their horses and the wounding of their men and, although their request for permission to charge was denied, two of them passed through the infantry at the Muslims, the rest of the Hospitallers following.

The next contingent of knights, the French, followed suit, and all along the line bands of knights charged out from the rear to the head of the column. Despite the spontaneity of the action, it worked as well as a planned attack and had much the same effect that Richard might have expected had the knights waited a bit longer for him to give the signal. Certainly the Muslims thought the attack was carefully planned, and they broke before the charge. The Crusaders did not make the mistake of pursuing them far, only for a mile, and then resumed their places. The Turks regrouped and closed about the Europeans again, and were dispersed by a second charge. They returned once more, were charged once more, and then fled without taking up the fight again.

But for all of Richard's success at Arsuf, Saladin had already irreparably harmed the Crusader states. Their disappearance was only a matter of time.

From a strategic point of view the Crusaders faced the same problem as their opponents—the protection of territory—but they were hampered by a shortage of manpower. The majority of their subjects were Muslim, and there were insufficient numbers of Christians and turcopoles to campaign aggressively. From a tactical standpoint, their methods were inapposite, although they retained them, probably as a matter of custom that was renewed by the influx of knights from Europe with each new Crusade. And they found a method to make their tactics work to some degree: infantry support until the critical moment of the charge, upon which they then gambled everything. The Crusaders did not have the steppe-style facility of maneuver, and while their armor gave them good protection, the Turks' freedom of action inevitably meant that some knights were shot and many horses disabled, leaving them vulnerable to further attrition or an utter rout if the Turks chose to close. In short, when the Seljuks came out of the steppe their tactics had allowed them to arrogate control of much of the Middle East. Only their disunity and occasional mistakes allowed the Europeans to win, for a time, a foothold along the Mediterranean coast northeast of Egypt.

NOTES

1. For a good discussion of this militarized society, see Archibald R. Lewis, *Nomads and Crusaders,* A.D. *1000–1368,* Bloomington, Indiana University Press, 1991, pp. 80–82.
2. C.W.C. Oman, *A History of the Art of War,* New York, G.P. Putnam's, 1898, p. 231.
3. *Gesta Francorum et Aliorum Hierosolimatanorum,* trans. and ed. Rosalind Hill, London, Thomas Nelson and Sons, 1962, p. 19.
4. Fulcher of Chartres, *A History of the Expedition to Jerusalem, 1095–1127,* trans. Frances Rita Ryan, Knoxville, University of Tennessee Press, 1969, I.XI.6, p. 85.
5. Oman, pp. 330–31.

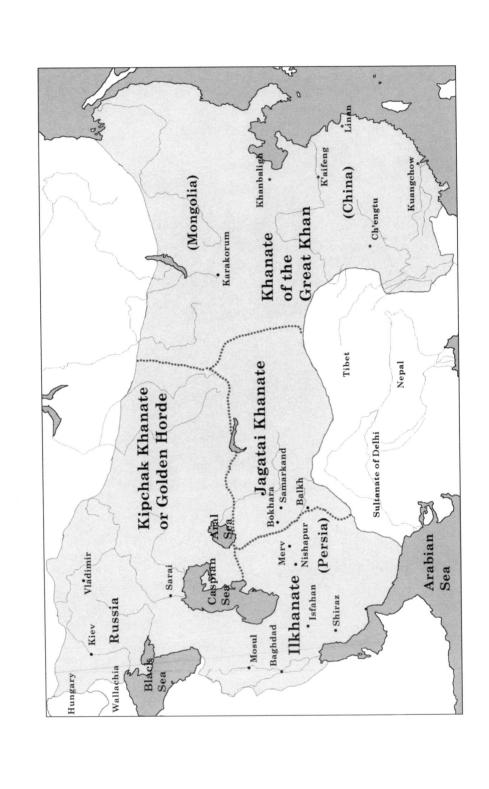

7

The Rise of the Mongols

The Mongols were by far the most successful of the steppe warriors; they created an empire that ultimately included all of Mongolia, China, Korea, Russia, Iran, Iraq, Afghanistan, Transoxiana, Syria and the Caucasus. It is for this, of course, that the expression "Mongol Horde" has passed into popular usage. And yet the Mongols were not so different from other steppe tribesmen. They were almost purely nomadic, they were illiterate, they were arranged in clans and tribes, they revered fire and followed shamans and they fought from horseback with the composite recurved bow using the conventional tactics of the steppe: encirclement, sweeps, feigned retreat and ambush.

In all of these things they were no different than their more numerous cousins the Turks, or their Indo-Aryan predecessors the Scythians. And they were not particularly numerous: in the thirteenth century, at the beginning of their rise to power, they numbered at most a million people. And yet, at the death of Mangu Khan in 1260 they held the largest land empire the world has ever known and it lasted for some three generations—not long by the standards of a settled people but a goodly time for a steppe empire. The question is, quite simply, why were the Mongols so much more successful than any other steppe tribe when, although they possessed the same military advantages over settled people that other steppe tribes did, they certainly do not appear to have had any greater advantages?

The answer to this question is inextricably woven into the history of one man: Chinggis Khan. While it was not solely through his efforts that the Mongols achieved what they did, he was certainly of the right character to play upon the natural advantages accruing to a steppe chieftain and to make the most of the political and military trends on the steppe at that time.

The Mongols proper and related Mongol peoples, the Tatars, Merkits and Naimans, lived on the Mongolian plateau and adjacent territories now part of modern Russia and China. A Mongolian chieftain named Yesugei of the Borjin clan had his encampment near the Onon River. He warred with the Tatar tribe and returned to camp one day, probably in the mid-1160s, with some captives including a Tatar chief. Yesugei's wife, Hoelun, had just born him a son whom he named Temujin after the captured Tatar. Another story suggests that he named the son as he did because of a tradition of ironsmithing in the clan, the word *temur* meaning "iron." This would account for the fact that one of Temujin's brothers was named Temuge while a sister was named Temulun. However this may be, the son would be better known by the title Chinggis Khan, which he assumed at the *khuriltai*, or council, of 1206.

Yesugei, as well as fighting the Tatars, had at one time helped the Kerait chief Toghrul, a Turk, when he had been ousted from power, apparently becoming tied to him with a bond of blood-brotherhood called *anda*, common on the steppe. He also sought an alliance with the Onggirat, a powerful tribe, and therefore set out to find Temujin, then eight or nine years old, a wife. He stopped to visit a certain Daisechen of the Boskur, an Onggirat tribe, and was charmed by his daughter Borte, to whom he succeeded in affiancing his son on condition that Temujin live with Daisechen's family— probably to help pay the high bride price required. Things did not go as planned: on his return Yesugei fell in with some Tatars and joined them for hospitality. He was recognized, however, and his food poisoned. Yesugei was able to reach his encampment, but died there after sending a follower to Daisechen to fetch his son back.

Upon Yesugei's death Temujin watched his father's followers melt away from him. Mongol (and Turkish) social organization was notoriously fluid and a given tribe depended upon the strength of its leader for stability and protection. Steppe nomads willingly joined other leaders whom they regarded as great warriors, and Yesugei's followers were unwilling to remain with the young Temujin and his brothers, who could offer them little in the way of either protection or booty. In fact, however, Yesugei's death, though initially dangerous for Temujin, presented certain advantages for a young noble with ambition. Since political power on the steppe stemmed from the person of individual leaders rather than from established institutions (as with settled peoples), with the death of the leader the power could vanish. Temujin had firsthand experience of this upon the death of his father.

However, even if there were a successful and orderly succession from father to son, or brother to brother, the successor was encumbered with his predecessor's close followers and this put a curb upon his power. Therefore, for a khan to rise to the high station of ruling absolutely—over his own tribe and others—he must needs become an absolute despot, depending upon his own personal followers who were unswervingly true to him. To achieve this he must start with a clean slate; a successor could never do this, and though he might begin higher, he could not, ultimately, rise so high. A corollary to this situation was the tendency to instability among steppe empires. As Joseph Fletcher notes:

> If the empire survived from generation to generation at all, it was because each successor tried not to be a successor in the agrarian empires' sense but rather a refounder. Without a refounder, who—ordinarily by struggle—brought his own personal retainers, administrators, and allies with him rather than inheriting those of his predecessor, it was unlikely that the empire would long endure.[1]

But such concerns were in the future. What immediately followed Yesugei's death were years of extreme hardship as the boy Temujin and his brothers and half-brothers eked out a living on the steppe through hunting marmots, steppe rats and birds and by fishing, held together by the matriarch, Hoelun. At some point, probably when he was about fifteen, Temujin fell into sharp conflict with his two half-brothers, Bekhter and Belgutai. These were Yesugei's sons by another wife and undoubtedly his elder brothers, as they had repeatedly robbed him and his other brothers of game and fish they had taken. In response, Temujin and his younger brother Kasar hunted Bekhter and Belgutai down in order to kill them. Bekhter, the elder of the two, saw what was about to happen and remained seated where he was, offering no resistance. He asked only that his younger brother, Belgutai, be spared. Temujin and Kasar then shot him to death with their bows. Although Bekhter's murder is no doubt supposed to have been justified by his theft, it was in reality a dynastic killing; Temujin, though the eldest son of Yesugei's chief wife, would take no chances in terms of his prospects of controlling the family, even in its present reduced circumstances.

We also see here for the first time a marked characteristic of Temujin: he would act violently for his own advantage, but always upon some moral pretext, often rather slender. The murder had one apparent repercussion: Temujin was taken captive by the Tayi'chiuts as punishment, and kept in the *cangue* (a heavy circular wooden collar which pinioned the hands on either side of the head) for some time. He made his escape with the help of some Tayi'chiut dependents whom he was able to win over by the strength of his personality, already displaying the attraction that would bring and hold followers. These people who had helped him subsequently deserted the Tayi'chiuts to join him.

The details of his captivity and escape are muddled in different sources and this suggests that Temujin was captured more than once, a commonplace on the steppe, where young men were often kidnapped for ransom or to serve as attendants or to settle scores. The obligation to exact vengeance was taken seriously on the steppe and even passed on from generation to generation—something which would affect Temujin later.

When Temujin was old enough to do so he visited Daisechen, to claim his fiancé, Borte. He wedded her and returned to his camp with his bride and the dowry of a sable cloak, a very expensive item indeed. His next step was to seek the protection of a patron, and he determined to join up with Toghrul of the Keraits, whom his father had helped years before. He was accompanied by his brothers and the first of his followers, including Bo'orchu (who had helped him recover stolen horses and would become one of his generals), and a handful of young men who had begun to join him. He also made a present of the sable cloak to Toghrul, reminding him of the service his father had done for him earlier.

Toghrul was delighted at the prospect of another supporter as he sat uneasily on his throne; relatives, including his very son, were maneuvering against him. The relationship was particularly valuable to Temujin who, because he had some personal followers, was able to enter Toghrul's service not as a mere retainer but as a leader himself, or *noyan*. And a noyan of Toghrul might expect to share in his generosity. Toghrul was a vassal of the Chinese and therefore commonly received gifts from them which, as khan, he was expected to divide among his noyans.

Shortly after this, a party of Merkits raided Temujin's camp and abducted his wife in revenge for his father's abduction of Hoelun many years before—Temujin's mother had been affianced to a Merkit before Yesugei stole her away. Temujin went to Toghrul to ask for help and was given it. The khan sent a large force of Kerait and ordered Jamuka, khan of the Jadarats, to contribute an equal number. Jamuka had been a childhood friend of Temujin, in fact his anda, or blood brother. Temujin was thus able to defeat the Merkits and recover Borte. She later gave birth to his eldest son, Juchi, whose paternity therefore was always in doubt, though Temujin never treated him differently than his other offspring.

After the Merkit defeat, Temujin and Jamuka remained extremely close, camping together for a year and a half before they separated. Their growing disaffection with each other was the natural result of each one's ambitions; both aspired to great power. But Jamuka attempted it through his office as khan of the Jadarats while Temujin, though of noble ancestry, attracted men from many different tribes and often from the lower orders of society. Thus, when the split between the two young men became marked, Jamuka was supported by the traditional steppe aristocracy (including the most important of the Mongol tribes) while Temujin's authority extended over a broader, if lower, stratum of people. This, however, would prove useful, even if not immediately. As Temujin created his following, he did so largely of men who owed their position to him personally, rather than to the accident of their birth. Thus, consciously or not, whether by plan or merely by taking the opportunities presented to him, Temujin began to create a power base beholden to him as a coterie of independent nobles would not have been. In the short term, however, Jamuka's confederacy comprehended more of the Mongols than did Temujin's and was the more powerful.

Nonetheless, after his success against the Merkits Temujin was widely seen as the rising star of the Mongols, and as a man who might restore to the Mongols the luster they had possessed generations earlier when they had been stronger. This view was supported by representations of the shaman Kokochu, one of Temujin's followers, who claimed that God had set aside the whole world as Temujin and his sons' domain. Among the superstitious and credible Mongols this may have contributed to his success. His rise, however, exacerbated the division between Temujin and Jamuka and war seemed likely. Accordingly, in 1186, Temujin was elected khan of the Mongols, and certain of his relatives who had until then supported Jamuka came over to him.

Temujin and Toghrul were both pleased, the former because he was now nominally co-equal with the Kerait khan and the latter because his ally had grown more powerful and could serve as a stronger prop to his own regime. While this was no doubt true, the Mongol khan was not as powerful as Jamuka, who took advantage of this in 1187 to attack him, ostensibly in reprisal for the killing of a tribesman by a Mongol during an attempted horse-theft. The Jadarat khan fielded an army of thirty thousand horsemen and launched a swift attack upon Temujin, who, warned of the action, scrambled to cobble together the men from thirteen "camps" in order to meet the attack. The Mongol khan was worsted in the Battle of Dalan Balzhut, following which Jamuka boiled a number of noble prisoners in cauldrons. This repugnant practice was intended to prevent the return of their ghosts, but seems instead to have turned a number of his followers away from him.

At this point the records are obscure and it appears that for the next ten years Temujin sought refuge among the Chinese. This seems the more likely since he had been a vassal of Khan Toghrul, himself a vassal of the Chin. In Temujin's absence his erstwhile protector Toghrul was driven from his throne and sought refuge among the Kara-Kitai, a sinicised steppe people to the south of Mongolia. He did not return until a year had passed and he had learned of Temujin's return and successful attack upon a band of Tatars.

Temujin next attacked his relation Sacha-beki, a Jurkin, because he had failed to join in the attack upon the Tatar band. After this he and Toghrul set upon Buiruk Khan, son of the late Inanch Khan, who had earlier driven Toghrul from power. Upon the death of

Inanch Khan the tribe had been divided between his two sons, who fell to quarreling, and Temujin and the Kerait Khan took the opportunity to attack Buiruk Khan, probably with his hostile brother's connivance.

The battle went well for the two allies: Buiruk Khan and his followers fled. But when Temujin and Toghrul returned from the foray they encountered a Naiman army. Temujin and Toghrul prepared for battle, but during the night Toghrul slipped away, leaving his ally to face the Naimans alone. His treacherous act may have been prompted by Jamuka, who is said to have spoken to him and maligned Temujin as potentially disloyal. It may be that Toghrul had begun to feel uneasy at Temujin's increasing power and prestige and thought to take the opportunity of letting him be drubbed, and hence weakened, by the powerful Naimans.

The situation, however, did not turn out to Toghrul's advantage. Temujin prudently retreated with his followers and the Naimans attacked Toghrul instead, seizing his son Senggum, Senggum's wife and half of the Kerait Khan's people and flocks. Faced with this turn of events Toghrul found himself forced to appeal to his nominal vassal for help in recovering his son. Temujin did not refuse him; he sent troops under four of his best lieutenants who managed to free Senggum, his wife and children and the khan's flocks. In light of Toghrul's behavior this is best explained as a proof by Temujin of their new relationship: he was now the stronger partner.[2] In a more subtle way too he may have wished to impress the Kerait people, since it soon became clear that he had decided to become their khan.

Toghrul had become aware of this goal by 1200, when he called a conference with Temujin at which he planned to capture him; but the Mongol Khan had been warned and nothing came of it. Outside of this narrow Kerait–Mongol sphere there was trouble brewing too: a confederation of Turco-Mongol tribes including the Katagin, Seljiut, Dorbet, Tatar and Onggirat had been formed to oppose Temujin. This confederacy fought and probably defeated Temujin, because he pulled back onto Chinese territory while Toghrul wintered along the Manchurian border.

There was more to come of this opposition to Temujin. In 1201, Jamuka was elected Gurkhan of another confederation of tribes determined to oppose the Mongol Khan; Naimans, Merkits, Oirats and Tayi'chiuts joined together. Temujin was warned by a member of the Korola tribe, and he sent word to Toghrul, who raised troops to support him. Toghrul had little choice—he was now effectively Temujin's vassal and the enemy confederation had marked him for destruction was well.

The two armies met on the Kalka River where Temujin and Toghrul were able to best the confederation. Jamuka fled after plundering some of his own followers, pursued by Toghrul, while Temujin chased A'uchu-bagatur of the Tayi'chiut toward the Onon River. The Oirats were drawn up on the far side and met Temujin after he crossed. He defeated them badly, driving away most of the warriors; and he slaughtered all the males he caught regardless of age. It was during this fight or in its aftermath that an enemy warrior shot and killed Temujin's horse. When the man was later trapped he admitted this and was pardoned and taken into the khan's service with the nickname "Jebe," or "arrow." Jebe rose to become one of Temujin's greatest generals.

This successful opposition was followed by an equally successful campaign against the Tatars in 1202 during which, it is said, this people was largely exterminated in revenge for the poisoning, years before, of Yesugei, Temujin's father. The survivors were distributed through the Mongol nation. The Mongol poem, *The Secret History of the Mongols,* purports to state Temujin's followers' words:

> Now to get revenge for all the defeats,
> to get satisfaction for the deaths of our grandfathers and fathers,
> we'll kill every Tatar man taller than the linch-pin on the wheel
>   of a cart.
> We'll kill them until they're destroyed as a tribe.[3]

Complete destruction seems unlikely because the Mongols became commonly known, especially in the West, as Tatars or Tartars and the successors of the Mongols in Russia and the Black Sea areas have kept the name until today. In view of this, it seems Temujin may have put only the nobility to death, without allowing them to join him voluntarily as he did with other tribes. This could account for the tale, which does not seem to accord with the persistence of the Tatar name. His success over them, however, was absolute.

There was still wrangling with Toghrul over the Kerait throne: Temujin sought a marriage between one of his sons and Toghrul's daughter, which would only have helped cement any claim he might have had to the throne. Though Toghrul reluctantly agreed, Senggum predictably opposed the match, and he gathered his allies and attacked Temujin by surprise. Temujin fled to the Chinese border and fought a battle, probably near the Kalka and Ulchin rivers, where he suffered a sound defeat and then escaped with a few thousand followers to the edge of Mongolia, where he might, if he needed, get help from the Jurchid. In spite of his position, numbers of Mongols joined him, even from Jamuka's alliance, showing the attraction Temujin exercised over people.

Toghrul, meanwhile, did not follow up his son's victory, and in fact, may not have wished to annihilate his former vassal. The Mongol Khan now holed up in a swampy area called Baljuna whose location is uncertain, though it may have been in southeastern Mongolia near the border of the Chin (Kin) Empire. Here Temujin awaited developments and, no doubt, tried to recruit followers. This was perhaps the most desperate hour in a career which, though it was one of gradual ascension, had been full of reverses. While Temujin passed his time in the Baljuna, Senggum and Toghrul's coalition dissolved—the usual centrifugal political tendencies asserting themselves, and Toghrul found himself the object of a murder plot. He plundered these former allies and drove them off.

In 1203 Temujin, having rebuilt his forces, left Baljuna for the Onon River. He sent messages to Toghrul as if for a parley, though it was a ruse: he surprised and attacked the Kerait army, defeating it. Toghrul fled west toward the Naimans, but was killed by one of them who failed to recognize him. After their defeat, and upon the death of their khan, the Keraits submitted to Temujin.

After Toghrul's demise, there was only a single power on the steppe left to challenge the Mongol Khan: the Naimans. This powerful tribe gathered as allies the remnants of tribes broken by Temujin and fought him in one last battle, in 1204. Among those who fought against Temujin was Jamuka, taking part in his last attempt to thwart the Mongol Khan in his try for supreme power on the steppe. The Naiman confederacy was defeated, however, and Temujin was at last the undisputed master of the Central Asian steppe. At the *khuriltai* of 1206 he was seated upon a swatch of black felt and acclaimed "Khan of All Who Dwelt in Felt Tents," that is, of all the Turco-Mongol peoples. It was at this moment that he took the name by which he is better known: Chinggis (or Genghis) Khan, which, though it is a subject of debate, likely means "All-Embracing Ruler."

Now Chinggis Khan held supreme power in the steppe, but as we know, steppe empires are intrinsically unstable; they exist as a consequence of the strength and acumen of the leader. Chinggis Khan was, however, more successful than any of his nomadic predecessors. Why? He recognized the fluid nature of the steppe tribes, their willingness to amalgamate voluntarily into larger units under the leadership of a man they respected, and he knew a corollary to this: defeated tribes could be effectively integrated into a steppe empire because they did not differ appreciably as a matter of culture. Thus he was able to build upon a base of those who joined him willingly, those who later submitted willingly and those whom he defeated. However, he did not simply take all of these different tribesmen into his army to create a mere congeries. Instead he employed the technique of decimal organization to set it in order. This was something familiar on the steppe, going back at least to the Hsiung-nu during the third century B.C.,[4] and could be used as effectively to establish political control as to ensure military discipline.

Under this system, every soldier belonged to a squad of ten men called an *arban*. One of the arban was its commander and ten arbans formed a unit of a hundred called a *jaghun*. Ten of these formed a unit of a thousand, or *mingghan*, and ten of these formed a *tumen* of ten thousand. Chinggis Khan divided the soldiers of his armies, who came from different tribes, into these units, being careful not to allow entire units to be made up of men from a single tribe. There were of course exceptions where tribes had been voluntarily loyal to him from the start of his career, and these he allowed to form national tumens—but it was uncommon. Families too were divided into decimal organizations, and thus Chinggis Khan tried single-handedly to form a new artificial nation called the Mongols which comprehended more than merely the Mongol tribe of old to which these amalgamated nomadic people would thenceforward belong. Tumens were invariably below strength and were classed into three categories with minimun actual strengths of seven thousand, five thousand and three thousand men; but the recognition and acceptance of this situation (common to most armies across history) shows that it was the fact of this formal organization that was important for both social stability and military efficiency.

And he did a second thing: he put people into power who owed their positions to him. This was natural since he had lost those people who would have been his traditional followers upon the death of his father. Such generals as Subotai, Jebe, Jelme and Bo'orchu, while steppe nomads, were not true Mongols and were unswervingly loyal to him.

As part of his military organization Chinggis Khan established a bodyguard, actually a personal regiment of ten thousand men, called the *kashik*, made up entirely of the steppe nobility. Service in this corps was often followed by command of another unit and these bodyguards were accorded high status; each common soldier of the kashik was deemed superior to the commander of a thousand men. When these men were distributed as officers throughout the Mongol army they could only reinforce their soldiers' feelings of loyalty to the khan.

Chinggis Khan's favorite shaman, Kokochu, had long before predicted that it was the will of heaven that Chinggis Khan and his family rule the earth, and this too was played upon to the superstitious nomads. With all of these means Chinggis Khan groped toward the creation of a sort of nation state that might survive him, and he had some success making a polity of great military power for his use and that of his descendants. An important part of this polity was a code of laws called the *yassaq*. Chinggis Khan is credited with drafting it, though much of it merely codified existing nomadic superstition. It went further than this, however. Among other things, the khan saw to it that the yassaq forbade slavery between Mongols and that it outlawed wife-stealing, a cause of incessant internecine warfare. The yassaq thus stabilized the Mongol nation by removing some of the causes of its instability.

The army, however, was the single most important institution of the Mongol state. In Chinggis Khan's time and that of his immediate successors it was divided into two groups: light and heavy cavalry, the light cavalry preponderating by perhaps two to one. The light cavalrymen were armed with at least one bow, often with two or even three, and with a quiver or two of arrows. They wore little armor: a helmet, a round leather-covered wickerwork shield and sometimes a padded, quilted coat whose defensive properties should not be underrated.[5] These men might additionally carry a light battle-axe or mace, a lasso and sometimes a saber. The heavy cavalrymen wore iron helmets with a leather flap hanging down behind and at the sides to protect the neck and a cuirass of lamellar armor. This armor was made of oblong plates, or lamellae, pierced in several places so that they might be laced together, each plate overlapping the plate to its side, and each row of these plates overlapping the row above. The plates could be made of either hardened leather or of iron. This was flexible armor and allowed for the natural bending of the body. Such armor has a long history in the East and can be seen, for instance, in the equipment of Japanese samurais. There is also evidence of a simpler leather armor made of hardened horizontal leather bands laced together which would have provided some flexibility, though less than lamellar armor. Giovanni di Plano Carpini described it in the thirteenth century:

> Their cuirasses and horse armors are of leather and made this way: they take strips of cowhide or other animal hide of one hand's width wide, and they glue three or four or these together and tie them to each other with laces or cords. In the top strip they put the cords at the edge, in the one below they put them in the center and they do this until the end. Therefore, when the soldiers bend, the lower strips slide up over the upper ones and so they are doubled or even tripled over the body.[6]

This armor would have resembled somewhat the Roman *lorica segmentata* of the first century A.D., though made in leather rather than iron. Marco Polo, who visited the Great Khan of the Mongols a few years after Carpini, described Mongol weapons and armor in a similar if less exact way:

> Their arms are bows, iron maces, and in some instances spears; but the first is the weapon at which they are most

expert, being accustomed, from children, to employ it in their sports. They wear defensive armor made of the thick hides of buffaloes and other beasts, dried by the fire, and thus rendered extremely hard and strong.[7]

The Mongol cuirass was made of a front and back plate, shoulder pieces and arm pieces usually open on the underside. Again the cavalryman would have a shield, and his horse might be armored as he was in lamellar armor. Nonetheless, though the armor of such a horseman was quite complete, it was not as heavy as that of a Western knight, particularly when made of leather, and so the Mongol heavy cavalryman was much more agile than his Western counterpart.

Carpini described the Mongol helmet too: "The Tartar helmet has a crown made of iron or steel, but the part that extends around the neck and throat is of leather; and all these pieces of leather are made as described above."[8]

Such a cavalryman was armed with a lance and a saber, but also with a bow and arrows, allowing him great versatility in combat. After the conquest of northern China, the Mongols were issued silk shirts to wear under their clothing. Silk is tough and will generally follow an arrowhead into the wound without breaking. The silk can then be tugged gently from the wound, drawing out the arrowhead without enlarging the injury.[9] A further acquisition from the Chinese, and one of greater significance, was the siege train. The Mongols employed Chinese engineers to build siege engines and siege works with which to take cities—something that, until then, no steppe army could expect to do.

This difficulty in taking cities was a problem for Chinggis Khan during the Mongols' first campaigns against sedentary people, such as the Chinese. China, during this period, was divided into two states: the Sung in the south and the Chin in the north, with the kingdom of Xixia (a state of sinicized Tanguts) to the northwest of the Chin and bordering Turkestan. Chinggis Khan chose to make war upon Xixia, the smallest and weakest of these states, probably to make good the losses in livestock which the various steppe tribes had suffered during the recent wars in Mongolia.

Although he was able to overrun the countryside during campaigns in 1205–7 and 1209, he was not able to take the capitals of Ningsia and Lingchow; the Mongols were no more successful against fortifications than the Avars or Magyars had been in Europe centuries before. Still, the situation was dangerous for the Xixian king, Li An-Ch'uan, and he declared himself to be Chinggis Khan's vassal in order to put an end to the war. The respite, though, was temporary; in 1209 the Mongols invested Ningsia and went so far as to build a dam to direct the Yellow River against it. The civil engineering was beyond the Mongols, however, or perhaps the Tangut soldiers were able to breach the dam; it gave way, flooding the Mongol camp. They thus failed to take the city, but years later, with the help of civilized engineers, they would from time to time flood other cities in order to take them. In any case, Li An-Ch'uan was impressed and gave his daughter to Chinggis Khan as a wife.

With Xixia's status as a vassal state assured, Chinggis Khan turned his attention to the Chin, whom he would fight with more or less intensity until his death on August 18, 1227. In order to keep his restive people in hand Chinggis had to offer them plunder—this was one of the main duties of a khan to his following—and he had decided by 1210 to fight the Chin. In 1211 he refused to send the Kerait tribute to the Chin emperor, an obligation he had inherited from Toghrul, whose people he now ruled. Chinggis had chosen his moment with care: the Chin were in some disorder upon the death of their emperor, to whom Chinggis Khan was a vassal, not only due to his connection with Toghrul but because Chinggis himself had been forced from time to time to seek refuge with the Chinese during his rise to power.

The old emperor had been succeeded by his son, Chung-hei, whom the Mongol Khan held in contempt. Furthermore, there were internal divisions between the Chinese proper and their rulers, the Jurchids, who had come off the steppe themselves to seize power years before. In addition, the Chin state was threatened by the Sung to the south, and all of this worked in Chinggis' favor because he had decided to attack what was ostensibly a much more powerful state. Some estimate that the Chin army of the period had, at least officially, 120,000 horse archers and half a million foot soldiers.[10] The army may not have been so large, and it would have been dispersed throughout the Chin Empire—large numbers no doubt stationed against the Sung—but it would still have presented a great threat to Chinggis Khan, whose total forces numbered about 65,000, some of whom he had to keep in Mongolia to prevent uprisings.[11]

Notwithstanding the disparity of forces, he repudiated his station as vassal and began to wage war. He was favored by the military situation of the Chin at this stage. The marches along the northern border with Mongolia were guarded for the Chin by Onggut Turks. One of their khans, Alaqash, had been interested in developments in Mongolia and had known and supported Chinggis Khan during his rise to power. He continued to favor the Mongol and opened the marches to him against the Chin, even going so far as to turn some of his soldiers over to the Mongols to fight for them. Alaqash's emirs were not so favorably inclined, though, and murdered him. Still, from the Chin standpoint the damage had been done. Chinggis was further able to incite the Khitans, a Mongol-speaking people along the southwest Manchurian border, to revolt.

In spite of benefiting from the treachery of Chin allies, which had allowed the Mongols to enter Chin territory, the Mongols again found it difficult to take fortified positions and this problem was compounded by the fact that the Chin not only had capable Chinese engineers, but were also fine soldiers. However, there were numerous desertions, even of officials from the Chin court itself, which highlight the riven condition of the state. When, with the help of the Ongguts, Chinggis had advanced into Chin territory and taken the cities of Xuande-fu and Fouzhou, Emperor Chung-hei sued for peace, though Chinggis refused it. All of this was followed by Jebe's seizing of the important Juyong Pass while another Mongol leader (and former Chin official), Ila Ahai, swept with his forces into the territory where the Chin's spare horses were kept, driving them off and denying the Chin remounts.

Things did not go completely Chinggis's way; he was struck by an arrow at Xijing and forced to relinquish command to his son Tolui while he recuperated. During this time the Chin were able to recover the Juyong Pass, though the Mongols, with the help of their Muslim ambassador Ja'far (actually a spy) were able to retake the pass. Ja'far had learned of a secret path while at the Chin court and a force of Mongols were able to approach the pass in stealth and slaughter the sleeping garrison. This was followed by the revolt of a certain Liuge against the Jurchid. He raised an army and, with Mongol support, established the Liao Empire, a vassal state.

The Jurchid rulers of the Chin Empire continued to suffer as much from internal disunity as from the external Mongol threat. The Jurchid general Hushahu, the powerful commander of a private army, deserted to Chinggis, thus allowing him to breach the Jijing Pass and defeat yet more Jurchid troops. Compounding this treachery he then advanced to the capital, Zhongdu (Beijing), where he murdered Emperor Chung-hei and set the latter's nephew on the throne as Emperor Xuan-zang. Hushahu's obnoxious progress was finally halted when a fellow commander, Shuhu Gaoqi, perceiving him as a threat, surrounded his house with troops and killed him.

By 1213–1214 the Mongols controlled most of the territory north of the Huanhe River and they invested Zhongdu, although they were unable to take the fortified city. They also began to suffer famine and sickness so that Chinggis began peace talks with the emperor, who sent him a Jurchid princess for a bride, along with silk, gold and three thousand horses. Feeling insecure, however, the emperor removed to the southern capital, Nanjing. Chinggis Khan took this as a canny strategy to gather reinforcements and then attack him. In response, he took up the war again in the winter of 1214.

During this campaign one of Chinggis' commanders, a Khitan named Yesen, determined to seize the city of Liaoyang, which he knew was to receive a new military commandant. With a few men, he lay in ambush along the road and surprised and killed the new appointee. With his letters of authority Yesen entered Liaoyang and masqueraded as the new commander. He spent three weeks thus disguised, effectively neutralizing the defenses, and when the Mongol general Mukali arrived, he took the city without a blow.

Zhongdu was then taken, in 1215, after a relief force had been defeated, and the Mongols pillaged it for a month, killing thousands of townspeople. Chinggis Khan now demanded that the emperor cede him all of the territories he had taken and henceforth call himself not emperor but "King of Hunan," as his territories had been reduced to little more than that province. When the emperor declined to do this, Chinggis Khan left the campaign in the hands of the Chinese Shi Tianni, who, like his father before him, had come over to the Mongols. The khan returned to Mongolia in 1216 and spent some time putting down an insurrection by the Merkits and by a discontented Naiman chief who had earlier fled to the lands of the Karakhitai; he also waged a not entirely successful campaign to bring the forest tribes to heel. Chinggis Khan was now master not only of Mongolia, but also of Xixia and most of northern China, from whence he could draft engineers and educated men to help him in any future campaigns against sedentary peoples.

In the course of his conquests, Chinggis Khan had taken the kingdom of the Uighurs, a somewhat settled Turkic steppe people with a capital at Karakorum. They, unlike the Mongols, were literate and Chinggis Khan took an important step in adopting their script for the writing of Mongol; also, he had his children taught to read. The Uighur Kingdom was near that of the Karakhitai, or Black Khitai, a sinicized steppe people whose kingdom had been established by a runaway Chinese prince. It too fell to the Mongols and they now had a common border with the Empire of Khwarezm, which had been expanding from the west.

There is no modern state corresponding precisely to Khwarezm. It was the eastern part of the Muslim world and might be considered as roughly comprising what is the modern state of Iran and part of Iraq; it had expanded north and west past the Caspian Sea into Turkmenistan, Uzbekistan and parts of Kazakhstan, and east into what is today Pakistan, thus including the area formerly known as Transoxiana. Its principal cities were Baghdad, Samarkand, Bukhara, Merv and Khorasan, still famous today.

It was a large empire, and very wealthy, although it was a new state at the time it began to share a border with the Mongol Empire, the result of recent conquests by its sultan, Muhammad II. In this sense it was not so very different than the Mongol Empire, albeit it was a much less stable state. Muhammad had a somewhat inflated view of his military abilities since his conquests had come over relatively weak neighbors, although in fairness to him he did have a huge army. It was composed chiefly of Kankhali Turks recruited from the steppe, a natural result of Muhammad's ancestry. His mother was the daughter of a Kankhali chieftain. Unfortunately, the Kankhali formed a military caste quite separate from the subjects of the empire and were not liked. Furthermore, Muhammad was in conflict with his mother, who retained great political power, and he had alienated his fellow Muslims in the west by abusing the Caliph of Baghdad, thereby losing an ally that he could well have used.

In 1218 a caravan of about one hundred Muslims from the Mongol Empire arrived in the Central Asian city of Otrar near the border on the Syr Darya River, accompanied by a Mongol envoy, Uquna. Trade relations had been established about a year earlier and the delegation was a natural result. The governor of the city, Inalchiq, also known by the title Qadir-khan, however, had the visitors all murdered with the complicity of Muhammad, on the grounds that they were spies. While it is likely that some of the traders were in fact there to act as spies (a common practice of the Mongols), it seems an incredibly stupid action for Muhammad to have connived in. Regardless of how he felt about his own strength, he could not have been unaware of the military successes of his neighbor. There would be consequences.

Chinggis Khan, reasonably enough, asked through an embassy that Inalchiq be handed over for Mongol justice. Muhammad refused. He murdered two of the Khan's envoys and sent the third back with his beard shaven. It was to be war, and Muhammad would soon lose everything.

This campaign against Khwarezm is one of primarily strategic interest because the armies fielded against each other fought similarly—the Khwarezmian army was made up largely of Turks, who fought like the Mongols. Furthermore, the Mongol army was now equipped with Chinese siege engineers as a result of their campaigns and conquests in northern China. As a result, this war included extensive and successful siegecraft, a feature absent from the warfare of the Mongols' predecessors.

In the summer of 1219 Chinggis Khan gathered his forces on the upper Irtysh and arrived in Quayaligh, where he gathered some allied troops from subject kings southeast of Lake Balkhash. Some estimate that the Mongol army now numbered between 100,000 and 150,000 men.[12] Still outnumbered by the Khwarezmian forces, they were nevertheless better disciplined and in better spirit. Muhammad had stationed his forces at strategic points along his frontier with the Mongol Empire. His army was huge, but it was spread dangerously thin and was subject to breakthroughs.

Chinggis Khan penetrated the frontier near the city of Otrar on the Syr Darya, where the original Khwarezm provocation had taken place. He divided his army and invested Otrar by a force under the command of his sons Jagatai and Occodai, who took the city after a prolonged siege. It was defended by the very Inalchiq who had killed the merchants and sparked the war, and he was killed by molten silver poured into his eyes and ears. The important point here is the fact that the Mongols, unlike the earlier Huns, Avars or Magyars, could expect to conduct a successful siege. This was an advantage that rendered them even more dangerous to settled people than they might have been. They had coupled the military skills of the steppe with one of the most important military skills of civilization: siegecraft.

During this siege, Chinggis Khan sent the balance of the army under his eldest son, Juchi, down the Syr Darya, along which he captured the cities of Signakhi and Jend. A smaller force of 5,000 Mongols were sent up the upper Syr Darya, took Benaket and besieged Khodzhent, whose garrison managed to escape down the Syr Darya in boats. Meanwhile, Chinggis Khan and his youngest son, Tolui, advanced directly to Bukhara, reaching it in February 1220. Its garrison of Turkish soldiers, numbering about 20,000, tried to break out of the city and escape, but most were killed in the attempt. Bukhara surrendered and its inhabitants were driven out while it was plundered for several days and burned completely, except for a mosque and some brick palaces. This done, Chinggis Khan marched on Samarkand, taking prisoners from Bukhara to do the siege work. His sons Jagatai and Occodai had taken Otrar and marched independently to meet him there. The independence of operation of different Mongol armies should be noted; it was a feature of their strategy, remarkably successful in an age of difficult communication, and it will be seen repeatedly.

Samarkand's Turkish garrison deserted to the Mongols and the city surrendered in five days. The population was driven into the plain outside the city which, for several more days, was methodically looted. Of its people, many were killed, while the artisans were largely deported to Mongolia. A quarter of the population was left to reoccupy the city. The Turkish turncoats were issued Mongol uniforms to allay their suspicions, and then surprised and killed. Although Chinggis Khan had made good use of traitors in the past, the garrison of Samarkand seemed to have provoked in him a certain contempt.

The Khwarezmian city of Urgench, formerly the capital, was the next to fall. It resisted a prolonged siege conducted by Jagatai, Juchi and Occodai in which prisoners from Samarkand were used. After it had fallen, the Mongols broke dams and submerged the city under the Amu Darya.

Muhammad was shocked at what had happened to Transoxiana, and he fled to the city of Balkh further south. He became rightly suspicious of the loyalty of his Turkish troops and took to sleeping in a different tent each night. He moved on to western Khorasan, then to the city of Nishapur, then to Kazvin in the province of Iraq'Ajami, always chased by a pair of tumens under the command of two of Chinggis Khan's greatest generals, Jebe and Subotai.

A handful of other towns were sacked during the pursuit, but the chase was the main thing: the Mongols had superstitious scruples against allowing a defeated enemy king to live. Muhammad was nearly caught at Karun, but the Mongols lost his trail. They destroyed Zenjan and Kazvin while Muhammad hid on an islet in the Caspian Sea, now probably the peninsula of Gumish Tepe, where he died of exhaustion.

The campaign, however, was not over. Chinggis Khan proceeded to conquer Afghanistan and Khurasan, fighting what was left of the Khwarezmian army in the spring of 1221. Balkh surrendered to him, but he massacred the townspeople and burned the city all the same. Tolui rounded up peasants from near Khurasan and besieged Merv, which surrendered too; but the entire population was slaughtered. Tolui then took by storm Nishapur, where the Mongol general Toquchar had been killed in an assault. Again the entire population was killed. The general's widow presided over the executions on a plain outside the town. Tolui then moved on to Herat, where the garrison resisted though the citizens threw open the gates. They were spared this time, but the garrison was killed. Terror had become an effective tool—purposeful terror could be just as useful as siegecraft, and caused fewer Mongol losses.

Chinggis Khan next took Thaleqan, passed the Hindu Kush

Mountains, and besieged Bamian—where his favorite grandson was killed. When that city was taken, everyone was killed, including the dogs and cats. The city was leveled and no loot was taken.

Muhammad's energetic son, Jelal ad-Din, had managed, during all of this, to escape into the mountains of Afghanistan at Ghazni where he raised an army and defeated a Mongol force commanded by Shigi-qutuqu. Chinggis Khan immediately advanced upon him and trapped him along the banks of the Indus, where he destroyed Jelal ad-Din's army. The young shah managed to escape only by stripping off his armor and riding his horse off a twenty-foot cliff into the Indus under a hail of Mongol arrows. He swam his horse to the opposite bank and took refuge in the court of Delhi. Chinggis Khan, who had seen the feat, commended him to his sons as a model of courage. The Mongols had no real interest in parts of the empire they had destroyed, and Jelal ad-Din later returned to reclaim some of it and face the Mongols again. He fought and failed, and without a country the prince became a bandit and adventurer in Afghanistan. He was later murdered there.

The destruction that took place during the Mongol campaign was appalling; Balkh still shows signs of the invasion and eastern Iran, according to Grousset, never completely recovered.[13] Parts of the empire became desert because there was no longer enough population to keep them properly irrigated. Centuries of careful effort had been ruined.

The Mongols' campaign points up certain aspects of their strategy with particularity: the use of siegecraft to take walled cities and the subsequent, calculated use of terror to cause other cities to capitulate without siege, as well as the use of prisoners to conduct sieges, thereby allowing small Mongol forces to attack cities that would otherwise have been too strong for them. These prisoners were also driven forward during the attack carrying Mongol flags to give a city the false impression of greater numbers, and to further exhaust the defenders without endangering as many Mongol lives. The maneuvering of entire armies, and lesser bodies of troops, with great independence and yet successfully, is reminiscent of much more modern armies, and their joining into larger bodies, as needed, to conduct parts of the campaigns, recalls Napoleon's maxim: "March dispersed, fight concentrated."

NOTES
1. Joseph Fletcher's "The Mongols: Ecological and Social Perspectives," in *The Harvard Journal of Asiatic Studies*, 46:1. See Ratchnevsky below, p. 49, who makes a convincing case for this and points out that it was common for nomads to seek refuge in China.
2. Paul Ratchnevsky, *Genghis Khan, His Life and Legacy*, trans. Thomas N. Haining, Oxford, UK, and Cambridge, MA, Blackwell, 1991, pp. 58–59.
3. *The Secret History of the Mongols, and Other Pieces*, trans. Arthur Waley, London, Allen and Unwin, 1963.
4. Thomas T. Allsen, *Mongol Imperialism: The Policies of the Grand Qan Miongke in China, Russia, and the Islamic Lands, 1251–1259*, Berkeley, University of Califormia Press, 1987, p. 193.
5. Bashford Dean, a former curator of arms at the Metropolitan Museum of Art and former Chairman of the Committee on Helmets and Body Armor of the Engineering Division of the National Research Council, tested British fabric armor designed for the First World War: "This is a heavily padded waistcoat weighing about six pounds, and, judging from a test made under the writer's direction in Washington, capable of stopping an automatic pistol ball, jacket in alloy, at a velocity of about 300 foot seconds"; Dean, *Helmets and Body Armor in Modern Warfare*, New Haven, CT, Yale University Press, 1920, p. 112. This armor was made of scraps of linen, cotton and silk hardened with a "resinous" material. While medieval padded armor would not have been made to the same specifications, it ought not to have been difficult to make a defense that was proof against arrows and sword cuts.
6. Giovanni di Plano Carpini, *The Story of the Mongols Whom We Call the Tartars*, trans. Erik Hildinger, Boston, Branden Books, 1996.
7. Marco Polo, *The Travels of Marco Polo the Venetian*, Marsden translation, ed. Thomas Wright, New York, AMS Press, 1968 (reprint of 1854 Bohn edition, London), pp. 133–34.
8. Giovanni, op. cit.
9. Otherwise, arrows are customarily removed by breaking the shaft off at the wound site and driving the arrow head through the body and out the other side to produce a cleaner wound than results from drawing it back through the wound channel.
10. Ratchnevsky, p. 108.
11. Ibid.
12. René Grousset, *The Empire of the Steppes*, trans. Naomi Walford, New Brunswick, NJ, Rutgers University Press, 1991, p. 238.
13. Ibid., p. 243.

8

The Mongols Reach the West

Upon the death of Chinggis Khan in 1227, the office of Khagan, or Great Khan, went to his second-eldest son, Occodai, in accordance with his wishes. He gauged that this son would make the best ruler, as he was liked by his brothers and would work well as a conciliator. Chinggis Khan's eldest son, Juchi, had been of uncertain parentage (possibly fathered by a Merkit when his mother had been kidnapped), and in any case he had predeceased his father in 1227 while on bad terms with him. Juchi's son, Batu, had succeeded to his father's appanage, the westernmost area of the Mongol Empire.

Chinggis Khan's youngest son, Tolui, was given an appanage far to the northeast in Siberia, north of Manchuria, while Jagatai was given lands south of Mongolia down to and incorporating Transoxiana. In spite of having their own huge appanages, or *uluses* as they were known, these members of the Golden Family and their lands were subordinate to the Khagan Occodai. The division of the father's estate—which included people, flocks and herds as well as territories—was, of course, the normal and expected thing. What Chinggis Khan hoped for, though, was that his empire might endure and spread. He is said to have stated expressly to his sons that they were to conquer the entire world, that the world had been given to them by Teb Tengri, the Blue Heaven. Therefore, it was important that each of his sons recognize Occodai's supremacy and that they each attend any subsequent khuriltais. Any who failed to do so would disappear like a "an arrow shot into reeds." The conqueror was quite aware of the tendency of steppe states to disintegrate and he had worked diligently to make his durable.

As the Great Khan had wished, all had attended the khuriltai at which Occodai had been elected, and this was followed by a decision to expand the empire—a move also consonant with their father's wishes. It was decided that Batu's domain, which was the smallest appanage, should be expanded to include Russia and Hungary, and Chinggis Khan's greatest general, Subotai, was chosen to plan and direct the campaign for the young Batu, who was the nominal leader.

The Mongol campaign against the Russian principalities exhibits a number of the features seen in the Khwarezmian campaign. However, the Russians were even less prepared than the Sultan of Khwarezm and were not, in any case, as powerful. They were also divided under a number of princes who generally disagreed among themselves. This situation was exacerbated by the peculiar medieval Russian method of lateral succession whereby when a powerful prince died his son did not generally succeed him. Instead the dead prince's brother would move from whatever city he was prince of, and take over the reins in a more important town. The vacant place at his former principality was then taken up by the next prince in succession, perhaps a younger brother. Sons of princes were given small cities to rule, like Moscow, until their turn came to move up.

Some scholars suggest that the Russians acquired this odd practice from earlier steppe nomads such as the Petchenegs. In fact the Mongols themselves practiced it: Chinggis Khan was succeeded by his son Occodai, but Occodai was succeeded by his brother Guyuk, and Guyuk by his brother Mangu. The Russians may have picked up this habit from earlier steppe peoples.[1] Whatever its source, it tended to disunity. Russia in the thirteenth century was comprised of many states: Suzdal in the northwest, the small state of Riazan divided between four princes, Chernikov further south, Novgorod, Pereiaslav, Smolensk, Kiev, Volhynia, Galicia and Plotsk.

To conquer this congeries of states, the Mongols decided it was best to divide the northern principalities from the southern and beat them individually. Subotai knew something of the Russian steppe because he and Jebe had been charged with the pursuit of Sultan Muhammad II of Khwarezm, and after his death on a Caspian islet they had decided to rejoin Chinggis Khan in the Central Asian steppes not by heading directly east, but by making an excursion along the western edge of the Caspian Sea and then passing through the Urals into the steppes along the Don River. It was hugely out of

At left is a 4th century graffito of a Persian or Roman cataphract scratched on a wall at Dura Europas in Syria. He is equipped in the manner of a Sarmatian heavy horseman, the model for this type of soldier. Above right is a modern artist's depiction of a Sarmatian warrior.

Below, a gravestone from the Greek Pontic (Black Sea) Kingdom shows a warrior equipped to fight in Sarmatian style. During the 2nd and 3rd centuries A.D. this Greek kingdom became Sarmatized in culture and mode of warfare.

The Scythians, like the barbarian Celts of Europe, were expert metal-smiths. The belt buckle above depicts a hunt.

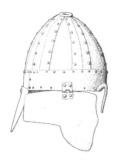 

Helmets of the kind probably worn by Huns, once large numbers of them had entered Roman service.

This scene from Trajan's Column shows Sarmatians from the Roxolani tribe fleeing a Roman onslaught. Although the horses appear to be ar-mored all the way to their hooves, in practice they wore coats of mail.

This nomad encampment was painted by Vasily Vereshchagin in the late 19th century, however it is a scene that might have been witnessed at any time over the past thousand years in Central Asia.

Crusaders arrived at the end of the 11th century to seize back the Holyland, which by then was occupied by the Seljuk Turks. Below, Turks storm a city, possibly Constantinople.

Perhaps the greatest conqueror in history; born with the name
Temujin he later became known as Chinggis Khan.

Successors to Chinggis Khan: his son Occodai, left, and his
grandson Kubilai.

This plate depicts a battle between the defenders of Khwarezm
and the invading Mongols.

"Ardashir fighting Bahman," a scene from Persian mythology showing men equipped in complete Mongol armor of the type worn during the 13th and 14th centuries.

Mongols storm a town during their invasion of the
Middle East.

Timur Lenk, known as Tamerlane. This sculpture was made from
the Great Emir's skull by Professor M.M. Gerasimov, a pioneer in
forensic reconstruction. The Soviet scientist braved the legend that if
Timur's body were exhumed the worst disaster ever to befall the
world would take place. Gerasimov performed the work in 1941.

In this Persian print, Timur's army assaults a city.

The mosque and tomb of Hodja-Ahmed Yassevi, which Timur Lenk built near Turkestan. This is an example of Timurid architecture whose beauty contrasts sharply with other aspects of Timur's life.

"The Apotheosis of War," by Vasily Vereshchagin, below, depicts the kind of architecture for which Timur Lenk is more commonly known.

"Tamerlane's Door," by Vasily Vereshchagin. At his height the Great Emir had the artisans and engineers of entire civilizations at his service to create whatever monements he chose.

As Central and Eastern Europeans fought against the Tatars they adopted much of their equpiment and technique. Above, Russian knights on the way to battle. Below, Rembrandt's "The Polish Rider," a light cavalryman of the 17th century dressed as and equipped like a Crimean Tatar, with recurved bow, saber and mace.

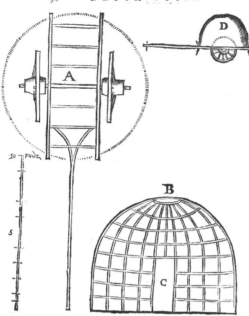

Two illustrations from Beauplan's *Description de L'Ukranie* showing a Crimean Tatar house mounted on a cart, left, and a Tatar strategy for hiding a troop of horsemen in the steppe, below. 400 men would divide into successively smaller squads and then meet at a pre-arranged rendezvous. The trails of the smallest groups would soon disappear from the steppe grass leaving no trace for enemy scouts to follow.

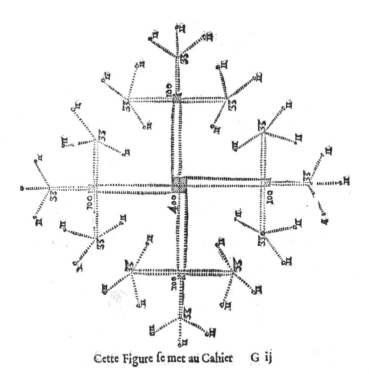

Cette Figure se met au Cahier   G ij

A turn-of-the-century French photograph of a Mongol. His clothing and equipment—recurved bow, belt-mounted bowcase and quiver, and his saber—are essentially unchanged from the days of Chinggis Khan.

This picture, usually labeled as that of a Mongol horseman from the late 19th century, may actually be of a Manchu, but in either case he rides the homely but tough steppe pony, sports a recurved composite bow, and carries a saber for close work. Whichever he may be, he is a perfect example of the steppe light-horseman as found throughout Central Asia across the centuries.

A European, Giuseppe Castiglione, painted the portait of Manchu emperor Qianlong, above.

A Chinese artist created the woodblock at right, which depicts a common Jurchid (Manchu) soldier. This was drawn shortly before the fall of the Ming dynasty.

the way, but this expedition of 1223 became the furthest reconnaissance west the Mongols had yet made.

Although they led only two tumens, or a nominal twenty thousand men, Jebe and Subotai had fought and beaten a Kipchak army under their Khan Khotyan, and many of the prisoners had been pressed into the Mongol army. They followed this with a signally successful action against a combined Russian army with Kipchak allies and then they returned home, fighting and defeating the Kama Bulgars on the upper Volga. Undoubtedly, the Mongols knew a good deal about the populations, geography and politics of the region, and they knew about the Russian forces. The Russians, by contrast, did not grasp much about the Mongols who had defeated them; in fact they did not really know their identity, much less their power. The Chronicle of Novgorod says this in its entry for the year 1224:

> In the same year, for our sins, there came unknown tribes. No one knew who they were or what was their origin, faith, or tongue, and some people called them Tatars, while others called them Taurmens, and still others called them Pechenegs [sic]. . . Only God knows who these people are or from whence they came. The wise men, who understand the Books, know who they are, but we do not. Here we record them in memory of the misfortunes of the Russian princes that came about at their [the Tatars'] hands.[2]

These misfortunes of 1224 culminated in a disastrous battle on the Kalka River between the Russians and their Kipchak (also called Kuman) allies and the Mongols. The Kipchaks, a numerous, Turkic-speaking steppe people, formed a vanguard that joined battle with the Mongols, but they were driven back upon the Russians, who were establishing a camp. In their haste and disorder the Russians were unable to organize themselves and many were killed. One of the Russian princes, Mstislav of Kiev, managed to pull back to the other shore of the Kalka and build a fortified camp or stockade from which his forces defended themselves until they were convinced by a band of Russian outlaws who had joined the Mongols that they would be taken prisoner and ransomed if they surrendered. Instead they were all killed.

Other Russians fled toward the Dnieper, chased by the Mongols. The Chronicle says:

> The other princes were pursued to the Dnieper, and six of them were killed there: Sviatoslav of Yahnev, Iziaslav, son of Ingvar, Sviatoslav of Shumsk, Mstislav of Chernigov and his son, and George of Nesvizh. But Prince Mstislav Mstislavich, Prince of Galich, escaped by crossing the Dnieper, and he cut loose the boats from the shore to ensure his escape. Only one Russian warrior in ten lived through this battle; in returning to their homelands, many of these were killed by the Kumans for their horses and clothes.[3]

The Russians had lost many of their princes and soldiers to these unknown "Tatars" and must have counted themselves lucky that they vanished to the east. Unhappily, however, they would return a dozen years later, work much more destruction, and dominate the land for two hundred years.

The Mongols were deliberate about the invasion and acted with typical foresight and practicality. They began operations in 1235 not against the Russians, but against their neighbors, the Kama Bulgars and Kipchaks. The former had built a city upon the Kama called Bulgar, a rich place trading in furs and honey. Some of these people had migrated west during the sixth century, as we have seen, to inhabit the land now known as Bulgaria.

The Mongol attack was launched on two fronts simultaneously. In 1236 Batu, Chinggis Khan's grandson, and Subotai went north against the city of Bulgar while his uncle Mangu and the general Budjek attacked the Kipchaks on the lower Volga to the south. Bulgar was utterly destroyed and the Kipchaks went to hide in the woods along the Dnieper River. Mangu and Budjek drew their troops into a huge circle and closed in on them as they did during a hunt. The Kipchak Khan Bachman and his ally the Alani leader Catchar were caught on an island and cut in two. Many of the Kipchaks were pressed into the Mongol army and began training. Others were sent to the Black Sea, where they were sold as slaves. Many of them, as it turned out, would find service as Mamluk soldiers for Egypt and some would fight the Mongols again, years later, at the Battle of Ayn Jalut in Syria. Other Kipchaks followed the old Khan Khotyan, who fled to the protection of Hungary. The Mongols' preliminary work was completed; with Bulgar gone their lines of communication and supply were safe and with the Kipchaks neutralized, or fighting for them, they could occupy the steppe of southern Russia at their whim. Now was the time to turn their attention to the Russians themselves.

Subotai decided to drive through the middle of the Russian principalities to stop the south from aiding the north. In the winter of 1237 he crossed the Volga into Russian territory through the small principality of Riazan, whose four squabbling princes could not stop him. It was a vassal state of Suzdal, but Grand Duke Yuri of Suzdal declined to help the Riazanians. The princes withdrew into their towns and prepared to defend themselves. Russian cities of the period were largely of wood, including the city walls. Just as the stone walls of Transoxiana and Khwarezm had been unable to stop the Mongols, so the wooden walls of the Russian cities failed as well. Not as strong, they could of course also be burned. Furthermore, the Mongols had by then supplemented their siege trains with Arabic as well as Chinese siege engineers.

While Prince Roman was away on an unsuccessful mission for help from Grand Duke Yuri, the Mongol army approached Riazan with their ambassador, a woman, who told the townspeople to surrender and give a tenth of their wealth and services to the Mongols. This woman was likely a Kipchak or other woman of the steppe who could speak Russian, but the townspeople regarded her as a witch and would not open the gates. They declined the Mongol offer. The Mongols then sacked the Riazanian towns Isteslawetz and Pronsk and wasted the countryside. The defenders of the city of Riazan met the Mongols on the field and were defeated, retreating back within their walls. The siege of Riazan began.

In nine days the Mongols built a wooden stockade completely around the city to prevent sallies from within or relief from the outside, and they battered it for five days with catapults. "The Tale of the Destruction of Riazan," a medieval Russian chronicle, describes the capture and its horrifying aftermath:

The accursed Batu began the conquest of the land of Riazan,

and soon approached the city of Riazan itself. [His forces] encircled the city and fought wthout surcease for five days. Batu changed his regiments frequently, replacing them with fresh troops, while the citizens of Riazan fought without relief. And many citizens were killed and others wounded. Still others were exhauseted by their great efforts and their wounds. On the dawn of the sixth day the pagan warriors began to storm the city, some with firebrands, some with battering rams, and others with countless scaling ladders for ascending the walls of the city. And they took the city of Riazan on the 21st day of December. And the Tatars came to the Cathedral of the Assumption of the Blessed Virgin, and they cut to pieces the Great Princess Agrippina, her daughters-in-law, and other princesses.

They burned to death the bishops and the priests and put the torch to the holy church. And the Tatars cut down many people, including women and children. Still others were drowned in the river. And they killed without exception all monks and priests. And they burned this holy city with all its beauty and wealth, and they captured the relatives of the Riazan princes, the princes of Kiev and Chernigov. And the churches of God were destroyed, and much blood was spilled on the holy altars. And not one man remained alive in the city. All were dead. All had drunk the same bitter cup to the dregs. And there was not even anyone to mourn the dead. Neither father nor mother could mourn their dead children, nor the children their fathers or mothers. Nor could a brother mourn the death of his brother, or relatives their relatives. All were dead. And this happened for our sins.[4]

The city was fired, the population largely slaughtered, and a small number allowed to flee so that terror would spread. The Mongols next moved on Kolomna. Grand Duke Yuri appreciated the menace now and sent his army to join Prince Roman in the defense of Kolomna; Yuri sent his son, Prince Vsevolod, with the army which was led by Ermei Glebovitch. He sent another son, Vladimir, to Moscow, only fifty miles distant from Kolomna, to assist in the defense of that town.

The Mongols met the army under Princes Roman and Vsevolod and General Glebovitch before it could enter the town and forced it onto a hillside to defend itself. Vsevolod and a band of men broke through the Mongols and escaped; Prince Roman and Ermei Glebovitch died, along with most of the rest of the army. Kolomna fell, and then Moscow, where Yuri's son Vladimir was captured. The killing in these towns was not as extensive as at Riazan; numbers of people were carried off to take part as laborers in the siege of Vladimir, Duke Yuri's capital in Suzdal.

The Duke had left Vladimir, which he thought strong enough to hold out, while he met with his brothers and nephews to raise an army elsewhere. With their typical speed the Mongol army moved quickly on Vladimir, a distance of about a hundred miles. They displayed their prisoner, Prince Vladimir, and demanded the surrender of the city in exchange for his life. This was necessarily refused and so the prince was killed in sight of his family. The Mongols then set up a palisade around the city with timber brought from Riazan; its siege had begun.

After the siege of Vladimir was started, Subotai sent half of his army to attack the city of Suzdal. It was taken at the first assault and the troops were back in five days with many prisoners to help in the siege of Vladimir.

Vladimir was assaulted on February 7, 1238, a Saturday, and on Sunday at dawn an attack was pressed on all four gates of the city at once. The defense became confused and ineffective. The Mongols stormed the city and found two of Duke Yuri's sons already dead. Yuri's wife, the Grand Duchess, had gone to the cathedral—where hundreds had fled—with her children and grandchildren. She and her family went into the choir loft and refused to descend when the Mongols asked. The church was set ablaze and collapsed.

With Vladimir taken, the Mongol army split into two. Subotai went north to search for Grand Duke Yuri and his army while Batu went northwest toward Novgorod. Both armies sacked cities on their way: Subotai took Yuriev, Rostov and Yaroslav; Batu took Dmitrov and Tver. Grand Duke Yuri, with his brother and nephews, had by now indeed gathered an army, but waited until February for a force from Novgorod that did not come. Yuri sent out a large reconnaissance only to find that he was surrounded. Battle was joined on March 4, 1238, and the Russian army was defeated. Meanwhile Batu, with the other half of the Mongol army, had been held up two weeks at the town of Torzhok, which defended itself sturdily. The spring thaw came and it was too difficult for the Mongols, with their thousands of horses, to penetrate the woods and swamps on the way to Novgorod, so that city was spared. Batu pulled back and joined Subotai on the Russian steppe west of the Don. The conquest of Russia was half completed.

The Mongols took up the conquest again in the summer of 1240, ravaging the country in the principalities of Periaslav and Chernikov and destroying both cities. Prince Michael of Chernikov fled to eastern Europe. In November 1240 a Mongol army under Chinggis' son Mangu arrived at Kiev, Russia's first and greatest city. Its ruler, Daniel, had fled to Poland with his brother, Prince Vasilko. The city was under the direction of a nobleman, Dimitri, posted there by Prince Daniel. Many of the citizens took the view that the city should be handed over to the Mongols in the hope of mercy, but Dimitri was determined to resist. When the Mongol envoys came to demand surrender he had them killed and their bodies displayed over a city gate, thus forestalling any efforts to treat with the enemy.

Batu arrived at Kiev and the Mongols began to barrage the Polish gate, a section of the defenses made of wood, with catapults. When the gate fell, cavalry rushed into the streets and the Mongols took the walls. The next day the Mongols completed the conquest of the city after hard fighting. Hundreds had fled to the Church of the Virgin, which they had fortified, but so many people climbed onto the roof that the building collapsed upon everyone inside. Dimitri was taken alive and, curiously perhaps, spared. Batu admired the man's loyalty to the absent prince who had left him in such a situation. Batu later gained a reputation as being favorable to Russians.

The fall of Kiev marked the end of serious resistance to the Mongols in Russia, though a number of other smaller cities were taken and destroyed shortly afterwards. Batu began to receive the submission of the minor Russian princes who had not fled. The Russian campaign was over.

Again we see in this campaign the Mongol hallmarks: speed in moving forces over great distance, coordination in the movement of separate forces to achieve strategic ends, successful siegecraft, and the calculated use of terror. We also see the amalgamation of other peoples, in this case Kipchaks, into the horde. This was something Chinggis Khan had done consistently in central Asia to swell his forces, although he wisely broke up defeated tribes and distributed them among loyal units so they would not pose a threat to him and so, over time, they would come to think of the Mongol state as the entity they should obey. As more than one writer has pointed out, Chinggis Khan created of the Mongols an artificial tribe made up of Mongols proper and the dozens of steppe peoples they had absorbed. His amalgamation was remarkably successful, and accounts for the solidity and longevity of his empire, which, by steppe standards, was impressive.

Batu's horde was known in the West as the Golden Horde, perhaps because of the color of its tents, but it was known in the East as the Kipchak Khanate because he had absorbed so many of the Kipchak Turks of the Russian steppe into it. In fact these far outnumbered the Mongols and the coins of the Golden Horde soon began to have Turkic inscriptions as well as Mongol. All the same, this horde was always loyal to the descendants of Chinggis Khan in spite of its mixed origins, and applied the "Tatar Yoke" to the Russian people for two hundred years.

As might reasonably be expected, in consequence of their subjection to them, the Russians adopted the Mongol style of warfare themselves. They fought with the compound bow from horseback, wore Mongol armor and rode with the short stirrup. As one historian noted:

> In the field Mongol armies were arranged into an advance guard, a main regiment, left and right regiments, and a rear guard. Because of the superiority of the right in shamanist tradition, the right guard was ranked above the left. Muscovite armies took the field in the same formation, even to the point of having the right guard dominant.[5]

The Central European campaign which followed, in 1241, shows with greater clarity than the Russian campaigns the tactics as well as the strategies most commonly used by the Mongols. On the eve of the Mongol invasions of Poland and Hungary, Europe was in a state of disorder. Pope Gregory IX and the Holy Roman Emperor, Frederick II, were at war with each other, Poland was divided among four related dukes and in Hungary King Bela IV was at odds with his nobles. Duke Frederick II of Austria, Bela's personal enemy, would take advantage of events at the Hungarian king's expense as well. In spite of this, when Mongol scouts were spotted in Poland and Hungary, the European nobility began to muster armies.

Those Mongol scouts were the first of an army of about sixty thousand that left Russia in February 1241 and crossed the frozen rivers into eastern Europe. The Mongols meant to take Hungary, but to do this they intended to isolate that country from any help its neighbors might give. In this regard, their approach is similar to that taken in their conquest of Russia, where a pre-emptive campaign was first fought against the Kama Bulgars and the Kipchaks.

The Mongol army divided into two parts. The smaller consisted of two tumens and started off first at the beginning of March, heading north into Poland. The Mongols knew that the nobility of eastern Europe were related by blood and marriage, and Subotai, who had planned the campaign, did not want to see any support from the Polish nobility for the King of Hungary. The northern column was to keep the Poles occupied, and then, when the time was right, sweep down from the north to assist in the defeat of Hungary. Baidar and Kaadan, two of Chinggis Khan's grandsons, commanded this column. They described a northward arc past the edge of the Carpathians and into Poland and began to look for resistance.

A few days later, Subotai and Batu broke the larger army of forty thousand into three different contingents. Each of them entered the Carpathians by a different route on the way to Hungary.

The Europeans were not unaware of the threat—news of the depredations in Russia had already caused tremors, particularly in Poland which had little in the way of geographical barriers—but their disunity kept them from effective mobilization. Count Boleslav IV (who claimed to be King of Poland) raised an army of Polish knights, foreign knights (including some from France and Germany) and members of the military orders.

The military orders, as we have seen, had already proven themselves as elite fighters during the Crusades against the Seljuks. These establishments of armed monks such as the Knights Templar, the Knights of the Hospital of Saint John of Jerusalem, the Teutonic knights and the Brothers of the Sword fought for the protection of the church. As Europe's most disciplined and professional soldiers they were an important addition to the Polish army, though in this case they were not numerous. They were, however, trained for shock combat—they wore full armor and charged the enemy with a heavy lance. Further encounters would be decided hand-to-hand with broadsword, axe or mace. While these men were extremely obedient to their captains (unlike secular knights), and very brave, they had no training to help them cope with horse archery and they were not capable of intricate or flexible maneuver on the battlefield. Their horses were necessarily heavy, and European tactics of the day were based upon the idea of winning at the first shock. This army numbered about thirty thousand.

Duke Henry of Silesia, then part of Poland, drew up a similar, somewhat larger army. Meanwhile in Hungary, King Bela gathered his forces, but got little cooperation from his nobles; they mistrusted his power and were unable to grasp the seriousness of the Mongol threat.

The northern Mongol column under Baidar and Kaadan looked for the enemy in Poland. Snow slowed them, but on March 18 they met the combined armies of Boleslav and the Russian prince Mstislav of Galicia. The Mongols defeated this army and drove the Poles south and the Slavs west. The Mongols then advanced to Kracow, which was abandoned, and burned the city. Afterward, they put a bridge across the Oder and took Breslau, where they found that Duke Henry had assembled his army near Liegnitz (modern Legnica). Henry's army numbered about forty thousand and awaited support from an army of fifty thousand under King Wenceslas of Bohemia. The Mongols were outnumbered by Duke Henry as things stood, and they knew of Wenceslas' approach. They decided to attack before the two armies could join.

Meanwhile to the south, Subotai and Batu's forces approached the guarded Hungarian passes of the Carpathian Mountains. King Bela had thought to stop the Mongol advance by cutting trees across the mountain paths and by strengthening the fortress garrisons that guarded the passes. Bela reasonably thought that he had gained time to prepare for the Mongol attack, and he needed time to spar with his nobles and convince them to support his efforts to resist. Bela's father had ceded a good deal of power to his nobles, and when Bela had taken the throne he had determined to gain it back in order to be an effective ruler. The nobles resisted this generally and were dangerously uncooperative in the face of the Mongol invasion. And then there was Khan Khotyan.

Khotyan, it will be remembered, had fled with a number of his Kipchaks to safety in Hungary during the Mongols' first onslaughts in Russia. He had accepted Christian baptism (Bela was his godfather) and he offered to field forty thousand Kipchaks against the Mongols. Bela was understandably delighted with this and settled the Kipchaks in Hungary, where the peasants regarded them as a nuisance. All the same, Bela stood by Khotyan, recognizing the invaluable help a steppe warrior with experience of the Mongols could give him. The nobles saw it differently: they regarded the Kipchaks as a support to the throne over which they had no power. Bela was therefore obliged to put Khotyan under house arrest in Buda to placate his nobles. Meanwhile, Duke Frederick of Austria, a personal enemy of Bela, had arrived with his forces, ostensibly to help, and promptly took the nobles' side. It was against this background that Bela received the news on March 10 that the Mongols had begun to attack the Carpathian passes. Four days later the commander of the passes arrived in Buda to say they had fallen.

Now Duke Frederick fanned the enmity of the Hungarian nobles against the Kipchaks, but Bela stood by them as they were the only force openly willing to fight the Mongols. Frederick and a handful of nobles went to the house where Khotyan and some of his Kipchak lieutenants were under house arrest and murdered them—their heads were thrown into the street to the cheers of the crowd. In a fury, the Kipchaks fled across Hungary into Bulgaria, pillaging as they went. Bela had lost a valuable ally. Frederick returned to Austria.

The passes having fallen quickly, the Mongols advanced with incredible speed, even by modern standards. They covered forty miles a day in the snow, something an army today would find difficult. The Mongols' disparate columns all rendezvoused outside Buda by prearrangement. Bela marshaled his army in the German town of

Pesth across the Danube from Buda.

At almost the same time in Poland, Duke Henry and his Polish-German army left Liegnitz. It was the morning of April 9. Their aim was to join with Wenceslas and his large Bohemian army which was only a day away. Instead they were confronted by the Mongols on a plain south of Liegnitz. This place has since been known as the "Wahlstatt," or chosen place. Henry's army took up positions on level ground with the mounted soldiers in the van and the infantry behind.

As the battle began, the Europeans noted that the enemy moved without battle cries or trumpets; signals were given by flags, and it was difficult to judge the size of the Mongol army because its cavalry formations were denser than those of the knights and they seemed only half as many as they were.

The first of Duke Henry's divisions charged and was beaten back by flights of Mongol arrows. The heavily armored knights could not close with the lightly equipped horse archers. Henry's men mounted a second charge which, unlike the first, drove the Mongols into flight. The knights were cheered and pressed the attack, and the enemy continued to melt away, evidently unable to face them.

Unfortunately, things were not as they seemed to the knights, for the Mongols were using the steppe tactic of the feigned retreat and they drew the knights into a line separated from the infantry. This move recalls what Marco Polo would write of Mongol tactics a few years later:

> When these Tartars come to engage in battle, they never mix with the enemy, but keep hovering about him, discharging their arrows first from one side and then from the other, occasionally pretending to fly, and during their flight shooting arrows backwards at their pursuers, killing men and horses, as if they were combating face to face. In this sort of warfare the adversary imagines he has gained a victory, when in fact he has lost the battle; for the Tartars, observing the mischief they have done him, wheel about, and make them prisoners in spite of their utmost exertions. Their horses are so well broken-in to quick changes of movement, that upon the signal given they instantly turn in every direction;

and by these rapid manoeuvres many victories have been obtained.[6]

The Mongols then swept to either side of the knights as they became strung out, and shot them with arrows from their composite bows. Other Mongols had lain in ambush—to meet the knights as they advanced into the trap. The Mongols sometimes found the knights' armor proof against their arrows, but then simply shot horses. Once dismounted, the knights were easy for the Mongols to run down with lance or saber, offering little danger to themselves. And the Mongols used another tactic: they produced smoke that drifted across the battlefield between Henry's infantry and his charging knights, thus screening one force from the other. Mongol horse archers advanced beyond the smoke and shot the infantry to pieces.

In this horrific battle the Mongols defeated the Europeans completely—on their own terms—and virtually annihilated them. Duke Henry was killed trying to escape with a handful of men, and the Mongols sent nine large sacks of ears to Batu and Subotai in Hungary to show them the extent of the victory. Contemporary records set the European losses at between twenty-five and thirty thousand. Duke Henry's head was set on a pike and displayed before the walls of Liegnitz, which the citizens had burned, withdrawing to the citadel. The Mongols forewent an assault, recalling Wenceslas and the Bohemian army.

Learning of Henry's defeat, Wenceslas and the Bohemians prudently halted their approach and retreated to a defensive position. Baidar and Kaadan felt too outnumbered to attack Wenceslas in his defensive position, and in any case they were satisfied there was no longer any support for Hungary to be found in Poland. They headed south to rejoin Batu and Subotai.

The Europeans consoled themselves with the thought that at the "Wahlstatt" they had been beaten by a force of Mongols that hugely outnumbered them. Aside from the horrific results of the battle, this idea was reinforced by the common notion that the Mongols numbered several times more than they did; their speed on the march of course caused their numbers to be overestimated. The same army or troop would be counted repeatedly as it moved; it did not occur to observers that apparently different Mongol forces were often the same forces seen repeatedly at different points far apart.

King Bela left Pesth, moving north, on April 9, 1241, the very date of the Battle of Liegnitz, although he was unaware of it. His army was very large, perhaps eighty thousand, and was, by European standards at least, quite good. Bela had a great number of mercenaries, and his nobles could no longer ignore the Mongols; they agreed to fight.

As the Hungarians advanced, the Mongols retired slowly ahead of them for several days. The steppe warriors were successfully leading the Hungarians to the plain of Mohi near the confluence of the Sajo and Tisza rivers, a spot that, with typical foresight, they had already chosen for the battle. When they reached Mohi, the Mongols crossed the Sajo by the only bridge and disappeared into the woods, camping some ten miles further on. The Hungarian scouts could find only their horse tracks.

Bela camped in the plain of Mohi and drew his wagons around the camp, chaining them for protection. Wherever the Mongols were, if they wished to attack they had to cross the river to his front and there was only the single stone bridge to allow this. Bela sent his brother, Koloman, a capable soldier, to hold it with a thousand men.

Before it was light Subotai had begun to move a column of horsemen upriver on the far bank of the Sajo, out of sight of the Hungarians. He intended to bridge the river behind them and attack while they were engaged by Batu and the balance of the Mongol army. Batu attacked the stone bridge, but Koloman and the Hungarians drove him off; the Mongols then returned to the bridge, this time equipped with catapults. These cast flash pots and smoke pots that disturbed the Hungarians and drove them off the bridge. The Mongols immediately took it, thousands swarming over.

Bela now mounted a charge into the Mongols. The horse archers had little room for maneuver and sustained significant losses from the shock. The fighting was hard and the Mongols resisted the Hungarian assault for two hours by heavy shooting, although Batu grew anxious as time passed. At one point Batu maneuvered his men toward the Hungarians' left flank and the enemy line turned. It was at this moment that Subotai appeared in the Hungarian rear. The Europeans, completely outmaneuvered, pulled back to their camp in good order, and the Mongols completely surrounded it. However, it was impractical to attack such a strong army within the protection of its wagons. Instead the Mongols attacked once more with catapults, throwing burning tar and naphtha.

Fire and smoke spread through the camp and it became more difficult to remain there. The Mongol army showed a gap to the west. With caution, a few of the Hungarians left the camp and tried to escape through it. The first were allowed to pass. Others followed, many throwing down their weapons and equipment to lighten their horses' loads. As more men fled, the flight became uncontrolled; they tried to race back to Pesth, three days' distance. As they ran, the Hungarians became strung out just like the knights chasing Baidar and Kaadan's army during its feigned retreat in Poland, and the Mongols handled them similarly: they rode along their flanks and shot them or rode them down with lance and saber.

Some say the killing went on for two days. In the end as many as sixty-five thousand men had died. Bela escaped, unrecognized, and fled ultimately to the Adriatic coast. The battle for Hungary was over. The Mongols began to systematically depopulate certain areas, promising peasants protection if they would take in the crops; then killing them once the work was done. The Mongols also used Bela's seal, which had fallen into their hands, to issue forged proclamations to the Hungarian authorities, telling them not to resist; they began to strike money. And then, eight months later, they pulled out and left, never to return to Central Europe in force. The withdrawal was of immeasurable importance to the West: another attack would likely have been as disastrous as the first.

The Mongols pulled out of Hungary ostensibly because the Great Khan Occodai, son and successor of Chinggis Khan, had died thousands of miles away in Karakorum, and the Mongols were needed at the kurilitai to choose another khan. This was true enough as far as it went, though there were already divisions forming within the Golden Family which would, in time, lead to the breakup of the Mongol Empire into a number of autonomous khanates. Batu was aware of these divisions and likely felt that, if his political influence in Karakorum were diminished with the election of a khan who was indifferent to him, he would no longer have the imperial tumens from Asia needed to extend, or even hold his conquests. He pulled out of Hungary, the imperial tumens returned to Mongolia, and Batu contented himself with Russia. There may have been other practical considerations as well, to be discussed later.

The campaign in Central Europe showed all the earmarks of Mongol steppe warfare—feigned retreat, ambush, encirclement, and the use of missiles (that is, arrows)—to wear an enemy down until his defeat was almost certain before closing in for hand-to-hand combat. Against this kind of warfare, and ignorant of the theory behind it, the heavily equipped knights and unsupported infantry of Europe were no match.

The election of Mangu as Great Khan may not have resulted in a resumption of hostilities against Europe, but it did produce a shattering blow for Islam. Since Chinggis Khan's defeat of the Khwarezmian Shah Muhammad II in the campaign of 1219–1221, the Persian territories had been left in an uncertain state; they were governed along the marches by generals with civil powers, but taxation had been left to other officials. No one was in general authority over the whole, while the kings of Georgia, Armenian Cilicia and the lords of Mosul were dependents. Mangu changed this in 1251 by appointing his younger brother, Hulegu, Regent of Persia and by charging him with the extermination of the Ismailis, a noxious Shia Muslim sect whose practice of political murder and use of hashish has left us the word "assassin." Mangu was further to subjugate the Caliph of Baghdad, the supreme religious leader of Islam, annex Syria and then conquer the last remaining power in the Near East, the Mamluk Sultanate of Egypt.

Hulegu set out from Mongolia and crossed the Amu Darya from Transoxiana into Persia in January 1256, there receiving the homage of the King of Herat, the Lord of Fars and the chiefs of the Seljuk Turks. He then went on to attack the mountain castles of the Ismaili Assassins at Mazanderan, Meimundiz and Alamut. During this campaign Hulegu used catapults served by Chinese engineers to batter the Assassins' forts. Round stone shot used as ammunition for Hulegu's catapults can still be found at the sites of the sieges. The last fortress, that of Alamut, surrendered on December 20, 1256, and the Assassins' Grand Master, Rukn ad-Din Kurshah, who had surrendered the fortress of Meimundiz was dead: he had been murdered as a prisoner en route to Mangu Khan in Mongolia. This sect, which

had withstood all previous efforts of extermination by Muslim powers, was finally extirpated by a nomad from the steppe, but one who
employed civilized technology. This was one of the keys to the
Mongol success: the coupling of steppe warfare with the technology
needed to take walled cities and strong places by means other than
blockade.

Although Hulegu's destruction of the Ismailis must have been
seen as a service to the Muslim world, his next move was not: he
proceeded against the Caliph al-Mustasim and called upon him to
hand over to the Mongols his temporal powers. The Caliph seems
unable to have grasped the danger that the Mongols presented, and
he declined. Hulegu recalled to the Caliph that the Mongols had
brought low a number of powers such as the Khwarezmians and the
Seljuks, who had formerly exercised their authority over the
Caliphate. How could it be any different now?

The Caliph would not be moved; he threatened Hulegu with a
great uprising of the Muslim world if he should attack. Hulegu was
not impressed. In November 1257 the Mongol general Baiju advanced on Baghdad by the Mosul Road. Hulegu's greatest general,
the Naiman Kitbuka, proceeded along the Luristan Road. Hulegu
himself led a third division from Hamadan. The Caliph's little army
sallied forth from the city to engage the Mongols on January 17,
1258, but was utterly destroyed. By the following day the Mongol
forces had joined together on the outskirts of Baghdad.

On January 22, a force of Mongols under three generals established themselves west of the Tigris River in a suburb while Hulegu
and Kitbuka completed the encirclement of Baghdad from the other
side. Now the Caliph wished to parley, and he sent out his vizier and
the Nestorian Christian bishop—but to no effect. The city was taken
by assault on February 5 and 6 and its garrison killed. On February
10, Caliph al-Mustasim came to Hulegu and, on the latter's orders,
commanded the people to come forth from the city without weapons. They obeyed and were killed; the Mongols then entered the
city and massacred those who had disobeyed. The dead from these
slaughters is said to have numbered ninety thousand altogether.
Hulegu was a Buddhist with two Nestorian Christian wives. His
mother had also been a Nestorian Christian and he was well disposed toward them, so that he spared the Christians of Baghdad as

he did those in other places. But the lot of the Muslims was horrific. The Caliph was then killed too—probably rolled into a carpet and trampled, because the Mongols were superstitiously uneasy about shedding royal blood except in battle.

Hulegu then moved north into Azerbaijan as the Muslim world reeled at the destruction of the Caliphate. By the time he left Azerbaijan his army contained Christian auxiliaries: Armenian troops of King Hethum I of Cilicia, one of Hulegu's vassals. As a nomad, Hulegu's court was not stationary, though it was often near the cities of Tabriz or Maragheh. At these cities he received the congratulations of the lords of Mosul and Fars and those of the sultans of the Seljuk Turks. His next duties were the conquests of Syria and Egypt.

The Syrian campaign began with the siege and capture of Maiyafariqin, justified as retaliation for its prince's execution of a Nestorian Christian priest traveling under Mongol protection. Upon the city's fall the prince was tortured to death. This was followed by the capture of Nisibin and the submission of Haran and Edessa.

The Mongol prince next crossed the Euphrates and, joined by additional Christian auxiliaries, he besieged Aleppo, Prince Bohemund VI of Antioch and Tripoli having joined him with troops. Upon its fall, Aleppo was subjected to a massacre of several days duration, and Hulegu gave Bohemund and Hethum territories that had been stripped from them by Muslims over the years.

Other terrified Muslim rulers in Syria submitted of their own accord. On March 1, 1260, Damascus surrendered at the approach of Kitbuka, accompanied by Bohemund and Hethum; there were no defenders. Only the citadel held out, and then for only a month, after which Kitbuka beheaded the governor as he had been ordered.

Three weeks more completed the conquest of Syria; only Egypt remained. No power in the West, either Christian or Muslim, had effectively resisted the Mongols. Hulegu was now Ilkhan of Persia, the suffix "Il" suggesting in the Mongol language that he was subservient to the Khagan, or Great Khan, Mangu. The Ilkhan now looked toward Egypt, the next area of military operations.

NOTES
1. Perhaps this tradition of lateral succession accounts for the Soviet Politburo's tendency to replace aging leaders with their fellow aging leaders. Note also

China in this regard, subject to a number of steppe invasions. Perhaps the scholars have missed something here.

2. "The Battle on the River Kalka," from the Novgorodian Chronicle in *Medieval Russia's Epics, Chronicles, and Tales*, trans. Serge A. Venkovsky, New York, Meridian Books, 1996, p. 194.

3. "The Battle on the River Kalka," p. 195.

4. "The Tale of the Destruction of Riazan," in *Medieval Russia's Epics, Chronicles, and Tales*, p. 202.

5. Charles J. Halperin, *Russia and the Golden Horde*, Bloomington, Indiana University Press, 1987, p. 91.

6. Marco Polo, *The Travels of Marco Polo the Venetian*, Marsden translation, ed. Thomas Wright, New York, AMS Press, 1968 (reprint of 1854 Bohn edition, London), p. 136.

9

The Mamluks

The Crusaders knew the Turks well enough. As Raymond of Aguilers wrote: "And indeed it is the custom of fighting among the Turks that, no matter how few they may be, still they always try to surround their enemies."[1] And they did this in order to shoot at them—a tactic which made as much of their numbers as possible, even when they were few. They also were known for flight before an enemy charge and regrouping to attack when the enemy charge broke down. What Odo of Deuil said of their fighting is consistent with this: "they are schooled and apt at flight," and he noted of King Louis VII that "he could have neither peace nor war."[2]

The pattern is familiar now. When Crusaders fought Muslims they often encountered steppe tactics because even though the Arab contingents of the Muslim armies fought in ways more closely resembling those of the Crusaders themselves, the Muslim armies commonly included Turkish units among their orders of battle or might be made up entirely of Turks. Anna Comnena, daughter of the Byzantine Emperor Alexius Comnenus (ruled 1081–1118) and a contemporary chronicler of the First Crusade, knew about Turkish tactics too:

> He [Alexius Comnenus] knew from very long experience that the Turkish battle-line differs from that of other peoples ... but their right and left wings and their centre formed separate groups with the ranks cut off, as it were, from one another; whenever an attack was made on right or left, the centre leapt into action and all the rest of the army behind, in a whirlwind onslaught that threw into confusion the

accepted tradition of battle. As for the weapons they use in war, unlike the Kelts [Franks] they do not fight with lances, but completely surround the enemy and shoot at him with arrows; they also defend themselves with arrows at a distance. In hot pursuit the Turk makes prisoners by using his bow; in flight he overwhelms his pursuer with the same weapon and when he shoots, the arrow in its course strikes either rider or horse, fired with such tremendous force that it passes clean through the body. So skilled are the Turkish archers.[3]

Her knowledge is no surprise. Using tactics such as these, the Seljuk Turks under Alp Arslan had stripped most of Anatolia from the Byzantine Empire after defeating Romanus Diogenes at the Battle of Manzikert in 1071, a blow from which the empire never recovered. Other Turks under their chief Osman would enter Anatolia upon the dissolution of Seljuk power to establish the state which ultimately became Ottoman Turkey. In the meantime the Arabs and Egyptians continued their longstanding practice of buying Turkic slaves to train as soldiers for use in their armies. By this practice they did somewhat as the late Romans had done: they adopted steppe warfare into their military approach. The Romans had done this by, for example, hiring entire bands of Huns, but the Arabs and Egyptians in contrast bought nomads as individuals and inculcated into them a loyalty for the state that the Huns had naturally lacked with regard to Rome. This allowed the Arabs and Egyptians to field armies of adept horse archers prepared to use the tactics of the steppe against the Byzantines, the Latin Crusaders or against other steppe nomads themselves. Thus, these settled civilizations had, in a sense, institutionalized the tactics of the steppe.

The introduction of slaves, called Mamluks,[4] into Arab armies likely began in the eighth century and was certainly well established by the ninth as a response to Islamic teaching and the fragmentation of the Islamic world after the death of Muhammad. The choice of caliphs, or successors, to Muhammad quickly became disputed as did the method of their selection, echoes of which are still found in the division between the Sunni and Shia sects. Further, territorial squabbles developed between the Islamic states, and both of these problems naturally invited a military solution. But there was a difficulty: the Koran discourages warfare between Muslims, and the devout often felt obliged to avoid conflicts and fighting with their co-religionists.

The solution taken by the Muslims was military slavery—the purchase of boys and young men, largely from the Turkic nomadic tribes of the southern Russian and Black Sea steppes, to be employed as soldiers. There was a particularly large influx of such Turks in the years following the Mongol invasion of Russia in 1236–1238. While the Mongols conquered the Kipchak Turks of the steppe and absorbed many of them into their state and hence into the army, they also sold large numbers of them to Egypt and the Arab states as slaves, and these men often began careers as professional soldiers in the Near East.

These men were invaluable. They fought the Mongols of Il-khanid Persia to a standstill and continued their earlier work in dislodging the Crusaders from their territories in the Middle East. It was directly as a result of the Mamluks that the Crusader states of Syria and Palestine were finally expunged from the Arab lands, and the nomads from the steppe prevented from carrying their depredations further into the Muslim world. The Mongols were stopped at Ayn Jalut, and though they pressed Egypt and Syria for a decade, the Mamluks stood fast and held them away.

Because these Turks were converted to Islam themselves and fought with armies composed of other Muslims, it is less than clear how the injunction against internecine Muslim warfare was really to be solved by this stratagem. It smacks of the technical and recalls the use, by medieval warrior-clergymen in Europe, of maces to avoid shedding blood.[5] Be that as it may, the Muslim world touched the steppe in many places and could not help but know of the skill of the nomad in warfare. Even the boys and young men purchased from the steppe, if not as accomplished as their elders, would have been excellent horsemen and practiced archers, extremely tough and largely inured to killing by virtue of their experience as herdsmen. They were perfect material for soldiers and, further, were open to the Muslim religion.

It is difficult to conceive of slaves whose duties were military, specially trained to develop and hone their skills as soldiers. The

Mamluks, however, were different. Though slaves, they enjoyed high status in Egypt and Syria; they were the best of the troops and knew it. A mark of their importance is that Turkic-Arabic grammars were written to encourage Arabs to learn their language. Some of these grammars survive and reflect from their vocabulary that most Mamluks were of Kipchak origin, while a few were Turkmen. Of more interest, from a military standpoint, is a different kind of book associated with the Mamluks: the *furusiya* manuals. Furusiya refers to the skills to be mastered by mounted soldiers, and these textbooks set out drill and instruction in the necessary skills for the Mamluks. This would have been useful because it allowed for formal training of these nomads who, for all their natural ability and practical experience, would not have been drilled in the sense that sedentary people used the term.

Of course, success led inevitably to power. Because they were proven soldiers, the Mamluks were depended upon by the sultans of Egypt and Syria as the backbone of their armies. Mamluks rose to advise the sultans in military matters, as was only natural, and in time they grew more powerful than their masters. Eventually the Ayyubid Sultanate, founded by Sultan Salah al-Din Yusuf ibn-Ayyub—the Kurd better known in the west as Saladin—was overthrown, and in 1250 Aybak became the first of the Mamluks to gain supreme power over Egypt. This Mamluk domination of the sultanate was to endure for centuries. A central figure in this revolution was the Mamluk Baybars al-Bunduqdari whose origins were typical of his class. He himself later rose to sultan, so his rise illustrates most aspects of the Mamluk's life.

Born a Kipchak Turk on the steppes of southern Russia around 1228, he lived there only until he was about fourteen. It was then that the Mongols advanced from Central Asia into this area to stay. The armed reconnaissance in 1223 under the generals Subotai and Jebe had defeated and badly frightened the Kipchaks, and their later incursion of 1236—this one an invasion proper—resulted in their subjection and incorporation into the Mongol Empire. These Turks were numerous, however, and after they had been pressed into the army, made up the larger part of the Mongol invasion force sent into Europe. They made a good fit with the Mongols, of course, because they were so like them in way of life and way of war, and it was not long before the *revanche du berceau,* or "cradle's revenge," had transformed the Golden Horde: it was soon known as the Kipchak Khanate and, though ruled by the descendants of Chinggis Khan, the horde's language became Turkish.

Baybars, however, did not become part of the horde. Instead, like thousands of others, he was sold into slavery and sent to Siwas, a city in Asia Minor, to be sold once more. Baybars was taken from there to Aleppo, in Syria, where he was sold to Imad al-din, a goldsmith, for 800 dirhams, but was sent back because he had a cataract in one eye. This caused him to be refused by the Princess al-Malik al-Mansur as well.

In the meantime, the Sultan of Egypt, Al-Malik al-Salih, had imprisoned one of his own Mamluks, Ala al-din al-Bunduqdari. This man learned of the Kipchak Baybars and purchased him. It appears likely that this was because al-Bunduqdari, as a Mamluk, was himself a Kipchak, and it was from al-Bunduqdari that Baybars acquired one of his names.

Al-Bunduqdari was eventually pardoned and then took Baybars with him to Cairo, but he fell into disgrace again and was imprisoned once more, forfeiting all his goods, including Baybars, to the Sultan. Another story indicates that Baybars showed such promise that it seemed he should become a Royal Mamluk, one of the Sultan's own, rather than the Mamluk of an emir, and it was on these grounds that the Sultan took him. This must have occurred after he had graduated from his training as a Mamluk.

Such training was disciplined and arduous and in the course of it a Mamluk was to perfect his skills as a rider, archer, lancer and swordsman. A group of young Mamluks would train together, and after years of this practice they would graduate as a class to be freed and enrolled in their masters' households as his personal soldiers. They might be Royal Mamluks attached to the Sultan himself or Mamluks of the lesser nobility, the emirs of various ranks. The training of the Royal Mamluks was better than that of the emirs' Mamluks, but both were marked by methodical practice.

The combat training was various, and we are fortunate in the survival of a number of medieval furusiya manuals such as the *Munyatu'l-Ghuzat,* or "Wish of the Warriors of the Faith." It dates from the fourteenth century, but the skills it touches on would have been those required of earlier Mamluks. Those skills were horsemanship, tilting, use of the shield, swordsmanship, archery and polo. The last skill should not be dismissed as frivolous; polo was developed to help cavalrymen hone their horsemanship and it requires useful skills. As the *Munyatu'l-Ghuzat* states:

> Know that playing polo is one of the most beneficial skills of horsemanship. This is essential for whatever skill of horsemanship you wish, especially for using the lance, sword and arrow, that is to say, in [all] these skills, because such things happen a lot in this [game]: charging, snatching away [the ball], turning, defending, running around, confronting each other, riding the horse and training the horse. In my opinion it happens in the training course, that is to say the horse and the horseman prepare for the war, they have a practice and their hearts get accustomed to war. . . . It is serious practice for war.[6]

Of the other skills it is tilting—the use of the lance from horseback against a mounted opponent—oddly, which is treated at much greater length than any other. It is difficult to say why this should be unless the Mamluk, a nomadic Turk by origin, was already expected to be competent at archery. Indeed, although the *Munyatu'l-Ghuzat* may be missing part of its archery section (this is uncertain), the remainder spends some time in explaining how to shoot up at walls, or down from them at attackers—something not encountered on the steppe, but a necessary skill in settled regions.

Furthermore, the lance was important to the Arab armies, for they had been patterned on the heavily armored Byzantine cavalry they had encountered, and they relied upon the lance and broadsword much as a Western knight did. Their equipment was lighter, however; it was generally agreed that Arab cavalry could not easily withstand the shock of a Frankish charge. Still, the Arab taste for tilting would account for its prominence in the furusiya manuals—it was a skill they clearly wished to impart to their Mamluk horse archers. Further, the medieval scholar David Ayalon suggests that lance work was so emphasized because it was demonstrated to the crowds during certain biennial processions. While this is no doubt true, only a handful of the Mamluks rode in these processions and performed these exercises, while the whole mass of them were expected to be proficient at them. The conclusion seems inescapable that they were meant to know how to the use the lance well, and to use it well in battle, even if it were not their principal weapon.

The *Munyatu'l-Ghuzat* describes four different methods of tilting: the old Khorasan style, the new Sagr style, the Damascus style and the Daylam (or Yaman) style. The first two, the old Khorasan and the new Sagr style, refer to two-handed methods of tilting. In the former, the lance is held near the butt with the right hand and behind the head with the left while the rider turns and leans slightly to the left to gain some protection from the horse's body. The lance is to be held with the blade near the horse's right cheek. In the new Sagr style the rider reverses this hold with the left hand near the butt and the right behind the head, and is to thrust it sharply at his opponent and then pull it back. It is difficult to see how the rider could effectively use a shield with these techniques, and indeed the *Munyatu'l-Ghuzat* considers them a nuisance in tilting.

The Damascus style of tilting is familiar to the Westerner: it calls for the lance to be held in the right hand and couched under the armpit for a more rigid hold. This technique was that favored by Western knights and it became practical with the introduction of stirrups.

In the Daylam, or Yaman, style the lance is held in the right hand alone. "You should hold the lance with your palm under it. The lance should be held so that it is resting on your right wrist." This method would, of course, not allow for the shock of the other, but would be the most delicate approach and useful for reaching out to vulnerable targets.

As for the lance itself, the *Munyatu'l-Ghuzat* states:

And the lance should be of medium size [in thickness] because if it is thick, it will not easily remain in one's hand. And also the fingers will not grasp [tightly] around it. No matter how strong you are, let your lance be as light as possible, because a light lance with defects is [still] better than a heavy lance without them. If you are strong and able to wield a heavy [lance], you will still do better with a light one, and you will be able to perform with it as you wish. No matter how strong you are, make your weapon as light as possible, especially your lance, and that is that.[7]

This emphasis on different lance techniques and the employment of a light lance for ease of use suggest an altogether more refined approach to tilting than that used by contemporary Western horsemen, and this is consistent with the fact that the *Munyatu'l-Ghuzat* describes certain tricks to perform with lances. For example: "If the opponent chases you, put your lance suddenly between the two front legs of his horse and bend down a little so that he will surely fall down." This is not a maneuver associated with Western shock cavalry tactics and would require a light lance, as would the various "transfers" found in the book which explain how to handle the lance when changing from one tilting style to another.

Shooting from horseback, though not so thoroughly treated, is addressed and this furusiya manual describes an exercise to help become proficient in this skill: the horse archer places five targets on his left side and five on his right, and shoots at them while galloping past. As he becomes more accomplished he is to move the targets closer to one another so that the horse will take only seven steps between each shot. Seven steps, the book assures us, is the limit between shots.

Thus, the skills of horsemanship, tilting, archery, swordsmanship, use of the shield and polo were the concern of Mamluks such as Baybars. These Mamluks were naturally well equipped as befitted soldiers of their position; they wore armor, usually chainmail coats or brigandines (short jackets with plates riveted to the inside), as well as conical iron helmets with mail coifs. Their shields were small and round. Mamluk swords were straight and double-edged like European swords and a mace was sometimes carried with the shaft slid under the saddlegirth.

While the practice of purchasing Turks from the steppe for the army went back centuries, in 1240 the Egyptian Sultan had established a unit of Mamluks of which he was particularly proud: the Bahri Regiment. This regiment, named for its fort on the island of Rawda in the Nile at Cairo, was recruited entirely of Kipchaks. One of the reasons given for its establishment was the threat that Al-malik al-Salih correctly perceived from the Mongols as a result of their expansion in the Middle East. It was not against the Mongols, however, that Baybars fought his first major battle; it was against the Crusaders at Mansurah in February 1250.

The Battle of Mansurah followed the landing, at Damietta, of Louis IX of France in November 1249. The French king led a crusade to win back Jerusalem from the Muslims, who had captured it some years before with a combined army of Mamluks and Khwarezmians. The pope had agreed to the preaching of the crusade in France and Louis had left for Cyprus, where he spent a good deal of time marshaling his forces, though he delayed rather too long and storms destroyed much of his fleet. Nevertheless he pressed on toward Damietta on the Nile delta, convinced that the defeat of Egypt was necessary to the recovery of Jerusalem.

Many of the ships were also scattered during the voyage, yet Louis and the French were able to land against Egyptian resistance and take Damietta, from which the Egyptian general Fakhr al-Din withdrew without a fight. Louis did not press his victory—and perhaps could not as he had to wait for the reinforcement of his scattered army as it found its way by ship to Damietta. Still, he might be said to have dawdled, for he waited six months in the city and the Egyptians were able to gather against him. Furthermore, the Nile rose, as it does seasonally, and denied the French the easy crossing they would have had earlier—needed for a rush on Cairo. Still, Louis was lucky: on the night of November 22–23, 1249, Sultan al-Malik al-Salih died. His death caused a vacuum in leadership which his son, Turanshah, was summoned to fill, but he was acting as viceroy in the north of the Ayyubid Empire and could not arrive quickly. The Sultan's death was kept a secret both from the French and from the Egyptians. The queen, Shajarat al-Durr, gained the support of the generals Fakhr al-Din and Jamal al-Din Mushin, and knitted things together.

King Louis and the French continued to advance, heading south until they reached Buramun, across from Mansurah, where they were trapped between the high waters of the Nile and one of its branches. There they stayed until February, when an Egyptian traitor, or perhaps a Bedouin, betrayed a ford to the French in return for payment. Louis sent his brother, Robert of Artois, with a detachment of knights and Templars to cross the river and hold that point until the main body of the army could follow. The lack of Crusader discipline then came to the fore. Robert saw a chance to surprise the Egyptian camp and did so, driving them off in a panic instead of holding his position at the ford. He was to do worse. Against the advice of the Templars, who wished to await the rest of the army, he pressed after the fleeing Egyptians all the way to the walls of Mansurah, where he found a gate open.

The Templars, famous for their discipline, followed Robert as their leader and the detachment penetrated the town as far as the citadel. There, however, they encountered troops who did not panic: Bahri and Jamadari Mamluks. The Latin knights with their heavy equipment and horses found they could not maneuver in the streets and alleys of Mansurah and were largely slaughtered by their more nimble opponents. Robert himself was killed, along with some three hundred knights, eighty Templars and a number of crossbowmen and mounted sergeants.

King Louis had, meantime, crossed the ford with the balance of the army and he beat off a counterattack by, it is said, four thousand mounted troops.[8] The figure is doubtless much exaggerated, although they must have been numerous. To the Crusaders, chronically short of men, this action exacted a terrible cost, and the French army was no longer strong enough to attack Mansurah. Louis and his men therefore hunkered down in an armed camp fending off Egyptian attacks. The king had sought to bring supplies in by river, but the Egyptians established their own flotilla and intercepted them. Eventually disease, the common scourge of armies, broke out and King Louis headed back toward Damietta, the army in some disorder and shadowed by the Egyptians, who took their opportunity to attack and destroy the French at Fariskur. Louis himself was captured and the price of his ransom was the return of Damietta.

While Baybars is sometimes wrongly credited with commanding the Mamluks at Mansurah (he was only about twenty-one at the time and could not have attained sufficient rank), he was certainly an officer of some sort by then, and almost certainly fought there with the Bahris. He had other, more important battles, however, ahead of him.

Turanshah, the new sultan, did not long survive King Louis's crusade. He has been accused of laziness and dissolution, but his chief
fault, in the eyes of the Bahri Mamluks, was his efforts to place his
own Mamluks from Hisn Kayfa into positions of power at the
Bahris' expense. He alienated Shajarat al-Durr, failed to reward an
important supporter and determined to make a quick peace with
King Louis so that he would not be dependent upon his father's
Mamluks. All in all he moved too quickly and on May 2, 1250, he
was killed by the Bahris. Prominent among the plotters was Baybars,
who initially struck him with a sword and perhaps later dispatched
him when Turanshah dove into the Nile.

The murder was observed by Jean de Joinville, biographer of
King Louis, who was held prisoner on a galley moored at the scene.
Aybak, a Mamluk of the Bahri regiment was soon installed with
Queen Shajarat al-Durr and ruled with a young Ayyubid prince to
give the regime legitimacy. Aybak purchased a number of personal
Mamluks to counterbalance the strength of the Bahri Regiment and
succeeded finally in driving the Bahri emirs from Egypt; a number of
them fled, with Baybars as their leader, to Al-Nasir, ruler of Aleppo
and Damascus.

Aybak, too, eventually fell victim to murderous Egyptian politics; his Queen, Shajarat al-Din, killed him. The throne then came to
Qutuz, another Mamluk, who repulsed an attack on Cairo by
Baybars and a small number of horsemen intent on taking advantage
of the unstable situation. Baybars had spent some years as a hired
soldier and adventurer, but by 1259 Qutuz was alarmed by the
Mongol threat and was willing to welcome him and the Bahris back
to Egypt—the Mongols were once again to play an extremely important part in Baybars' life.

The Mongol Hulegu's bloody conquest of Persia had begun with his
attack on the mountain strongholds of the Assassins. He largely
exterminated the sect, which most Muslims found justly repugnant,
but his advance did not stop there. By 1258 he had taken all of Persia
and killed the Caliph of Baghdad for failing to submit. By 1259 it
was clear that he had designs on the Mamluk states of Egypt and
Syria; in view of this, Qutuz charged Baybars with the defense of the
empire against the apparently indomitable Mongol hordes.

In 1260 Mongol envoys visited Qutuz with a letter from Hulegu demanding submission and insulting him: "He is of the race of the Mamluks [that is, Kipchaks] who fled before our sword into this country, who enjoyed its comforts and then killed its rulers."[9] Qutuz acted decisively: he got the agreement of his emirs and committed the state to war by murdering the envoys—an unpardonable crime in Mongol eyes. Their heads were put on display in Cairo. Qutuz then set out for Salihiyya, about seventy-five miles northeast, to organize the army, now augmented by Syrian troops, Turkmen, Bedouins and Kurds. It is not possible to determine the size of the army, but estimates of late Ayyubid armies suggest that it contained ten to twelve thousand horsemen, and if this were supplemented by the others mentioned above, then it probably was larger than the Mongol army under its commander Kitbuka.

The Mongol general was in the unenviable position of holding the frontier with a reduced force, about ten thousand men, while Hulegu pulled away many of the troops and headed back to Karakorum in Mongolia for the election of a new khan. Mangu had died and Hulegu had an interest in the outcome: although he had only a slender chance of being elevated as Great Khan himself, it was important to him who held the office. Hulegu did not get along well with his cousin Berke, Khan of Kipchak, and if there was to be war he did not want to find that his opponent had the favor of Karakorum. In this way the Mongol invasion of the Near East, like that of Europe twenty years before, was adversely affected by the death of the sovereign thousands of miles away.

Kitbuka's army was not made up entirely of Mongol troops, even in the loose sense that it contained large numbers of Kipchaks, Tatars or other steppe peoples. In Syria, Kitbuka also had some Armenians given by King Hethum of Cilicia and a number of Ayyubid Arab soldiers from Syria under the emirs Al-Ashraf Musa and Al-Said Hasan, now unwilling subjects.

Qutuz determined to advance against the Mongols in Syria. His emirs were generally opposed to this and preferred to wait for the Mongol advance into Egypt in the expectation of fighting them at Salihiyya; such an advance might confer an advantage upon the Mamluks by tiring the Mongol army as it passed through an arid region. Furthermore, there was always the chance that the Mongols would not in fact attack. Qutuz remonstrated with the emirs and finally announced that he would fight the Mongols alone, a tactic that finally provoked their cooperation. It seems he gambled that he had a chance to defeat the Mongols now that their forces were severely reduced, and also believed that this would enhance his position as sultan. He seems further to have feared that his emirs would grow less willing to resist the Mongols the longer they waited for action. He therefore sent Baybars ahead with a detachment of troops as a vanguard to find the Mongols.

Kitbuka was in the Bekaa Valley when he learned that the Mamluks had gone into Syria. He considered a retreat but ultimately decided to meet them. In doing so he approached a place known as Ayn Jalut, or "Goliath's Well." In the meantime Baybars reached Gaza, where he found a Mongol vanguard that pulled away upon seeing the Egyptian force. The leader of this Mongol force, one Baydar, sent word to Kitbuka at Baalbek, who told him to stand fast. There is a confused account of Qutuz driving Baydar away from this area to the Asi River near Ayn Jalut, which is probably a description of Qutuz's later approach with the main army toward the battlefield.

Qutuz came up to Gaza with the main army and then went on to Acre, one of the Crusader states. These Latins were in a difficult position. While the Mongols were open enemies of the Muslims and it might be hoped that they would effectively remove the Mamluk menace, the Crusaders were likely under no illusions about the ferocity of the Mongols and their cold self-interest. No doubt the Crusaders recalled what had happened to Poland and Hungary at the hands of the Mongols twenty years earlier. They remained neutral, slightly preferring the Mamluks, and furnished Qutuz's army with supplies.

Baybars soon found the Mongol army encamped near Ayn Jalut. He had ascended a height, probably Mount Gilboa or the Hill of Morah, to make a reconnaissance when he was spotted. The Mongols moved quickly to surround the hill and trap him but Baybars was able to descend and escape. There was skirmishing. Baybars sent word to Qutuz that he had met the enemy and then he fell back until he had joined Qutuz and the main army.

The battle itself began on the morning of September 3, 1260, after the Mamluk army had ridden in from the northwest through the Jezreel Valley. The Mongols had already taken up their position and the armies were probably drawn up, north to south, along a wide front, given their numbers.

As the Mamluks advanced the Mongols attacked, crushing the Mamluk left wing, which fell apart. At the beginning of the battle Al-Ashraf Musa deserted to the Mamluks with his men—surely a cause of distress to the Mongols, though these Syrian troops could scarcely have been trusted. The Mamluks were able to counterattack with good effect and this provoked a second Mongol attack that nearly caused a Mamluk defeat.

It was at this point that, according to tradition, Qutuz rallied the Mamluks with the cry "O Islam!" and charged into the Mongols. Military historian Hans Delbrueck has rightly pointed out that the human voice does not carry far, especially over the noise of battle, and that tales of leaders inspiring and rallying their men by voice, as claimed here, simply cannot be true, despite their universal currency. Still, Qutuz did in some way lead a second counter-charge and this decided the fight in the Mamluks' favor.

Kitbuka was killed, as were many Mongols—as many as fifteen hundred—while the rest scattered in flight. Local peasants killed numbers of others and the Mamluks fired fields of reeds in which Mongols were known to be hiding, burning them alive. The remnants of the Mongol force retreated and sought the protection of their ally King Hethum of Armenia in his territory. The Mongols had been decisively checked for the first time since the son of the Khwarezm Shah had won a brief victory against a small Mongol force in mountainous territory some eighty years before. The view that the Mongols could never be successfully resisted had been empirically disproved—albeit by troops who, for the most part, fought as they did.

There has naturally been a great deal of discussion of the Battle of Ayn Jalut, with some analyses of how the Mamluks were able to do what the Chinese, Khwarezmians, Russians, Europeans and Persians had been unable to do. Each case is, of course, special: the Chinese were internally divided as were the Europeans; Khwarezm was unstable, the Russian states small and busy quarreling. Chinggis Khan unquestionably had made his appearance at the right time. Still, nomads were always historically opportunistic and took advantage of any weakness in their neighbors. There must have been many such opportunities over the centuries for hundreds of minor khans, and yet, for all that, Chinggis Khan's victories and those of his immediate successors were far greater than anyone else's. They were clearly the most redoubtable of the nomad hordes, and no one had much success against them until the Mamluks. Further, the Mamluks were to have other successes: the Battle of Homs, for instance, ten years later, showed that their success was not a fluke.

One theory is that the Mamluks were simply better equipped than the Mongols coming off the steppe.[10] While this might have been true in given instances, or even generally, the difference could not have been that marked. The Mongol Empire now included Persia, from which a good number of weapons and armor must have been seized, and the Empire was now a well-established fact, with the power to tax huge numbers of people in order to equip the army. The Great Khan even had storehouses of weapons, mostly lances and swords, that were to be given out in time of war. And besides, every Mongol soldier, however poorly equipped, would have had at least his primary weapon: the bow. We know from many sources that he often carried two or even three, as well as a great many arrows, some of different lengths for shooting at long or short distance.

Differences in the quality of weapons alone do not, as a rule, give one army such a decisive advantage that it will tend to prevail; where there is even rough equality in such things, intangible factors such as morale, discipline and a tradition of winning will tend to decide the issue. James Dunigan gives a parallel from this century:

The Soviet Army in 1941 was one of the most lavishly equipped in history. Poorly led and poorly trained, and not very well motivated, the Soviets melted before the onslaught of the Germans. The Wehrmacht was not only outnumbered, but also had inferior weapons.[11]

The answer must be simpler: the Mamluks, like the Mongols, were horse archers, and professionally trained ones at that. By virtue of this they could fight them on something like equal terms as regards skill and technique. Secondly, the Mamluks benefited from the decisive leadership of Qutuz and Baybars, and were in a desperate situation, often a sufficient provocation in itself to produce the utmost effort. Further, the Mamluks seem to have outnumbered the Mongols. Although, as we have seen, a larger army was no guarantee whatsoever of being able to defeat an army from the steppes, in this case, the numbers may have been decisive: the Battle of Ayn Jalut was determined by a series of charges.

These charges were no doubt performed by numbers of mounted archers who shot at each other as they approached in order to soften the target. However, in this battle, in which two armies of mounted archers faced each other, the matter had to be settled at some point by closing and fighting hand-to-hand. The Mongols were prepared to do this of course, so long as their opponents were broken or a least softened. The Mamluks, however, could treat the Mongols to a dose of their own medicine, as Kitbuka knew, and he may have determined to close sooner than he would have otherwise against an army of shock cavalry since, in the end, that is where the decision would lay, whether there was extensive archery beforehand or not.

It is a truism, however, that cavalry cannot stand on the defense and receive a shock; only infantry can do this. Cavalry, by contrast, will be driven back and disordered. This is a point generally not recalled these days, but was common knowledge in pre-industrial armies depending upon cavalry as a combat arm. The response to a cavalry charge by its intended target is a counter-charge, and this is what the Mamluk response must have been. In fact, this basic rule of cavalry tactics dictates that the Mamluk response could have been nothing different; otherwise even a small body of Mongols would have disordered their target by plowing through them. Furthermore, increasing the depth of the attacking column does not increase the effect of a cavalry charge, because horsemen, unlike infantrymen, do not support each other in the charge. Successive waves of single lines of horsemen are, in theory, the best way to employ cavalry in a pure charge. Therefore, the army with the largest body of men, or the last reserve, will have a great advantage. It was likely this that Qutuz relied upon in the last charge which broke the Mongols.

All of this is not to suggest that the Mamluks did not fight this battle as steppe warriors might have done; the point is that the Mamluks, by perfecting the techniques of steppe warfare on a tactical level, were able to force the Mongols to fight at Ayn Jalut (and later elsewhere) on terms that favored their numbers, training and possibly superior armament.

Baybars did not forget the value of such training. Within a year Qutuz was dead; Baybars had been one of the chief plotters, and he assumed the throne as Sultan of Egypt and Syria. He was active against both the Mongols and the Crusaders, and built two famous hippodromes in Cairo, the Al-Maydan al-Zahiri and the Maydan al-Kabak, for the purpose of accommodating furusiya exercises—he encouraged others to practice by doing them himself twice a week. The Mamluks, though soldiers of a settled culture, were well trained in the techniques and tactical points of steppe warfare, and their institutional approach to it had saved Egypt and Syria from an enemy no one else could face.

NOTES

1. Quoted in R.C. Smail, *Crusading Warfare*, New York, Cambridge University Press, 1995, p. 79: "*Etenim id moris pubnandi apud Turcos est, ut, licet pauciores sint, tamen semper nitantur hostes cingere suos.*" (The above translation is by Erik Hildinger.)
2. Ibid., p. 78, n. 8: "*. . . docti et faciles ad fugam*" and "*. . . pacem no posset habere, nec pugnam.*"
3. Anna Comnena, *The Alexiad*, XV, iii, trans. E.R.A. Sewter, Hammondsworth, UK, Penguin, 1982.
4. Mamluk is simply Arabic for "slave."
5. An example is Bishop Odo, brother of William the Conqueror, who fought at the Battle of Hastings with a clubin order to avoid shedding blood.
6. *Munyatu'l-Ghuzat, A 14th Century Mamluk-Kipchak Military Treatise*, trans. Kurtulus Oztopcu, Cambridge, MA, Harvard University Press, 1989, p. 77.
7. Ibid., p. 58.
8. Coming from French sources, this is almost certainly an exaggeration tending to aggrandize this skirmish—one of the bright spots in the Mansurah disaster. The entire Egyptian cavalry seem to have numbered only ten to twelve thousand; it is doubtful that this many would be free for such an action.
9. Quoted in Reuven Amitai-Press, *Mamluks and Mongols: The Mamluk-Ilkhanid War, 1260–1281*, Cambridge, UK, Cambridge University Press, 1995, p. 36.
10. Amitai-Press, op. cit.
11. James F. Dunigan, *How to Make War*, 3rd ed., New York, William Morrow, 1993, p. 306.

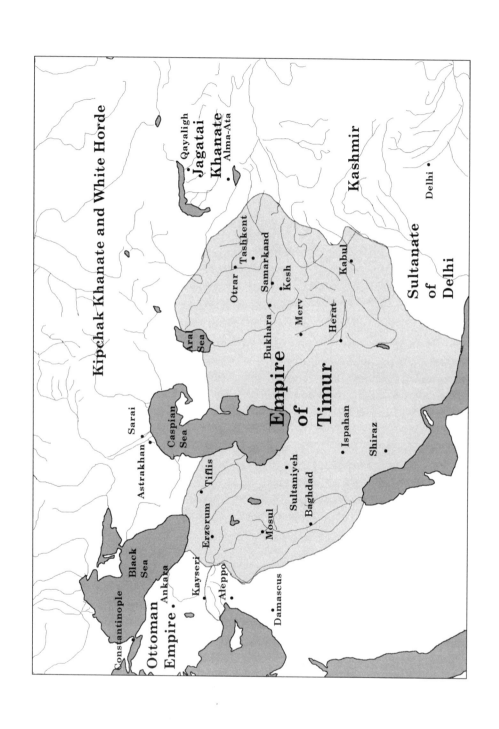

10

Timur Lenk

When the Mongol Empire was divided at the death of Chinggis Khan in 1227 into appanages for his children, Jagatai, the eldest surviving son, was given the most central—defined by the territory south of the Aral Sea to the borders of India and from the borders of Mongolia to those of China. Because of its proximity to the court of the Grand Khan at Karakorum it was, for a while, the least independent of the khanates, though it later achieved great freedom by supporting Kubilai during his war with Arikboka for the supreme crown. Kubilai prevailed and moved his capital to China, leaving the Jagatai Khanate free to do as it wished.

The Jagatai Khanate remained the most traditional, even primitive, of those making up the empire and the Mongols living on the steppe in the north of the appanage remained much as they had in Chinggis' day: pastoral in lifestyle and animistic in religion. Unable to appreciate cities, they would ocasionally sweep into the civilized south and sack cities that belonged to them.

By contrast the southern territories and cities were inhabited mainly by Muslim Turks. The Jagatai Khanate was achieving a Turkish cast in the south as the Kipchak Khanate had already done. In 1334 the khanate split into the territories of Mogholistan, a land of steppe and mountain to the north, and Transoxiana in the south. A Jagataite khan ruled each khanate, that of Transoxiana having been elected by the local Turko-Mongol aristocracy. This Transoxianan khan, Kazan, son of Yassawur, met his end in 1346–1347 when Emir Qazghan marched against him in response to his efforts to control the aristocracy. Qazghan then installed another Chinggisid as khan, this time a descendant of Occodai named Danish-

Mendiya, though Qazghan soon repented of the decision and murdered him, placing another Jagataite, Buyun-Quli on the throne in 1348. This khan pleased him and ruled for ten years.

By contrast, the Khan of Mogholistan, Timur Tughlugh, was more successful than his cousins. He astutely accepted Islam as part of a plan to recover Transoxiana and reform the old Jagatai Khanate, knowing that this would remove religious objections to his claims. He made ready to invade the south.

It was in the midst of this upheaval that Timur, son of Taragai, was born. A generation after his death the Arab historian Ahmed ibn Arabshah wrote this of his birth:

> They say that on the night on which he was born something like a helmet appeared, seemed to flutter in the air, then fell into the middle of the plain and finally was scattered over the ground; thence also live coals flew about like glowing ashes and collected so that they filled the plain and the city: they also say that when that evil man saw the light, his palms were full of freshly shed blood.[1]

Of course, the story should not be taken literally; at that time all the world believed in portents at the birth or death of great men. However, the elements of this display, fictional though they may have been, do tell us how he was regarded in his lifetime. The helmet, obviously the sign of a soldier, the glowing coals foretelling widespread destruction and the blood on the infant's hands recalling the folktales of Chinggis' birth. The first Khagan was said to have been born grasping a clot of blood in his fist. Tamerlane was not of the house of Chinggis Khan, but he emulated and tried to surpass him. In fact he conquered more territory than Chinggis, although it was only in sheer cruelty and bloody-mindedness that he exceeded the Mongol khan.

Timur was born on April 8, 1336 in Kesh, south of the city of Samarkand in Transoxiana. He is generally known in the West as Tamerlane, a corruption of Timur Lenk, or "Timur the Lame." During his rise to power he had suffered arrow wounds to an arm and leg, and he limped throughout his life as these injuries progressed, until near the end he was largely crippled. But even then he could not be stopped, and still less did his gait hinder him when he was younger. Timur was a noble Turk born into the Barlas clan, which may ultimately have derived from a Mongol tribe, early followers of Chinggis Khan. He seems to have claimed kinship with the World Conqueror; and Arabshah states:

> And I have seen, in the appendix of the Persian Chronicle called Muntakhab, which is brought down from the creation to the times of Timur with truly admirable effort, the genealogy of Timur traced without a break to Jenghizkhan through females, snares of Satan.[2]

Timur did not rely much on this genealogy, however: he ruled through puppet khans of Chinggis' line while merely styling himself the "Great Emir."

At age twenty Timur entered the service of Emir Qazghan, the real power behind the puppet khan of Transoxiana. The emir appreciated Timur's qualities so much that he married a granddaughter to him and put him in command of a military unit. But Qazghan was a hard man and dangerous; in 1357 he was murdered by a discontented vassal and Transoxiana disolved into chaos as the emirs warred with each other. Timur Tughlugh, Khan of Mogholistan, saw his chance approaching.

Timur son of Taragai returned to Kesh where he found his uncle, Hajji Barlas, now chief of his clan. Their reunion could not have been cordial as Timur wished to head the clan himself—something not lost on the uncle. There was no chance, however, for the struggle to play out; Timur Tughlugh invaded Transoxiana in 1360 and marched upon Kesh. Hajji conducted a fighting retreat to Khorassan, while by contrast Timur acknowledged Timur Tughlugh as his lord, thus saving Kesh from sack and achieving his desired position as leader of the Barlas clan.

The Mongol khan was soon forced to return to Mogholistan to settle unrest there, and Hajji Barlas marched upon Kesh to attack his nephew. Timur initially defeated him but was forced to make up with his uncle all the same when his troops deserted. Still, the situation was recovered by Timur Tughlugh's return in 1361 at the head of the Mongol army, causing Hajji to flee once more to Khorassan while his nephew resumed his earlier position. Timur Tughlugh insisted that the Transoxianan emirs pay court to him, among them Hajji Barlas. To display his power over them the Mongol khan arbitrarily executed one of their number, Mir Bayazid, and this put Hajji Barlas into a panic. He fled to the village of Khorasha in Buluk-i-Juvin, subject to the state of Sebzawar, where he and his brother Idegu were killed by bandits.[3] Timur was free of his rival.

Timur served the Jagatais loyally and the Mongol Khan gave him the office of advisor to his son, Ilyas-khoja, who ruled Transoxiana for him. If Timur thought that this would lead to the exercise of supreme power, though, he was to be disappointed: Timur Tughlugh nominated the emir Begjik to share power with Ilyas-khoja. This provoked Timur to quit Timur Tughlugh's service and ally himself with his brother-in-law, Mir Hussein, king of Balkh, Kunduz and Kabul. They went off together with a troop of men and served as mercenaries in Persia and neighboring Seistan. Though successfully employed by the Prince of Seistan to put down a revolt, Timur and Hussein's army was then ambushed by the prince's own troops since he found them threatening and, in addition, did not wish to pay them. Timur fought strongly against superior numbers, but suffered two arrow wounds, one in the shoulder and the other in the thigh. These were the wounds that would lead to his popular nickname, Timur Lenk.

Returning from this unhappy adventure, Timur and his brother-in-law came to the River Vakhsh on the opposite bank of which they observed a Mongol force considerably larger than their own. A clever trick was soon decided upon: Hussein was posted with most of the men to hold the only bridge in the vicinity while Timur and a smaller force crossed the river secretly and climbed among hills above the Mongols. Once in position Timur's men lighted a great number of torches and began to beat upon drums, the traditional Turkish martial instrument. The Mongols thought themselves outflanked by a large force and were unable to force the bridge. To avoid envelopment they began to flee, disordered, along the riverbank while Timur and Hussein attacked from the rear during their flight, inflicting heavy casualties.

Timur and Hussein then led their men toward Kesh. And Timur determined on another ruse: he ordered his advance parties to drag bushes and bundles of twigs in the dirt behind their horses. The resultant clouds of dust appeared like those of a much larger army and the townspeople of Kesh opened the gates to him, surrendering their town without resistance.

There followed another battle, that of Kaba-matan, which resulted in the expulsion of Ilyas-khoja from Transoxiana, and now Timur and Hussein were masters of the country. Observing the custom that only a Chinggisid could rule, they chose the Jagataite Kabul-shah as Khan of Transoxiana—the action also serving to undercut Ilyas-khoja's claims to the region, which was now being governed (nominally) by a descendant of the Golden Family. Nonetheless, in 1364 Ilyas-khoja made a last try at imposing himself as ruler of Transoxiana: he invaded and defeated Timur and Hussein, who were forced to go into hiding while the Mongols besieged Samarkand. The city put up a vigororous defense, however, and—of equal importance—an epidemic broke out.[4] Ilyas-khoja and the Mongols lifted the siege and retreated to Mogholistan, pursued and harried by Timur and Hussein as far as Tashkent. Transoxiana was now unquestionably theirs.

Both men were ambitious, however, and could not happily share Transoxiana between them. Hussein appeared the more powerful of the two and he lorded it over the Transoxianan emirs. Timur cannily sided with the nobility, even lending them money to pay the taxes Hussein levied upon them, and with the death of Timur's wife (Hussein's sister) there came a complete breach. In 1370, following a good deal of diplomacy and subtle double-dealing, Timur marched suddenly upon the city of Balkh, where Hussein was installed. Surprised and unprepared, Hussein was forced to surrender the city and agree to make a pilgrimage to Mecca. Nonetheless, he was murdered, supposedly without Timur's knowledge, and the people of Balkh were likewise by and large massacred.

Khan Kabul-shah, nominal suzerain of Transoxiana, had supported Hussein; Timur murdered him and set up another Chinggisid, Soyurghatmish, as khan. In spite of his shallow pretensions to a distant descent from Chinggis Khan, Timur would never feel confident enough to establish himself as khan. Though he rose to become the undisputed master of Central Asia, he never took a more elevated title than "sultan," in 1388, and continued to rule through the descendants of the Golden Family.

Timur was now sole master of Transoxiana; he next shifted his capital to the city of Samarkand, which was elegant and strategically better situated than Kesh, thus preparing himself for the endless campaigning that would mark his reign. The campaigning, however, differed in a marked way from that of Chinggis Khan, whom he emulated: it failed to display any signs of design. Where Chinggis struggled for years to achieve mastery over Mongolia, and then methodically overpowered Khwarezm and fought to consolidate gains in China, Timur simply romped from one end of his world to the other, facing each situation as it appeared and anticipating them very little. So, while he fought as Chinggis had done with a cavalry composed of steppe warriors, or those modeled upon them, he found that he often had to wage campaigns repeatedly over the same territories where, in his place, Chinggis would have done the job only once.

As a result of Timur's reaction to various situations, his military history is chaotic and, from a strategic standpoint, formless. The amorphous quality of his campaigns has even caused some historians to describe his activities geographically instead of chronologically.[5] His campaigns against Mogholistan and Khwarezm furnish an example of haphazard campaigning while at the same time employing an army organized and equipped in the steppe fashion: Timur's army, like all Turco-Mongol armies, was one of mounted archers. This was to be expected and would follow from the speed with which he established his empire: empires won on horseback tend to be large and taken quickly. Timur himself established what each of his soldiers should carry, and he recorded in his Institutes:

> For the private soldiers I ordained, that on an expedition every eighteen men should take one tent; and that each man should be supplied with two horses, and with a bow, and with a quiver of arrows, and with a sword, and with a saw, and with an axe, and with an awl, and with thread, and with ten needles, and with a leathern knapsack.[6]

Here again we see the use of more than one horse to allow the

rider to rest one mount while riding another. There is no armor specified, and the weapon first mentioned is, of course, the bow. The
only other one specified for the common soldier is the sword, no
doubt a saber, to be used when it was necessary to come to blows
directly with the enemy. The equipment is that of a light-armed
horseman, and such a soldier would have made up the majority of
his troops. Timur provided that elite troops wear helmets and armor,
and refers in his Institutes to soldiers of a certain rank carrying
maces, clubs and lances as well. Part of his forces, then, would be
considered heavy cavalry, and in this way his army resembled that of
the Mongols as did its decimal organization. The Timurid army was
divided into regiments of 10,000 men called *tuman*, troops of 1,000
men called *binlik* and squadrons of 100 men called *koshun* or *iuzlik*.

Armor consisted of round shields, helmets, and coats of chainmail or armor made of plates. This armor must have been similar to
lamellar armor with the plates overlapping their neighbors and the
plates above, but whereas lamellar armor uses plates or lamellae
laced to each other, Timur's choice of armor consisted of plates overlapping each other but fixed to and behind a fabric facing. It was
described, along with helmets, by the Spanish ambassador Ruy
Gonzalez de Clavijo, who visited Timur at Samarkand. Timur was
inspecting work done by his armorers.

> Among the rest they brought to show him three thousand
> new suits of plate armour, which is of the sort stitched on a
> backing of red canvas. To our way of thinking this appeared
> very well wrought, except that the plates are not thick
> enough, and they do not here know how properly to temper
> the steel. At the same time an immense number of helms
> were exhibited, and these each with its suit of plate armor
> were that day many of them given as presents by his
> Highness, being distributed among the lords and nobles
> there in attendance. These helms of theirs are made round
> and high, some turning back to a point, while in front a
> piece comes down to guard the face and nose—which is a
> plate, two fingers broad, reaching the level of the chin
> below. This piece can be raised or lowered at will and it
> serves to ward off a side stroke by a sword. These suits of

plate-armour are composed very much as is the custom with us in Spain, but they wear a long skirt, made of a material other than that which is plate-armored, and this comes down so as to appear below, as might be with us a jerkin.[7]

When Clavijo says "as is the custom with us in Spain" he is evidently referring to a brigandine—a jacket lined with overlapping plates that are fixed by rivets coming through a covering fabric. These jackets can be identified in illustrations by the pattern of rivet heads coming through the material. They were popular in Europe, particularly among the less well-to-do, and were both lighter and more flexible than plate armor. Such armor was understandably popular with the Eastern horsemen too. Coats of mail survive from eastern Turkey often with rows of metal plates set as panels into the front and back, and it seems likely that many of Timur's soldiers wore these as well.

Surviving Timurid helmets belonged to nobility and even royalty and are very elegant indeed; there are specimens in the Istanbul Military Museum, the Metropolitan Museum of Art in New York and in the Tower of London. They bear religious inscriptions chased elegantly into their surfaces and their crowns have decorative channels or cannelures running vertically or on a curve to the peak. The helmets of the common soldiers were probably similar, though less elaborate.

We return now to the first of Timur's extraterritorial campaigns, that against the Khan of Mogholistan, Kamar ed-Din. Though Timur had some success in his engagements against the khan, he was unable to bring him to bay, for the Mongol used the expanse of the steppes to withdraw and hide from him. These engagements were followed by activities in neighboring Khwarezm. Its king, Hussein Sufi, had taken advantage of the earlier disorder in Transoxiana to seize the cities of Kiat and Khiva, which he declined to surrender upon Timur's request in 1371. In response Timur marched upon the Khwarezmian capital of Urgench and besieged it. Hussein died during the siege, to be succeeded by his brother, Yusuf Sufi, who agreed to deliver the towns in exchange for the lifting of the siege.

Upon Timur's withdrawal, however, Yusuf tried to seize back the towns. Timur had already returned to Mogholistan to deal further with Kamar ed-Din, but he sped back to confront Yusuf who managed to save his head and position by betrothing his beautiful daughter Khanzade to Jahangir, Timur's son. The wedding over, Timur returned to the steppes of Mogholistan, but he broke off the campaign abruptly, it is said, when he had a premonition that his son was dying. In fact, it turned out to be true: Jahangir had died of a sudden, brief illness at Samarkand. When the period of mourning was over, Timur again returned to Mogholistan and Yusuf again decided the time was right to seize Kiat and Khiva.

As before, Timur rushed down from the steppe and trapped the Khwarezmian king in Urgench. Displaying great bravado, Timur challenged Yusuf to single combat, but when the emir appeared before the city armed and mounted, the king was struck by sudden fear and refused. He died a few weeks later of despair. Unhappily, the affair was not yet over for the townspeople of Urgench; it was here that Timur initiated a feature of his use of calculated terror. He called for the city to surrender on the terms that, if it did so, the people would be largely spared, there would be a heavy indemnity charged and the townspeople would recognize Timur's suzerainty. When the city refused to capitulate, he prepared for an assault and once again called for surrender, but this time on harsher terms: there would be killing, though some of the population would be spared, there would be wholesale pillaging and the walls would be leveled. The dwellings would, however, be spared firing. Again the townsfolk refused to surrender. The city was then taken by force and a wholesale massacre followed. Any survivors were enslaved and the dwellings burned. With this, Khwarezm was finally taken into the Timurid realm.

The Great Emir next turned his attention to eastern Iran, then a series of contending principalities which he subdued between 1382 and 1385, following this with the conquests of western Iran and of what is today Azerbaijan in 1386. The winter of 1386–1387 found Timur engaged in a "holy war" against the Kingdom of Georgia, "holy" because these people were Christians. This campaign was as successful as his others, notwithstanding the fact that it was fought in mountains during the winter. King Bagrat V was compelled to profess the Muslim religion.

Timur then wintered further south in Karabakh, where he received the alarming news that Toktamish, Khan of Kipchak, was marching against him. The relationship between these two went back some years and had given Timur no cause to expect anything but gratitude from the khan. In 1376 Toktamish had fled to him for protection—a refugee from the White Horde—of which his uncle was khan.

As the Mongol Empire had continued to splinter into separate powers, the southeastern territories of the Kipchak Khanate bordering Transoxiana had split off to form the White Horde. Timur had seen an opportunity in Toktamish's plight and he eased the Tatar's predicament by granting him three fortified towns along the Syr Darya River, Timur's border with the White Horde. In 1377 the old khan was succeeded by his son, Timur Malik, who shared his father's animosity toward Toktamish. The two Tatars waged intermittent warfare until Toktamish, with Timur's support, defeated his cousin and assumed the position of Khan of the White Horde. Timur Lenk must have felt that his plan succeeded nicely: he now had for a neighbor a Chinggisid khan obliged to him for his position, and he likely felt safer from that quarter than he had in the past.

This belief was no doubt enhanced when Toktamish attacked and defeated the Kipchak Khanate in 1381. The latter had recently suffered its first defeat at the hands of the Russians under Prince Dmitri, henceforth called "Donskoi" for this victory on September 8, 1380 at Kulikovo Field on the Don and Nepryadva rivers. The horde was disordered and susceptible to Toktamish's opportune attack. This victory made him the Khan of Kipchak as well, and united all of its former territories as they had been under its founder, Batu. Toktamish naturally called upon the Russian princes to submit and render him the tribute they had refused since the battle on the Don, but they, flush with their recent unprecedented success, refused. Toktamish engaged the Russians, defeated them and on August 13, 1382 he burned Moscow, the city of Prince Dmitri. The Tatar Yoke would be imposed for another hundred years.

Toktamish's star was clearly rising and he no longer felt himself beholden to Timur, whom he characterized as an "upstart Turk." In fact, it seemed the time had come to strip him of a few provinces. Therefore, that winter of 1386–1387 Timur found himself unexpectedly facing his protegé who had marched into Karabakh through the Derbent Pass on the western shore of the Caspian.

Timur took full advantage of the mobility of his steppe-style army; he sent a small detachment to hold a ford where he expected the Tatars to cross. His son, Prince Miran Shah, meanwhile flanked Toktamish with the larger part of the army. The Tatars, outmaneuvered, withdrew past the Caucasus. For a time, the crisis was over.

Timur did not pursue the enemy; there were difficulties in Iran and he seems to have been impressed with Toktamish's lineage: he was a Chinggisid and therefore to be given some deference. Accordingly Timur even sent Toktamish's captured soldiers back with a letter asking that he and Toktamish be reconciled. Quite at odds with this suggestion, Toktamish readied a large army against him.

Timur, meanwhile, fixed his attention on Armenia, at that time divided between a number of warring Turkmen lords. One of them, Tahirtin of Erzindjan, lost his city of Erzeroum to Timur in a single day; he submitted and accepted Timur as his overlord. Timur confirmed him in his position and it was as Tahirtin's protector that he would be drawn into war years later to fight one of the great battles of history, with Sultan Bayazet of Turkey.

As usual with Timur's campaigns, one thing led to another. The Armenian expedition put him into conflict with the Black Sheep Turkmen, so called for the black sheep on their banners. This led to a good deal of fighting with their khan, Kara Muhammad Turmuch, but neither Timur nor his son Miran Shah was able to completely defeat them as they would flee across the steppe and hide in deep forests if need be. Armenia, however, was secured with the capture of Van.

There followed actions against the new king of Fars in Persia. His father had submitted to Timur, but the son failed to show submission. Timur marched upon Isphahan intent on making a show of force and exacting a heavy indemnity for the disobedience. The indemnity was in fact agreed upon, but during its collection the townspeople rose against the Transoxianan soldiers, killed three thousand of them and shut the city gates to Timur, who was camped outside. A few citizens hid some of the soldiers who had survived, and awaited the outcome. It was a blood bath. Timur stormed the city and had all its inhabitants killed with the sole exception of the Muslim clergy and those who had protected his survivng soldiers. To

ensure that his wish was kept he ordered each of his troops to bring
in a quota of heads. All told, 70,000 are said to have been cut off
and placed in piles outside the city to discourage further uprisings
elsewhere. Timur then marched upon Shiraz, where the news had
preceeded him: the city threw open its gates.

While staying at Shiraz, Timur learned of Toktamish's latest
actions; the Khan of Kipchak had just attacked Transoxiana and was
marching upon Tashkent assisted by soldiers from Mogholistan.
Timur's son Omar Sheik had gathered what forces he could in the
north, but had been driven back to Ardijan. Toktamish could not
take the town, but he ravaged the countryside and blockaded
Bukhara. Timur, meanwhile, rushed to Samarkand—which convinced Toktamish to withdraw to the steppe.

And still Toktamish was not finished. In the winter of 1388 he
marched against Timur once more with his army of Tatars, supported by Russians, Bulgarians and Circassians; Kamar ed-Din, Khan of
Mogholistan lent him troops as well. In the face of this large army
Timur's counselors suggested that he pull back and put together an
army fit to face the Tatars. Instead, Timur took the small army he
could gather on the spot and rushed through the snow at his enemy;
scouts encountered Toktamish's advance guard near Khodjent.
Prince Omar Sheik was advancing from the north and his father
Timur was in communication with him; Timur ordered his son to lie
in wait upon the enemy's rear until commanded to attack. On the
morning of the battle Timur drove Toktamish's vanguard back and
charged into his center. The Great Emir's audacity unsettled the
Tatars. Still, a bloody fight ensued during which Omar Sheik
attacked the Tatar rear and caused a panic; Toktamish's troops fled
across the Syr Darya into the steppe.

After these encounters it is hardly a surprise that Timur determined to put an end to the Khan of Kipchak. To protect his flank, he
first advanced north into Mogholistan in the spring of 1389 and neutralized it so that he would have no enemy at his rear when he ven-
tured into Toktamish's domain.

On January 19, 1391, Timur departed with his army from
Tashkent. News arrived, however, that Toktamish had gone into the
territories of the White Horde; Timur accordingly changed his line of
advance. All the same, Timur wandered for three months across the

steppe without catching sight of his enemy. Supplies ran low and the army was in danger of starvation, so Timur organized a great hunt, or *battue,* like those of the Chinggisid Mongols. The game fed the soldiers and doubtless helped keep them in training. He also organized a military review such as he was accustomed to hold at Samarkand; the army was large and it took him two days to review all the troops.

Scouting parties were sent everywhere across the steppe until finally, at the Tobol River in Siberia, the traces of a camp were found. Timur's scouts tracked Toktamish's and, when found, they were tortured to reveal that their khan was on the other side of the Urals. Timur set out west to find him, and as he drew nearer his army was subject to constant ambush and harassment. Nonetheless, Timur advanced quickly, finally engaging Toktamish's rearguard. On the following day, June 13, 1391, the battle began in earnest.

The battle probably took place near the site of the modern Russian city of Orenburg near the Ural River. Toktamish arrayed his army in the conventional crescent formation with a view to encircling Timur who, by contrast, had broken his forces into seven separate divisions that were allowed to move independently. The Tatar army's wings were not able to complete an encirclement and Timur's center rushed to attack Toktamish's. As his center failed, Toktamish gathered some forces and broke away, to be followed by Timur's seventh division, serving as a tactical reserve, which pursued him from the battlefield.

The Kipchak Khan's men thought him dead and lost heart; they were chased and cut down all the way to the Volga, a distance of roughly four hundred miles. It is this long pursuit that may have given rise to the statement that the battle lasted three days—something that would otherwise seem an exaggeration, for pre-modern battles seldom lasted more than a day, depending as they did solely on the strength of men and animals. A pursuit of this distance, however, undoubtedly took several days and recalls rather the movements of modern, mechanized armies than those of the preindustrial period. No sedentary force of the age could have covered a small fraction of that distance in either flight or pursuit—the character of steppe warfare reveals itself once more in this example. What is remarkable is that Toktamish let himself be engaged when he might have continued fleeing ahead of Timur's army until want and exhaustion made it susceptible to counteroffensive and destruction.

His task accomplished, Timur camped beside the Volga and held a festival for twenty-six days. He did not, however, do much in the way of consolidating his gains. He divided Kipchak between three Chinggisid princes (two of whom quickly showed themselves hostile) and returned to Samarkand.

This campaign against the Kipchak Khanate was followed by further operations in the Middle East, punitive expeditions really, against certain Iranian provinces in revolt. Timur led his army past Bukhara, where he was laid low by, probably, an infection of the leg. Although he prepared himself to die, in six weeks he was back on the march. Throughout 1393 the almost-sixty-year-old warrior campaigned in Iran with his accustomed success; when he summoned the Sultan of Baghdad, the ruler was so frightened that he temporized and then fled to Egypt to the protection of Sultan Barkuk of the Mamluks. There followed fighting in Kurdestan and a revolt was put down in Georgia.

The irrepressible Toktamish had meanwhile regained his station, necessitating yet another—and, as it turned out, final—expedition northward. In the spring of 1395 Timur led his army through the Derbent Pass and on April 15 engaged Toktamish for the last time.

During the battle a band of Toktamish's Tatars managed to surround and menace Timur and his immediate companions, although his men rallied to him and beat back the enemy. As the battle turned in Timur's favor, Toktamish fled north, ultimately seeking refuge with Vitovt, Grand Duke of Lithuania. His army was again destroyed. Timur sent the booty on to Samarkand under guard, but this time took, looted and destroyed Kipchak's two capitals, Astrakhan and Sarai. The khanate was now broken and the path was cleared for the gradual rise of the Russians under Muscovite leadership, which would culminate years later in the liberation of the Russian people after Duke Ivan III's stand-off on the Oka in 1480.

Timur's next campaign, after what was for him a significant rest, was something that he had long entertained: an action against the Indian Sultanate of Delhi. The sultanate was Muslim, though many of its subjects were Hindu, and this offered Timur the transparent excuse of conducting a holy war against those who tolerated idolators. Furthermore, the sultanate was also conveniently much less powerful than it had been a few decades before when it controlled most of India. Now it consisted primarily of the territories of Punjab and Doab, as most of its other provinces had gained their independence.

Timur sent off his grandson Pir Muhammad with a vanguard at the beginning of 1398. He crossed the Indus and besieged the city of Multan for six months, finally taking it. Timur himself followed with the larger part of the army, crossed the Indus in September, sacked Talamba and joined up with his grandson. The army proceded toward Delhi, capturing forts and prisoners along the way. The Hindu prisoners, said to have amounted to one hundred thousand, became an encumbrance and so were executed.

On December 17, 1398 Timur fought the army of the Sultanate of Delhi on the Jumna River, the Indian army under the command of Sultan Mahmud Shah himself and his advisor, Mallu Iqbal. The Indians were beaten, their war elephants being completely ineffective in the face of the Timurid cavalry, and the Sultan and his advisor fled to Gujarat.

The citizens of Delhi were to be spared the treatment they might have expected of the Great Emir, but the townspeople soon rose up at the brutality of his soldiers. Thus, inevitably, Delhi was given over to pillage, killing and fire; piles of severed heads were set at the corners of the city.

Timur spent fifteen days in the burned city before heading home with an immense amount of loot, along the way taking the city of Kiraj, where he subjected Hindu prisoners to horrific torture: he flayed many alive as idolators. Holy war though he claimed it to have been, he had irreparably harmed the Muslim state and made no arrangements concerning the future of the sultanate; he left the state in chaos. Timur's grotesque claim that he had been engaged in a holy war only serves to point up how utterly crass his behavior had been: the expedition had been no more than a giant plundering raid such as any petty steppe khan might have conducted if he had had the power. But whereas Timur, with a veneer of culture, tried to color what he had done, his simpler, rougher ancestors on the steppe would have known the raid for what it was and spoken of it without hypocrisy.

Next to suffer Timur's attentions were the Mamluks. This military aristocracy which ruled Egypt and Syria had long been at odds with Timur: Sultan Barkuk had sheltered the Sultan of Baghdad and had protected other fugitives from the Great Emir. Barkuk's son and successor, Sultan Faraj, was no more favorably disposed to Timur. The Mamluks, however, suffered from internal dissension as their emirs contended with each other over their landholdings, and the empire, albeit a military state, was not as powerful as it had been when it had withstood the Ilkhanid Mongols in the thirteenth century.

Timur entered Syria in October 1400, defeating the governor of Syria in battle on October 30. The Great Emir took Aleppo and then seized Hama, Homs and Baalbek. The Mamluk sultan Faraj attacked Timur's army on December 25, 1400, as it shifted camp, but the attempt was unsuccessful. Faraj retired to Egypt and Timur took Damascus on March 19, 1401. The city suffered pillage and fire as had so many before, as well as the enslavement and transportation to Samarkand of artisans, weavers and armorers. When he marched from Syria, Timur left no organization behind and the Mamluks reoccupied the territory he had mauled. Relics of Timur's presence in the area, however, were seen a few years later when the Spanish ambassador Ruy Gonzalez de Clavijo passed through Syria on a mission to Samarkand in 1406: he saw towers made from men's heads. He wrote:

> Outside Damghan at the distance of a bowshot we noticed two towers, built as tall as the height to which one might cast up a stone, which were entirely constructed from men's skulls set in clay. Besides these there were other two [sic] similar towers, but these appeared already fallen to the ground in decay.[1]

These grisly structures were built from the remains of thousands of Aya Qunlu Turkmen whom Timur had conquered and resettled in Syria. They had decided to return to their homeland but were caught by the Great Emir who was campaigning nearby. The townspeople of Damghan told Clavijo that "frequently flames, as of burning lamps, might be noticed flickering on the top of the towers of Tartar skulls."[2] Clearly Timur's efforts at terror had worked successfully in this area; supernatural after-effects had even been attributed to the mass killing.

A year later Timur was finally to engage an opponent who might be considered an equal: the Sultan of Turkey. During the summer of 1402 the Western World waited for the fall of Constantinople. This city, the final political vestige of Imperial Rome, had lasted nearly a thousand years as a sovereign state following the dissolution of the Western Roman Empire. For most of that time Constantinople, as capital of the Byzantine Empire, had been the most powerful state in Europe, holding sway over Anatolia, Greece, Macedonia, the Balkans, Sicily and southern Italy, and even, for a time, North Africa. It had been a civilizing influence as well: Byzantine missionaries had spread Christianity among the Russians and other Slavs, thereby drawing them into the Western fold, even drawing up the Cyrillic alphabet to write their languages. Constantinople was a rich city too, the home of architectural masterworks such as the Church of Hagia Sophia, reputedly the most beautiful in the world.

However, the empire had been declining a long while, particularly after the Emperor Romanus Diogenes' spectacular defeat at the hands of the Turk Alp Arslan at the Battle of Manzikert in 1271. Following this debacle the Byzantine Empire had lost its territories in Anatolia to the Turks—a loss it could not afford for it depended on these areas for the recruitment of soldiers. As Italian cities like Venice and Genoa became preeminent in trade, Constantinople became economically pressed and found it difficult to hire mercenary soldiers to make up for those she could no longer recruit.

And so, Christendom looked to the Bosphorus that summer of 1402 to watch the inevitable extinction of the Byzantine Empire at the hands of the Sultan of Turkey, Bayazet, surnamed "Yildirin," or "Lightning." His nickname was fair—he had won it for his speed and ability on campaign and he was generally regarded as one of the two great captains of the age. Western Europeans had already dealt with him: in 1396 Pope Boniface IX, in order to relieve the pressure on Constantinople, had called for a crusade against the Ottomans; however, at the Battle of Nicopolis this multinational force was disastrously defeated. Thousands of Western knights taken prisoner were lined up before Bayazet and beheaded.

Six years later, Bayazet sat before Constantinople and had invested the city for more than a year; its fall could only be a matter of weeks, or even days. Emperor Manuel II Palaeologus had fled to France under the sponsorship of the French Marshal Boucicault to petition for troops and money. Still, there was little reason to think that Constantinople could survive the Ottoman assault.

And yet, in June 1402, Sultan Bayazet hurriedly called off the siege and embarked his troops on a campaign to defend his own territories against that rapacious conqueror from further east, the Great Emir Timur Lenk. The city of Constantinople had won a reprieve of fifty years.

The contest was probably inevitable. With the decline of Seljuk power in the Near East and the rise of the Ottoman Turks under Bayazet's father, Murad, only they could seriously challenge Timur and the Turks of Transoxiana. The Europeans were aware of this, and as Bayazet extended his sway over the remnants of the Seljuk state and consolidated Ottoman power in the Balkans, the Byzantine Emperor Manuel II sent his ambassador, a Dominican Father called Francis, to Timur's court to explain that Constantinople would be content to pay him the tribute now owed to Bayazet.

The idea of a European vassal must have appealed to Timur. Furthermore, the Great Emir was constantly at odds with his neighbor Kara Yusuf, leader of the Khanate of Mogholistan whom Bayazet actively aided against him. More irritating still, Bayazet had taken advantage of Timur's Syrian campaign of 1400 against the Mamluks to provoke him; while Timur had been busied with the Mamluks, Bayazet took from him the vassal city of Erzindjan and forced its lord, Tahirtin, Timur's subject, to submit. When he learned of this, Timur gathered his troops and prepared to face Bayazet. All the same, he continued with his Syrian campaign long enough to take Aleppo—which incidentally served to open the way for Timur into Anatolia. Bayazet understood the situation; he began to prepare for war with the Great Emir.

While marshaling his forces Bayazet recognized that he needed to be able to cross the strait to his domains on the European side of the Bosphorus, particularly in the event that he lost his contest with the Great Emir. The need for flight to Europe, though a distasteful idea, was not something to be overlooked, however the Italian cities and Constantinople backed Timur in the developing conflict. In practice this meant that Italian and Greek ships were prepared to attempt to hold the Bosphorus and cut the Ottoman Empire in two. The army of Constantinople was no longer in a position to risk a battle outside the protection of its walls.

Bayazet left nine galleys and a number of smaller vessels at Gallipoli on the European side and armed twenty ships at Ayasoluk and Balat under the command of a Greek named Atessi. He then sent Timur's own erstwhile vassal Tahirtin of Erzindjan to talk peace with Timur. There is some debate whether this was a genuine offer of peace, or merely a ploy to buy time.[8] Given the value placed upon deception in the diplomacy of the period, it might well have been a mere ploy. On the other hand, Bayazet was facing the most danger-ous opponent of his life and might have been willing to consider peace if the terms were not too humiliating. Meanwhile, time would unquestionably be bought for him to gather his forces, which, unlike Timur's, were dispersed throughout his territories. Timur did not commit himself one way or another to the peace offer, but merely left Bayazet uncertain. Both sides continued to prepare.

The campaign did not begin precipitately; Timur knew Bayazet was a dangerous opponent. He spent the autumn of 1401 hunting with his army (always a popular training for cavalry) in the moun-tains of Georgia. He built barracks for his troops and announced quite falsely that he would invade the Kipchak Khanate in the spring. In the meantime reinforcements from Samarkand arrived under the command of Timur's favorite grandson, Muhammad Sultan. These troops were splendid and fresh and, in contrast to the rest of the army, each troop was equipped in a different color: their cuirasses, capes, shields, saddles, caparisons, belts, quivers and lances might be white, green, violet or red.[9]

Bayazet's forces contrasted sharply with Timur's army of steppe cavalry. The more cosmopolitan character of the Ottoman Empire saw to that. The fact of an Ottoman fleet is only one example; the army differed too. Historically, Turks had everywhere been steppe people: horsemen and mounted archers in their own right or as part of Chinggis Khan's world empire; as Mamluk soldiers for the Egyptians and Arabs in their internecine wars; or in defense of Islam from the Crusaders. With the Ottoman Turks there came a change. They had come off the steppe and settled in a small area of Anatolia under their chief, Osman—hence "Ottoman"—and had gradually extended their sway. As this happened they sought to quash the nomadic lifestyle which, although it lent them military strength, caused the government trouble in controling its people. They were therefore encouraged to settle, but they could still field effective mounted archers.

By the time of Bayazet's father, Murad, the Ottomans controlled an Empire extending even into Europe and it had been won with the help of Murad's "new soldiers," or "Yeni Ceri." These were a new force in a Turkish army: professional infantrymen—the janissaries. These wore a distinctive tall hat of square cross-section with a flap to cover the back of the neck, a red cape and baggy blue trousers. They were armed primarily with a recurved composite bow and arrows, but also carried a saber, a dagger, a round buckler and a two-headed battle-axe. Their devotion to their sultan was intense since each janissary had been captured as a young child of Christian parents or taken from Christian parents who were subject to the Ottomans, by a process called *devchirme* in Turkish. He was then taught Turkish and carefully raised as a devout Muslim and professional soldier. There are echoes here of the Mamluk approach to war, though their method of fighting was quite different.

Janissaries were subject to strict regulations isolating them from the rest of society. They could not marry, they were to pass their time learning and teaching the military skills, they could practice no other profession than soldier and no one could join the corps who had not been selected through the devchirme. They were regarded as invincible by Europeans; they were certainly tough, loyal and reliable.

The Turks, of course, had cavalry too, divided into two kinds. The light cavalry were generally irregulars used for scouting and harassing an enemy. The *sipahis* were more heavily equipped; they had mail jackets, helmets, lance and shield, battle-axe or mace, saber and dagger, and, of course, the composite, recurved bow and arrows. Sipahis held land from the sovereign, called in Arabic *iqta*. The land was to support them while they in turn were to provide military service. The system resembled the feudal arrangements of a knight, and the sipahis were obliged to supply a number of cavalry commensurate with the value of the land they held.

The Ottoman Turks also fielded numbers of infantry and irregular light infantry as well as troops from conquered nations, of which the Serbian cavalry were to do important service in this campaign.

As the campaign began in earnest that spring of 1402, Timur sent his son Muhammad Sultan to take the Turkish city Kemakh while he himself seized Erzeroum. This done, Timur captured the city of Siwas, where he received Bayazet's ambassadors, who presented him with gifts and asked him to consider peace. He showed no interest in any gift but a falcon that he briefly put on his wrist; he had nothing encouraging to say to the embassy, and he demanded that Bayazet surrender Kara Yusuf to him, or kill him himself. As Bayazet would not do this, it was to be war without question. By way of emphasis, Timur had Bayazet's embassy watch an impressive military review lasting from dawn until noon, with troops parading under the command of twenty sultans subject to him.

Bayazet meanwhile shifted his main force from the siege of Constantinople, thus relieving the city before what had seemed its inevitable fall, and augmented his army with soldiers from his various territories: Anatolia, Roumelia, Karaman and Gallipoli. He called up auxiliaries too: Tatar horsemen from southern Russia and cavalry from Christian Serbia led by Prince Stefan Lazaravitch, whose sister was Bayazet's favorite wife. Stefan supplied knights in black armor—armor left rough from the forge.[10] In spite of all of these contingents, however, it is agreed that Timur's army was the larger, though precise figures are naturally unavailable. One of the contingents consisted of Turkmen unhappily subject to Bayazet, to whom Timur had promised the right to elect their own khan if they allied with him.

Bayazet reckoned that Timur would decide to fight at Ankara so he marched there, putting his army together as he went. Spies informed him, however, that Timur was attacking Tokat so he changed position, leaving a few troops to reinforce Ankara's garrison while he advanced quickly to the River Kizil Irmak. Bayazet took up positions in hilly, forested ground west of Tokat and Siwas. This terrain favored the Ottoman army, which contained much infantry, because woods and hills would hinder the operations of mounted archers, making them particularly vulnerable to infantry bowmen with more powerful weapons who could use the terrain to avoid cavalry charges and dispersal.

Timur, however, did not cater to Bayazet by fighting there. Instead he rushed southwest to Kayseri, reaching it in six days, where his army rested and foraged. He followed this with a four-day march to Kir-Shehir, not far from Ankara (which he had obliged Bayazet to leave days before), and established a camp surrounded with a palisade and shields. This camp was only thirty-five miles from Bayazet's, close for a mounted army, although neither antagonist knew it. Timur could be sure of one thing, however: he would fight near Ankara, just as Bayazet had first guessed, but he had forced the Ottomans to march an exhausting circuit from that city and back again. Timur had also done more: he had sent pioneers ahead of his own army to dig wells along the route to Ankara. Once there he destroyed those wells he did not hold. When the Ottomans arrived they would be harassed by thirst as well as fatigue.

The camps, as noted, were not far apart, and a skirmish between scouting parties alerted Bayazet that Timur was at his rear. On July 28, 1402, the Battle of Ankara was joined. It began in the morning, probably around nine, when Timur's advance guards met the wings of the Ottoman army. Timur had disposed the army in his preferred way, in seven divisions. He himself commanded the center, made up of two corps, while one corps formed a right wing and one a left. Each wing was preceded by an advance guard, and it was these who had first met the Ottoman wings. Timur kept the fresh troops from Samarkand behind the center as a reserve.

Bayazet too commanded the center of his army, where he was surrounded by janissaries. Cavalry formed his right and left wings with a troop behind each one—an inversion of Timur's placement of cavalry ahead of his two wings. The sipahis were drawn up as a rearguard or reserve.

As Timur's advance guard met Bayazet's wings, the left Ottoman wing was forced back. The Ottoman right wing, containing the Serbian cavalry, likewise drove Timur's left advance guard back, though as always with such fights this may have been a feigned retreat to draw the Serbs after them. The Serbs did, in fact, become dangerously separated for some time from the rest of the Ottoman army. Timur then sent another troop of horsemen against the Ottoman left wing, which had earlier shown signs of collapse. This corps contained Bayazet's Turkmen auxiliaries, who saw that their opponents were commanded by a number of their own chiefs driven from power by the Ottoman ruler. Recalling Timur's promise to allow them to choose their own khan, these Turkmen promptly turned coat and joined their old leaders in the fight against the Ottomans. Timur had shown himself to be as apt politically as he was on the battlefield.

As the fighting continued to rage, Timur's nephew, Prince Hussein, led a foolhardy charge into the janissaries, who repelled him at great cost with flights of arrows. It can only be imagined what damage and havoc they produced among Hussein's men, because they had both the advantages of the foot archer: they stood steady on their own two feet to shoot accurately, and must have used stronger bows than the mounted men. The janissaries had earlier shown great steadiness in meeting a charge of French knights at Nicopolis—they did not break and they pulled the knights from their saddles. Horses will not charge infantry that stands fast[11] (something it must be trained to do, and something rare for the period), and if the janissaries did so this time, as they must have, we can imagine those of Hussein's men who had weathered the arrow storm dragged from their saddles and dispatched when their horses pulled up a few yards short of the enemy line.

The Ottoman left wing continued to collapse, however, a natural result of the first Timurid attack, the subsequent desertion of the Turkmens and the confusion that followed. This disintegration was stopped only by the action of Bayazet's son, Muhammad, whose efforts just stabilized the wing, though it was a close thing. In order to meet his opponent's attack, however, Bayazet had been obliged to use his reserves to support both wings, leaving Timur with the last reserve. As a rule, he with the last reserve prevails. Timur's, the troops from Samarkand, were sent into the Ottoman center under his grandson, Muhammad Sultan, and they broke it into fragments, each band of men fighting until dissolution or flight.

The sipahis left the field with the crown prince, who was ultimately taken across the Bosphorus to European Turkey. Bayazet, meanwhile, retired to a hill where he held out with his janissaries against repeated attacks. The rest of the Ottoman army had melted away upon seeing the flight of its higher officers, although the Serbs under Stefan Lazaravitch remained to fight furiously, their leader imploring Bayazet to flee. He refused to do so, however, until the janissaries were killed, when he took a horse; but the animal tripped during the flight and the sultan was captured by Mahmud Khan, Timur's puppet ruler who served as a general, and a party of his soldiers.

Bayazet might reasonably have expected execution from Timur, the emir known for his pyramids of human heads and towers built to immure crowds of living people. Oddly, perhaps, the Ottoman ruler was allowed to live. Timur received him graciously and then, true to form, holding Bayazet prisoner, left for Samarkand without giving a thought to the defeated Ottoman state. En route Bayazet tried to dig his way out of the tent in which he was held and, on account of this, was transported in a barred litter, an event which through exaggeration became the story of the "iron cage" in which the humiliated sultan is said to have been transported. Though spared, Bayazet did not live long. Utterly dejected, he died on March 9, 1403.

Of this battle there are two things to remark, the first of tactical and the second of political significance. The Ottoman army, although still reliant to a large degree on horse archery by such as the sipahis and allied Tatar and Turkmen units, was now a heterogeneous force including great numbers of infantry, both janissaries and irregular light infantry, either Anatolian or from subject peoples.[12] It contained heavy cavalry too, by which is meant cavalry suited to shock action whether they were in fact heavily armored, like Stefan Lazaravitch's Serbs, or more lightly, like the sipahis, who were prepared, if need be, to fight with the lance or mace.

This suggests that Bayazet might have used an effective combined-arms approach against Timur's purely steppe-style army. In fact, however, this turned out not to be the case, and there are a number of reasons. The terrain near Ankara was better suited to mounted archery, not being as hilly or forested as that near the river Kizil Irmak, where Bayazet had first thought to encounter Timur. Furthermore, as it developed, not all of Bayazet's contingents were to be trusted: the Turkmens deserted and their defection not only weakened the Ottoman army, but sowed disorder. Timur had none of these difficulties; he kept his army in hand and it was a larger one. Numbers alone will not tell, but it is true enough, as Napoleon said, that victory goes to the bigger battalions. Numbers do count and, all things being equal, they will prevail. Some historians rather confidently give the numbers of the contending armies: the Ottomans at 85,000 and the Timurids at 140,000 for example.[13]

Experience has shown, however, that accurate numbers for pre-modern armies are virtually impossible to establish and that contemporary accounts are generally subject to great exaggeration. These numbers seem extreme for the period (though possible) although we may be sure that it was for the time a huge battle and the numbers, if nothing else, probably do roughly express the disproportion between the two armies. This disproportion may have allowed the Timurid forces to withstand the shock from such troops as the Serb knights instead of relying completely upon movement and archery. Still, although the janissaries' archery ought to have been more effective than that of the mounted men, Timur's entirely mounted force was better suited to envelopment, particularly if the Ottoman wings failed, as Bayazet must have understood, putting his cavalry reserve in to support the wings and leaving Timur with the strength for the last blow. Thus, this battle was not purely a steppe-style affair—nor could it have been, given the composition of the troops involved. Things might have turned out differently a hundred years later when the janissaries had become musketeers, but even this is uncertain.

Politically, Timur acted true to form. He had destroyed the Ottoman army—and apparently the empire—and yet, fifty years later, in 1453, the Ottomans under Bayazet's great-grandson Mehmed II, "The Conqueror," would batter the walls of Constantinople with the largest cannon the world had yet seen. These monster guns had diameters of two feet and hurled stone shot weighing twelve hundred or more pounds apiece until the great wall, which had withstood a thousand years of sieges, collapsed. Half a century later Mehmed completed the work of Bayazet, and the Ottoman Empire would endure until after the First World War, to be replaced by its successor state the Republic of Turkey. Timur and his state, by contrast, have been almost forgotten.

Constantinople's reprieve was revoked because Timur, with no real interest in the Ottomans, turned his back upon them as he had on so many other nations he conquered. His great victory, in the end, had achieved nothing, because of a lack of consolidation. Timur never intended consolidation, however, either in this or any other victory. Content with his empire centered in Transoxiana and Khwarezm, he merely stormed about fighting his neighbors, just as any of a thousand petty steppe khans had done through history in thousands of forgotten wars.

Timur's only significance is one of scale: he acted on a grand scale indeed—though in the final analysis this meant little or nothing. He changed things as little as all of the half-forgotten or completely forgotten minor khans who waged war, as he did, for sport or plunder. He was in this, albeit larger than life, a perfect example of the steppe warrior. He was more cruel, certainly, and one of the more tactically successful, but in the end no more significant than Attila, whose empire, like that of Timur, could not survive his death. It is the dissolution of the Timurid Empire which has rendered Timur a rather obscure figure despite the scale of his conquests and the care he took to have his history documented. In spite of the large scale of his actions, and the accounts of them, he is nearly forgotten today; he has left little more in the popular imagination than a corruption of his name and a vague feeling of unease at his methods.

At the time of his death, Timur was contemplating an invasion of China, something historians generally believe would have been extremely damaging to the Chinese state. They do not doubt his ability to defeat the Chinese militarily and they suggest that a consequent forcible imposition of Islam would have done irreparable damage to Chinese culture. In view of Timur's failure to follow up most of his conquests and the inherent instability of his empire (amply demonstrated at his death), one could wonder—all questions of slaughter in battle aside—whether he could really have affected that Eastern culture to the degree the Mongols had earlier.

In any case, on January 19, 1405, at the age of seventy-one "Tamerlane" died at a town called Otrar in northern Transoxiana near his borders with the Kipchak and Jagatai khanates. He was at that very time marshaling his army for the invasion of China, an invasion which of course never took place. Timur was the greater part of the state and in his absence there was no campaign, just as earlier, when the Great Khan Occodai's death had suspended Mongol operations in Europe and the death of Mangu had ended those against the Near East. Although Timur lived in and governed from a city, he and his army—and his polity—had all of the essential characteristics of the steppe: great military power coupled with speed and the ability to project force over very great distances, but all of this utterly dependent upon the will of a single ruler. Upon his death his realm fell prey to the inevitable civil war and dissolution, an ironic postscript of which was the defeat of his cultured descendant, Babur, who settled in India and established the Mogul kingdom, whose name evoked memories of the great Tatar-Mongol states.

Though he operated on a scale greater then any other, Timur Lenk was not as significant a ruler as Chinggis Khan or any of his immediate successors; he had more in common with a petty khan whose only joy was in looting and conflict.

NOTES

1. *Tamerlane or Timur The Great Amir*, trans. Ahmed Ibn Arabshah and J.H. Sanders, Lahore, India, Progressive Books, 1976, p. 1.
2. Ibid., p. 4.
3. Mirza Muhammad Haidar, *A History of the Moghuls of Central Asia, Being The Tarikh-I-Rashidi of Mirza Muhammad Haidar, Dughlat,* trans. E. Dennison Ross, London, Curzon Press, 1972, p. 19.
4. The disease may have been an equine malady and this would have been hardly less serious. Given the nature of steppe warfare, for the Mongols to have been left without sufficient horses would have put them at the mercy of their enemies.
5. For example, Grousset and Edward Gibbon nearly two hundred years before him.
6. *The Political and Military Institutes of Tamerlane, Recorded by Sharfuddin Ali Yezdi,* trans. James Davy, New Delhi, India, Idarah-I Adabiyat-I Delli, 1972.
7. Ruy Gonzalez de Clavijo, *Clavijo, Embassy to Timur, 1403–1406*, New York, Harper & Brothers, 1928, p. 293.
8. Lucien Kehren, *Tamerlan*, Paris, Payot, 1988, pp. 117–18.
9. Kehren (above) sees it as a ploy; Marie-Mathilde Alexandrescu-Dersca, *La Campagne de Timur en Anatolie (1402)*, London, Variorum Reprints, 1977, sees the offer as genuine.
10. Black armor (unfinished after forging) was popular at this time, particularly in Germany, and helmets of it were often painted with designs.

11. Something observed as recently as at the Battle of Waterloo, in which French cavalry horses pulled up several yards from British infantry squares and suffered heavy casualties.

12. For some time after nomadism had been introduced by the Turks into Anatolia, the Turkish government had, after a while, discouraged the practice, encouraging instead a sedentary lifestyle to restrict ungovernable nomads. This was already apparent in the Ottoman army of the fifteenth century; Douglas L. Johnson, *The Nature of Nomadism: A Comparative Study of Pastoral Migrations in Southwestern Asia and Northern Africa*, Chicago, University of Chicago Press, Department of Geography Research Papers, 1969.

13. Alexandrescu-Dersca, p. 70.

11

Crimean Tatars

The Russian principalities, chiefly Moscow, struggled against the Tatar yoke, although with mixed and generally poor success until the fifteenth century, when the Mongols were beset by their greatest weakness: division. The first great victory against the Kipchak Khanate, or Golden Horde, was that of Dmitri, Grand Prince of Muscovy, in the later fourteenth century. His success, however, would not immediately shake off Mongol oppression.

Upon the death of Khan Berdibeg in 1359, the Kipchak Khanate became extremely unsettled as various of the descendants of Juchi sought the throne. Ultimately a certain Mamai took control of the horde, but over the years, beginning in 1371, the Russians refused to pay their accustomed tribute. Grand Prince Dmitri beat off a Mongol punitive expedition in 1373 and went so far as to campaign against them in 1376 and defeat Mamai's forces on August 11, 1378 on the Volga. This was followed in 1380 by another more important victory beyond the Don, in which Dmitri won the nickname "Donskoi."

In this instance Dmitri led a Russian army to meet Khan Mamai on the Don and used the terrain to protect his flanks from the encirclement he had every reason to expect from steppe forces. Dmitri's army consisted of horse archers like the Mongols, but he could not expect them to be as adept as the nomads, and the precaution was wise. The battle took place on September 8 on Kulikovo Field, where the Don and Nepryadva meet. It was hard fought, Mamai eventually breaking off when he perceived that he could not win.

Mamai went on to attack the Genoese, who had a trading colony in the Crimea, but failed to subject them and was forced to

197

recognize their possession. It looked as if the Kipchak Khanate would disintegrate then, but its slide was halted by Toktamish, Khan of the White Horde and protegé of Timur, the Great Emir of Samarkand. Toktamish had been watching events in Kipchak, and after Mamai's bad luck with the Russians and the Genoese he attacked the horde near the Sea of Azov by the Kalka River, defeating it. Mamai fled to the Genoese, who killed him, and Toktamish was now Khan of both Kipchak and the White Horde, thereby reconstituting the territories of the Golden Horde (or Kipchak Khanate) as they had been in the great days of Batu.

Toktamish, at the head of this revitalized Mongol horde, promptly demanded tribute of the Russians, who refused. Toktamish then ravaged the Russians' land, taking Suzdal, Vladimir, Yuriel, Mozhaisk and Moscow, which he completely destroyed. Vitovt, the Grand Duke of Lithuania, had been meddling in Russia at this time and Toktamish defeated a Lithuanian army too, at Poltava. There were to be one hundred more years of the Tatar Yoke.

However, the victory at Kulikovo Field had taught the Russians that the Mongols were not invincible, and in time they had another opportunity. Toktamish began to war with his former protector, Timur of Samarkand (sometimes conscripting Russian troops into his army), until the Great Emir finally and decisively defeated him in 1395. Toktamish then fled to Lithuania to enter the service of Grand Duke Vitovt, his erstwhile enemy, while Timur set Timur Qutlugh on the Kipchak throne, he being, like Toktamish, a Chinggisid of the White Horde. Timur Qutlugh then defeated another Lithuanian army, this time on the Vozakla River, after Toktamish had prevailed upon Vitovt to meddle further.

Upon Timur Qutlugh's death the Kipchak Khanate began its dissolution. His brother, Shadibeg, assumed rule over Kipchak proper while the eastern steppe was ruled by Koirijak of the White Horde, another protege of Timur of Samarkand. This was the start of those divisions that would ultimately free Russia from subjection. Shadibeg was powerful, but not nearly as strong as his predecessors of the century before. With the reign of his son, Khan Kuchuk Muhammad, the Kipchak Khanate broke up decisively when the khanates of Crimea and Kazan were founded in 1430 and 1445, respectively.

These khanates were still dangerous, however, as Grand Duke Vasili II of Moscow learned at the Battle of Suzdal in 1445. The Grand Duke was troubled along his frontier with Lithuania as well as further east where Ulu Muhammad (an unsuccessful claimaint for the Kipchak throne) and his son Mahmudek had founded the Khanate of Kazan. Vasili learned of a Tatar raid from this quarter and prepared to meet it. But a summons of his nobles was unsatisfactory; those on the Lithuanian frontier whose lands were subject to attack from that direction sent him only token forces and in the end he marched with only fifteen hundred men. Still, it must have seemed enough to stop the raiding Tatars and, besides, he appears to have expected reinforcement from an allied Tatar princeling, the "Tsarevich" Berdidad. With the dissolution of the Tatar power, it would become common for Russian armies to include contingents of Tatars, even to fight other Tatars. Berdidad, however, never appeared; he apparently was on post near the Lithuanian border defending the realm from there.

On the morning of July 7, 1445, the Muscovite army arose in its camp outside Suzdal to learn that the Tatars they were to face were more than a mere raiding party. In fact they numbered thirty-five hundred, significantly more than the Russians. Nonetheless the Russians attacked the Tatars vigorously and to their delight they drove them back—the Tatars broke and retreated and the Muscovites followed them. It was of course a feigned retreat, and once the Muscovites became disordered the Tatars wheeled about and attacked them, giving them a complete drubbing. What is more, Grand Duke Vasili was captured, making the defeat absolute.

But already times had changed: the Tatars of the Khanate of Kazan were not strong enough to follow up their victory. The old khans of Kipchak had had little hesitation about killing princes who opposed them and putting their lands and people under complete subjugation. In this instance, after a long delay during which the Tatars tried to interfere in Muscovite politics, they ransomed Vasili. They could no longer subject the Russians as their grandfathers had done; they could only prey upon them in the age-old steppe manner, taking advantage of opportunities.

The Russians could see this too; they had stopped paying tribute to the Kipchak Khanate in the 1450s and it was during the reign of Kuchuk Muhammad's son Khan Ahmed that the Tatar Yoke is popularly considered to have dissolved. In 1480 Ivan III was Grand Duke of Moscow, a clever politician who maintained friendly relations with Mengli Girei, Khan of the Crimea, an enemy of the Kipchak Khanate. In this way the duke was able to face the horde and at the same time menace it from behind with other Tatars. Ivan consistently refused to pay the tribute or to recognize Khan Ahmed as his suzerain. In response, Ahmed marched against Muscovy, advancing first to the Oka River, which Ivan guarded against his passage. The armies then pulled back to the Ugra, where they remained on opposite banks.

These opposing forces watched each other for several weeks, but neither side dared to engage and settle the question of supremacy— each had too much to lose. The weather grew cold in October and Khan Ahmed feared that Khan Mengli Girei would fall upon his lands while he was engaged with the Russians, so he withdrew to his territories. It had been shown that the Tatars could no longer exact their tribute.

A year later Khan Ahmed was dead, killed by the khan of a Siberian horde, and in 1502 Khan Mengli Girei of the Crimea sacked the Kipchak capital of Sarai. The Kipchak Khanate was finished. This left a handful of small khanates and hordes, though many were still dangerous to Russia, Poland, Ukraine and Lithuania. The more important were those of Kazan, Astrakhan and the Crimea. These states were all Muslim and this added to the antipathy which the Tatars and Slavs felt for each other.

Ivan III did a number of other things to protect his territories. He himself established the Khanate of Kasimov around the city of that name on behalf of the Tatar khan Qasim. This was a vassal state of Moscow from the start and was used to affect the internal politics of the other khanates. Ivan did many other things as well. His reign saw a tremendous expansion of territory as Muscovy took over the lands of its Russian neighbors through diplomacy, intimidation, purchase or conquest. Ivan enlarged the Muscovite army and demanded the services of those whose territories he acquired.

This enlarged army was not different from that of his predecessors: they were horse archers like the Tatars they fought. This was still the case in the early 1500s, as the German nobleman Sigismund von Herberstein observed when he visited Muscovy a few years after Ivan III's reign. He wrote that the Muscovite cavalry wore mail coats or silk coats thickly stuffed with wool to keep out arrows, and conical helmets. They rode small, tough horses and used small saddles with short stirrup leathers that let them turn easily in any direction to shoot a bow. Aside from this weapon they carried a lance, an axe and a saber if they were wealthy enough, as well as a kind of mace consisting of a shaft of wood capped by a copper, iron or even staghorn head. It was furnished with a long strap and used "to hit hard."[1]

The Russian cavalryman of the period was indeed, outwardly, a very Tatar-like soldier. Still, though much of the army did not differ in equipment or tactics from its nomad enemies, Muscovy could now field a much larger army than earlier and this alone posed a threat to the Tatars, who were now broken into smaller khanates and hordes that could not raise large armies as the Kipchak Khanate had done.

Like Vasili II before him, Ivan also employed troops of Tatars who were dispossessed from the steppe during internal struggles as the Kipchak Khanate collapsed. The Grand Duke further planned ahead to meet his Tatar enemies. He would post small forces on the approach routes of his lands in order to engage and slow the Tatars while reinforcements were brought up. As an example, because of fighting near Kazan in 1469, he established an outpost of three hundred men who were to be given, among other things, 300 bows, 6,000 arrows and 300 sheepskin coats against the winter cold.

Although these marcher outposts may not have been large at this time, the approach was still effective. By increasing the danger to Tatar raiders—in other words by increasing the cost of raiding—he could stem raids somewhat, as an example from 1472 shows. In that year Tatars from Gorodets tried to raid Muscovite territory near the town of Aleksin on the Oka. The garrison there, although inadequately supplied and armed, was able to hold off the raiders for a while before abandoning the town. During this time Muscovite forces were able to gather and prepare to meet the Tatars. When he learned of this, the khan returned to the steppes.

Ivan's defensive scheme recalled the castellated Bavarian frontier that the German emperors had earlier established against the

Magyars, and over time it would become more and more substantial.

And then there was gunpowder. Ivan encouraged the casting of cannon to be used in the defense of cities and citadels. The lack of decent roads meant that cannon were particularly difficult to move overland, and so, apart from sieges, they did not figure much, if at all, in engagements. Furthermore, the Russians employed steppe tactics anyway and would have found it difficult to use cannon in the field even under the best of conditions—a fact confirmed by Von Herberstein. He noted that cannon were kept in camp because in the field the troops (and here he meant the cavalry) moved too quickly. In fact, he observed, even foot soldiers and arquebusiers were not much used in field operations because the cavalry, whether "attacking, standing fast, or fleeing, did this suddenly and with haste."[2] All the same, cannon served to strengthen towns and cities and the Tatars found it more and more difficult to deal with these strong places.

On a level more concerned with policy than strategy or tactics, Ivan showed a penchant for granting military promotions to men of experience and proven ability, assigning his officers to small commands until they had proven themselves.

All of these things, joined to cordial relations with the Khan of the Crimea, allowed him to handle the various other khanates and hordes as no Russian ruler before him had done. The Tatars were still a serious threat and in fact they would manage to burn Moscow once more, but they would never dominate Russia again. Organization, diplomacy and gunpowder would finally, albeit gradually, marginalize them.

The Khanate of the Crimea, which Ivan used against the Kipchak Khanate, was established around 1430 by Hajji Girei, a descendant of Batu's brother, and his family ruled it until its conquest by Russia in 1771. With its capital at Bakhchisarai in the south, it lay between the lower Dnieper and Don and extended north as far as Yelets and Tambov. The Crimeans were still largely nomadic and lived on the steppe, though some were settled in towns in the Crimean peninsula. Nonetheless, they kept in touch with their nomadic roots and fielded dangerous forces; it was the threat posed by the Crimean Tatars that prompted Poland to create a standing army in the 1490s.

Upon Hajji Girei's death, the khanate's throne was contested by his sons. His sixth son, Mengli Girei, ultimately prevailed in part because the Genoese merchants of the Crimean town of Caffa held his rival and brother prisoner during the struggle. The city was besieged by the Ottoman Turks, and Mengli Girei, who supported the Italians, was taken prisoner. The Turks held him for two years, releasing him when he had agreed to become a Turkish vassal. This circumstance strengthened Mengli Girei and his successors rather than weakened them because, as a client state of the powerful Turkish Empire, the Muscovites and Poles had to treat the Crimean Tatars with some caution. It was a direct result of their dependency upon the Turks that the Crimean Tatars survived as an independent political state long after the other khanates had been defeated and forcibly annexed by Russia. Tsar Ivan IV, the Terrible, besieged Kazan with artillery and took it on October 2, 1552, with great slaughter. In 1556 he took the Khanate of Astrakhan when a puppet khan whom he had installed revolted. The Crimean Tatars, however, would last another two hundred years, raiding into Russia, Poland and Lithuania. In 1571 a Crimean Tatar army even took Moscow, except for the citadel of the Kremlin, and burned it.

Moreover, earlier, in 1502–1503, the Great Horde had submitted to the Khan of the Crimea and moved from their lands near the Volga to the peninsula. Noghay Tatars moved into the lands they had left, and many of these Noghay tribes also submitted to the Khan of the Crimea. The Crimean Tatars had protection, manpower and, through their ports on the Black Sea, trading connections with other nations. They were well positioned to trouble their neighbors.

In spite of their now having a number of towns or small cities, most of these Tatars were still nomadic, or largely so, and lived in small villages that moved about. It was from these villages that the Tatars were summoned for service, and when this happened they were organized decimally, just as were the Mongols of old. Each man belonged to a squad of ten called a *kos*, and the common Tatars of each *kos* had to appear when marshaled with their own mounts and equipment, which included a whistle, sundial, awl, flint and needles. One of the kos was responsible for the group's cooking equipment and drum. These kos were joined to form troops of one hundred, one thousand or even ten thousand. On campaign the men subsisted on little more than millet, powdered meat and garlic. They would also consume horses that went lame or died on the march, eating the flesh raw and warmed beneath the saddle. Like their predecessors they were tough men indeed.

The Tatar khans maintained a retinue of over a thousand men, and the officers of the court and lesser nobles maintained smaller ones. These men constituted something of a professional corps of soldiers to stiffen the militia levied from the people as a whole for a campaign. The loyalty of the common Tatars was given to their own nobles or princes, however, and not directly to the khan. This meant that in practice the khan had to gather the support of his nobles before he could embark on a war; he no longer had the absolute power of the great Mongol khans.

The size of a field army would vary considerably according to its aims, and forces of different sizes were commanded by different officers. When the khan himself led the army it could number eighty thousand or even more. The Kalga (usually the khan's brother) would command fifty thousand, while an army led by the Nur al-Din, the Kalga's assistant, would generally number forty thousand. However, because the Crimean Tatars so often exercised aggression in the form of pillaging raids, their forces were often much smaller than this.

Tatar armies, like those of their steppe predecessors, were made up of cavalry—with a concession to progress: arquebusiers were incorporated in small numbers. The khan had six hundred of them divided into twenty companies and he would raise that many again when he went on campaign. Though these men fought on foot they must have travelled on horseback for they could not otherwise have kept up with a mounted army. As a client of the Ottoman Empire, the Khan of the Crimea was from time to time furnished with a number of janissaries for expeditions he made on the Turks' behalf.

Each Tatar was to bring three horses on campaign. The French traveller Guillaume Le Vasseur de Beauplan, writing in the 1630s, described these as "ugly," recalling the Romans' opinion of Hun horses. His description continues, adding that they are tractable and the best horses for war—again echoing the Roman view of the

Hunnic steppe pony. Another traveler of the same period, Pierre Chevalier, observed:

> Their horses, which they call Bacmates, are long, ugly, and lean, have the Hair of their Neck thick, and great Tayls which hang down to the ground; but Nature hath very well repaired their ugliness by their swiftness, and their incomparable and indefatigable service they perform in traveling, being able to carry their Riders whole days journeys without drawing Bit; they feed at all times, and when in winter the Earth is covered with Snow and the Tatars make their incursions they live either upon what is under the Snow, or upon the Branches or sprouts of Trees, Pine tops, Straw, or any thing they can find . . .[3]

So, these late steppe warriors still commonly rode the tough, ugly pony which had served the nomads so well across the centuries. As for the nobles, Chevalier says: ". . . the chief of the Tatars have Turkish and Arabian Horses, and their Cham [khan] very good Race-horses."[4]

The well-to-do Tatars wore helmets and chainmail shirts, although the ordinary Tatar fought without much, if any, armor. The use of chainmail instead of lamellar armor or the brigandine-like armor of the later Mongols shows Western influence.

The Tatars' principal weapon was the recurved composite bow, and while Beauplan states that each Tatar carried a quiver of 18 to 20 arrows, it is reasonable to suppose that on campaign they would have taken more, 40 to 60 being usual for Mongols and Turks of the thirteenth century. A Tatar's armament would be completed by a curved saber and a knife or curved dagger at the belt. He might carry a lance and a shield too or, rarely, firearms such as pistols or an arquebus for, as Chevalier noted in the mid-seventeenth century, "they have begun to use firearms."[5]

The Tatars produced and exported gunpowder to Turkey without using it extensively themselves and this may seem curious, but the primitive firearms of the period were heavy, inaccurate, slow to reload and without much range. In particular, arquebuses were useful only on foot, unlike the bow. For the Tatars' mounted warfare, the bow was still the better weapon.

While the Tatar noble wore robes of colored cotton, most Tatar soldiers wore sheepskin jackets and caps, turning the fleece of both outward in warm or rainy weather and inward in cold weather. Because of this, Beauplan states:

> The commoners have on their shoulders only a sheepskin jacket, and put the wool outwards in times of heat or rain, and when seen so dressed when one encounters them in the country unexpectedly they give a fright because one takes them for white bears mounted on horses, but when it is cold and in winter they reverse their jacket and put the wool inside and do the same with their hat which is made of the same material: they are armed with a saber, a bow and their quiver is furnished with eighteen or twenty arrows, a knife [is] at their belt.[6]

The tents of a Tatar khan and his retinue were of the traditional *ger* type used by the Mongols and still seen today in the steppes of Central Asia: they were circular frames covered with felt or other fabric. When the khan himself campaigned there might be sixty of these.

Tatar horses were unshod, although the nobility might use leather stockings to protect their horses' hooves. Therefore the Tatars preferred to mount expeditions in winter, when the snow would protect hooves. For this reason they disliked dry winters; the lack of snow curbed their campaigning. Secondarily, winter also made it possible to cross frozen rivers more easily—a reason for the Mongol winter advance on Central Europe in 1241. However, the Crimean Tatars were known for their audacity in crossing rivers, no matter how wide or in what season. The men would make floats of reeds and put their equipment on them. These were tied to their horse's tail and the horse would be directed into the river to swim to the other bank, its master clinging to its mane. The principle was the same as that used by the Mongols of two or three hundred years earlier. A khan and his nobles, however, used boats wherever possible.

When beginning an important raid the Tatars would gather at the fortress of Perekop in the north, near the entrance to the Crimean peninsula. According to L.J.D. Collins, other "provincial" forces such as those from Azov and the Kuban would join the army when it went to the mainland.[7] He adds that tradition evidently required the army to carry out a campaign once it reached the mainland.[8]

The Tatars would conduct their approach march to the Ukrainian border by short stages of about six leagues (or eighteen miles) a day in order to spare their horses. When the army was to cross the border it broke into several columns and entered by moving through valleys to avoid detection. No fires were allowed at night for the same reason. But if the Tatars wished to remain unobserved, they still wanted whatever information they could get about the country. Accordingly, men were sent to capture Cossacks or peasants for interrogation. After questioning, the unfortunates were killed.

While the individual columns could continue to penetrate enemy territory, if there were enemy forces present they would regroup into a single force and advance in that way. An army of eighty or a hundred thousand men would advance with a front of one hundred soldiers and a depth of eight hundred or a thousand. Beauplan rather vividly describes this:

> Thus the Tatars advance with a front of 100 horses, that is to say 300, because each Tatar leads two by the hand as his relays, as we have said before, their front can be 800 to 1,000 paces and in depth they are 800 to 1,000 horses that take up three or four large leagues in length when they are drawn up because otherwise they make a column more than ten leagues long, which is a surprising thing to one who has not seen it because 80,000 Tatars make more than 200,000 horses; trees are not thicker in the woods than their horses are in the countryside, and seem to those that see them from far off to be a sort of cloud that rises from the horizon and grows larger as it rises which strikes terror in the most stalwart, I speak of those who are not accustomed to see such legions together . . .[9]

A cavalry army a thousand yards wide and thirty miles long would indeed be a stunning, frightening sight and all the more effective because it could be raised, if need be, within two to four weeks.[10] Furthermore its advance could be quick; Kaplan Girei's army covered 118 miles in six days over swampy terrain in 1698.

Such an army halted in its advance every hour to let the men and horses urinate. The animals were so well trained that they would do this as soon as the riders dismounted. The signal to halt, and other signals on the march, were given by whistle. When the army had reached deeply enough into Ukraine it would find a place to camp that offered some cover to make it difficult for the Polish army to discover it, and the men would rest for two or three days. Next, the army was divided into thirds. Two-thirds of it stayed at the camp to form a corps called, like a troop of ten men, a kos. The remaining third was divided evenly into two raiding columns basing themselves on the kos. Each party left the kos and traveled a few leagues before breaking into smaller raiding parties of about a hundred men, called *tschambouls*. These tschambouls would raid the countryside at a distance of about eighty miles from the kos. When they had gotten sufficient booty and captives they returned to the kos, from which a new raiding party was then sent out. In this way fresh troops were constantly sent on depredations while the bulk of the Tatar army was kept together in case it needed to face a major response from the Poles.

The Tatars surrounded a village by placing four parties around it to prevent peasants in the countryside from seeking refuge within. When it had been judged that enough plunder had been gotten, the kos decamped and headed home. The last raiding parties had no difficulty following the withdrawing Tatar army because the huge number of its horses left such an obvious trail across the country.

The Tatars' raids were quick; they might even be done before an army could be raised to oppose them and they were also extremely destructive. In 1667 the Crimean Tatars destroyed 300 villages and took 50,000 cattle from the estates of Jan Sobieski, the King of Poland. In 1672 Sobieski defeated a Tatar army and rescued 44,000 captives. It was, in fact, these captives who formed a large part of the raiders' booty. Called *yassyr*, they were to have been sold into slavery in the Turkish Empire, from which women might even be shipped to harems in India.

Rreturning home, the Tatars took a route back that was different from that which they took on their advance. This was of course the time of greatest danger for them because they were burdened by loot and slowed by captives. Beauplan states that when the Poles fought the Tatars they could defeat them handily:

> . . . because these bandits (so one should call these Tatars) do not enter Poland to fight, but to pillage and loot by surprise, but when they are met by the Poles they play them a good game and make them retreat more quickly than at a walking pace . . .[11]

Beauplan probably refers to encounters with the retreating and burdened nomads, since the Poles otherwise could not hope to catch them, let alone come to grips with them. Without booty to defend the Tatars could simply continue to fall back before a slower, more conventional army, either fleeing it entirely or else wearing it out during the pursuit before joining it in battle on their own terms—a battle of maneuver and archery until they had gained the upper hand. Chevalier confirms the need to trap the Tatars where their mobility is compromised, if they are to be beaten: ". . . and it is difficult to surprise them, they keeping strict watch all night, nor easie to defeat them, unless it be in some streight, or upon some pass of a River."[12]

When they had completed their withdrawal to the frontier, an area thirty or forty leagues wide, the Tatars would spend a week dividing the booty and replacing the equipment of men who had lost theirs in battle or on campaign. As noted, a great deal of the booty was made up of captives bound for slavery in the Turkish Empire. Beauplan details the horrors of families broken up at this time, husbands from wives and children from their mothers, and the rapes which would occur.

A Tatar raid was indeed a horrific event for the Ukrainians, Poles, Ruthenians and Russians, and it was something that was difficult to prevent, even by treaty. Tatar nobles felt themselves entitled to lead their own raids into the Ukraine and Poland, notwithstanding agreements to the contrary between Poland and the khan. The Polish state therefore tried, whenever possible, to reach treaties with individual Tatar lords to curtail this practice.

Smaller raids took place in the summer, the Tatar forces not generally exceeding ten or twenty thousand, ostensibly because a larger force would be more easily discovered. Sixty to ninety miles from the Polish or Ukrainian frontier the Tatar army divided into ten or twelve troops, each of about a thousand horsemen. Five or six of these troops would head one way over the border at a distance of a league or a league and a half from the other five or six troops, which would cross at different points. Beauplan states that one group went "right" and the other "left." This way the Tatars would advance on a front of ten to twelve leagues (or thirty to thirty-six miles), scouts going ahead of them to gather information. The army would have an agreed rendezvous near the frontier, but it would advance in these several columns so that any reports of them would underestimate their numbers. The Cossack sentries would be inclined to report the incursion of only the single column they observed. Beauplan comments:

> Because these Cossacks spot these Tatars from afar and they run off immediately to give the alarm to the whole country, and seeing only about 1,000 or so, they are not much frightened by this number, so they are surprised a few days later when they have news . . .[13]

In contrast to winter campaigns, advances during the summer were on high ground between rivers, where the way was easy and these raids would generally extend only six to ten leagues into the country under attack. The raids would be short and the Tatars would try to return home after merely a couple of days. The raids' speed was meant to achieve surprise and avoid confrontation with any force large enough to be a challenge.

The Tatars employed deception too, because it could protect the raiders and make estimation of their numbers difficult; the Crimean Tatars broke up into smaller units to give the appearance of small numbers. In contrast, the Mongols in Central Europe four hundred years earlier had traveled in very fast troops, which the terrified Europeans took to be different forces, thus intentionally giving the impression of huge numbers. Steppe people understood deception and used it readily. Beauplan noted a further Tatar technique used on the summer raids: A troop of four hundred Tatars left a visible trail in the grass of the steppe, and that trail remained for some time and could lead the Cossacks or the Polish army to them. However, the track of a handful of horses over the tall steppe grass would last only a day or so before the grass sprang back up. The Tatars knew this and used it to their advantage.

A troop of four hundred Tatars would divide into four, each of the four smaller troops going off for a league and a half in a different direction. This done, these troops of one hundred then divided again, this time into thirds. Each troop of thirty-three then headed off in a different direction, though not to the rear, and after another half league each troop divided again into three, and the process was repeated until the Tatars had divided into squads of ten. This was done at a full trot and took about an hour and a half. Later, the dispersed Tatars met at an agreed point over a period of several hours and the grass which the small squads had ridden over returned to its earlier state. A troop of Cossacks could find the original trail, but as it continually divided and became less distinct they would have to call off the search. Meanwhile, a sizable troop of horsemen lay in wait somewhere, undetected.

They were not always undetected, of course. By the seventeenth century the Polish and Russian armies were more effective in dealing with their raids and often came to grips with them. However, in such situations the Tatars had no illusions about fighting hand-to-hand if they expected to prevail. From Beauplan:

> In other words, if the Poles attack the Tatars and the Tatars do not feel themselves strong enough to resist saber in hand, they scatter like flies, each one in his own direction and shoot backwards with the bow which they handle so well that they do not fail at all at 60 to 100 paces to get their man, [and] the Poles cannot pursue them because their horses do not have such good wind as theirs, then the Tatars gather themselves again a quarter league away and begin to make a frontal charge on the Poles, and then when one joins them they scatter again and they always shoot from the left while retreating because they cannot do so from the right and in this way tire the Poles so that they force them to

make a retreat, . . .[14]

We can appreciate that Beauplan is revealing some prejudice against the Tatars when he goes on to tell us that they would not engage even in this kind of fighting unless they outnumbered their opponents ten to one. Nonetheless, it is clear that they resisted coming directly to blows with an opponent unless the advantage was clearly theirs. Beauplan's description of Tatar tactics is a wonderfully clear description of steppe warfare that could as easily apply to the Scythians, Huns or Mongols as it did to the seventeenth-century Crimean Tatars. Beauplan even mentions the "Parthian shot."

Another author makes clear the Tatar's capacity for surprise, even when he is looked for. During the early 18th century, Captain John Perry had been assigned Tatars who were in the service of Moscow to protect him in the country: two thousand mounted men, four thousand foot soldiers and twelve pieces of artillery. Outposts were set up on hills and these men watched for hostile Kuban Tatars. Captain Perry wrote:

> But notwithstanding all our Guards and Watches that have been placed, a Party of between 3 and 4,000 of these [Kuban] Tatars once came just as it was Day in the Morning, without our having the least Advice of them, up to our very Camp; and when they found that the Alarm was taken, and our Cannon began to play upon them from our Lines, they immediately retired with the same Speed they came on, before our Men could mount or get in an Order to attack them, it requireth some time before they could come with their Horses; besides, that many of their Horses that were some Distance without the Camp, were surprized and carried off by the Enemy. They carried off in all about 1,400 Horses, some of which belonged to the Army, and others to the Workmen; with several People that were looking after the Horses where they were feeding in the Meadows, at some Distance from the Camp; there being no Inclosures in that Country.[15]

Troublesome and expensive as such a raid was, it was nothing like the incursions of the thirteenth or fourteenth centuries. The Kuban Tatars, like all of those in the Russian orbit, had been marginalized. They were either dependent upon the Tsar and served in his armies or, if hostile, their incursions were ultimately quite limited in effect. The Kingdom of Poland, which at that time extended into today's Ukraine, while constantly facing the Crimean Tatars, tried to achieve the same result.

Because the Crimean Tatars went to war primarily for loot (or as an obligation to their protectors, the Ottoman Turks, who employed them in flying columns) they had the natural strategic advantages of the raider: surprise, uncertainty of object and the use of flight to avoid any serious contest. By the same token, however, their distaste for set battle and inability to take fortified positions with troops of moderate or even large numbers of cavalry intent on safety of movement meant that a clever general like Jan Sobieski, Hetman (or general) of the Polish army and later king, could meet them effectively by the use of forethought.

The Polish army of the seventeenth century was a heterogeneous force; it was in fact divided into two parts, called the "Polish Army" and the "Foreign Army," although both parts were made up of Poles. The Polish Army was the larger division, consisting nominally of 24,000 men, all cavalry, or about two-thirds of the army. This force in turn consisted of hussars, *panczerniks*, and *peteores*. Its purely cavalry character suggests medieval knightly origins with strong steppe influence, as will become apparent with further description.

The Polish hussars were the elite of the cavalry and not, as in Hungary where the term originates, light horse. These hussars were aristocratic armored lancers equipped with cuirass and helmet and heavy sword. They were described in a work by François-Paullin Dalairac, a Frenchman in the Polish diplomatic service under Sobieski:

> They are composed of handsome men, mounted on the finest Horses of the Kingdom, with divers other Led-Horses, richly capparisoned, their Bridles adorn'd with Plates and Nails of Silver or Vermillion gilt, embroidered Saddles with gilt Boys [saddlebows], great hanging Houzes [housses], according to the Turkish manner, with Fringes of Gold and

Silver: A Falchon or very rich Sword is fixed to the left side of the saddle under the Horseman's Thigh. Formerly the Polish Cavalry had not Pistols, but now they are used among those fixed troops. . . . The Equipage of the Hussars is as much distinguished as their personal habit. . . . The Hussars are armed with Back and Breast, a scaled Head-Piece adorn'd on the sides and behind with Pendants of Iron Plates quilted, which come down to their Shoulders, where they have another separate Piece of Armour, with Braces reaching over their Neck to which there is fixed a sort of Gantlet of Mail, which covers the back of the hand only. . . Over all this they wear a great Leopard or Tigre's Skin, in form of a loose Coat made in a Warlike Fashion, which is a very fine Ornament to the Gens d'Arms.[16]

The hussars' lances were long. Dalairac says three or four ells, or something over three or four meters—longer, in fact, than a Western infantry pike of the time—and the French diplomat, who had seen these men in action and on review, suggests that they were really too long to be extremely useful. These cavalrymen were also fitted with a pair of large wings made of eagle feathers strapped to their backs to make them appear more terrifying as they charged, this being their principal tactic. Each of these hussars was attended by a few armed and mounted servants, much like medieval squires, and these men, called *pacolets*, formed ranks behind the hussars and followed them in the charge.

The hussars were known for the shock they could inflict on the enemy with their heavy equipment and lances, although Dalairac noted that they did not easily re-form after a charge. It became the habit of Sobieski to flank squadrons of hussars with panzcerniks, cavalrymen somewhat less heavily equipped. These wore mail coats and helmets with mail coifs to protect the neck and lower part of the face, recalling certain Tatar and Turkish helmets. They were armed with sword and musketoon, a musket shortened for use on horseback. In earlier days they had carried bows. These troops were more agile and apparently able to recover themselves better after charging.

The employment of an entirely mounted army (which the fiction of calling the cavalry by the separate name of "Polish Army" implies) suggests steppe influence, as does the use of steppe-style cavalry helmets and, earlier, the bow from horseback. But for all the cavalry's color and dash, Sobieski relied more on the "Foreign Army" to curb the Tatars. This force consisted of those Poles who fought in the German manner, that is, as musket-armed infantry, light cavalry, dragoons (mounted infantry) or artillerymen using Western drill and techniques.

Understanding that the Tatars were after plunder, Sobieski would station troops of men near the various forts and other strong places along the Polish border. Tatar tschambouls were unable to take fortifications, but at the same time they were wary of passing them by either, or of putting themselves in a position to be met by Polish forces in their rear or on their line of withdrawal. This dispersal of troops along the frontier was quite effective in curbing Tatar raiding since these pillagers were not interested in the political issues or territorial acquisition that require decisive battles; even small bodies of soldiers could make the raids too difficult and potentially too costly to be worthwhile. Thus Sobieski employed the same strategy against the Crimean Tatars that Ivan III had used against the Kipchak Khanate; indeed, it was the same strategy the Germans had used against the Magyars before that.

From time to time, however, there was a major engagement, as when the Polish senate, or Sejm, due to political wrangling and willful incompetence, refused to respond to Tatar incursions by calling the army out. Under these circumstances Sobieski, as Hetman, employed his own troops and those of the government that were under his command. On more than one occasion he awaited the Tatars in prepared positions, as he did on October 6, 1667, at Podhajce. There he met a large Tatar army let by Krym Girei Soltan-Kalka composed of thirty thousand Tatars, twenty thousand Cossack allies, three thousand janissaries and 24 guns.

Two ravines ran the length of the battlefield, one of them down the center and the other off to the side, beyond which lay a wood. On the other side of the field the ground was swampy. Any attack upon Sobieski and the Poles, who had positioned themselves in two bodies before the Castle of Podhajce and its village, would of necessity be a straight advance upon the front with no possible maneuver. To improve his position further, Sobieski had a pair of demi-lune ramparts built on his flanks, on which to mount cannon. The rules of war had changed here: he had introduced modern European gunnery and military architecture into the age-old struggle against the steppe horseman.

The Tatars, vastly outnumbering him and determined to take the position, attacked, only to be met by murderous cannon fire and musketry from the flanks as they advanced. Still the fight was a close one and it was some time before Sobieski's troops, consisting of cavalry, hussars and *reiters* (German-style cavalry armed with pistols and swords), supported by infantry, succeeded in defeating the Tatar army. But close as Sobieski's victory may have been in this case, the victory was won by a smaller force against a larger one with the help of gunpowder and its attendant tactics. It was only one of many that would deliver the Tatars into the hands of settled powers. Less than a century later, Tsarina Catherine the Great's general Potemkin marched his army of musket-armed foot soldiers into the Crimea and formally annexed it to the Russian Empire. The year was 1771 and the era of the steppe warrior had ended.

NOTES

1. Sigismund von Heberstein, *Das alte Russland*, Zurich, Manesse Verlag, 1985, p. 136.

2. Ibid.

3. Pierre Chevalier, *A Discourse of the Original, Countrey, Manners, Government and Religion of the Cossacks with Another of the Precopian Tatars, and a History of the Wars of the Cossacks Against Poland*, London, printed for Hobart Kemp, 1672, p. 42.

4. Ibid.

5. Ibid., p. 41.

6. Guillaume Le Vasseur de Beauplan, *La Description d'Ukranie*, Ottawa, Les Presses de l'Université d'Ottawa, 1990, pp. 62–63 (translation by Erik Hildinger).

7. L.J.D. Collins, "The Military Organization and Tactics of the Crimean Tatars During the Sixteenth and Seventeenth Centuries," in *War, Technology and Society in the Middle East*, ed. V.J. Parry and M.E. Yapp, London, Oxford University Press, 1975, p. 264.

8. Ibid., p. 265.

9. Beauplan, pp. 65–66.

10. Collins, p. 264.

11. Beauplan, p. 67.

12. Chevalier, p. 53.

13. Beauplan, p. 68.

14. Beauplan, pp. 71–72. A right-handed man sitting on a horse can only shoot to the left side, and he will turn left to shoot backwards over the horse's rump.

15. John Perry, *The State of Russia Under the Present Czar*, London and Edinburgh, Thomas Nelson, Ltd. (reprint of 1716 edtion), pp. 89–90.

16. François-Paulin Dalairac, *Polish Manuscripts: or The Secret History of the Reign of John Sobieski, the III of that Name, King of Poland*, London, printed for H. Rhodes, 1700, pp. 15–16.

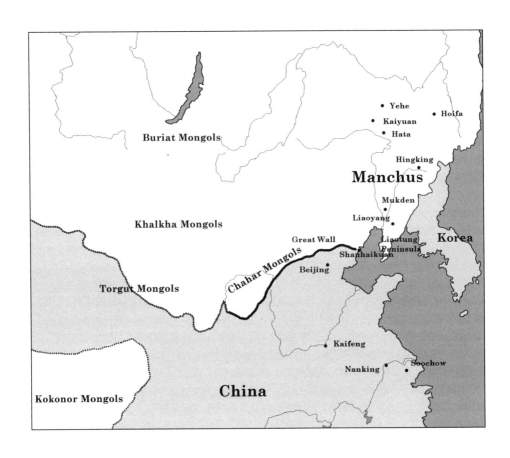

12

The Manchus

The last nomads to conquer and occupy a settled civilization were a nation of Jurchids who took the name Manchu. After forty-five years of conflict with Ming Dynasty China they succeeded, in 1644, in taking the capital of Beijing. In the following years they quelled local, disorganized resistance and their royalty ruled as the Ch'ing (Qing) Dynasty until 1912. Although they ruled China longer than did the Mongols, whose Yüan empire lasted from 1279 to 1368, they were never as expansionist or as powerful. Like their Mongol cousins they were, however, opportunists, and were just as ready to take advantage of any weakness in their neighbor. The Manchus were much like the Mongols, only writ smaller.

The Jurchid people were related to the Chin (Kin) who had conquered China in the twelfth century and fought the Mongols steadily to maintain their empire. The Manchus were nomads, though not pastoral nomads; instead they principally hunted, in distinction to the Mongols and Turks, and they differed from them in speech too: they spoke a Tungusic language, which is today rarely heard. Although these Jurchids were hunting rather than herding nomads, they shared the pastoralists' toughness and skill at mounted archery. While scholars make a distinction between the Manchus and the Mongols, it is instructive that modern Chinese regard them as being essentially the same people. Again, the broad similarities between different nomads is evident, although the Manchus were more familiar with the Chinese than the Mongols, because they had lived for centuries along their northern border. They were therefore not so alien to the Chinese and, after conquest, they were more readily—and completely—assimilated.

Modern-day Manchuria is essentially the territory these Jurchid tribes occupied; it was the country north of the Great Wall as far west as Mongolia, as far east as the Yellow Sea, north to Siberia and southeast to the border of Korea. In the sixteenth century it contained a number of settlements, small states and petty kingdoms and was divided between seven Jurchid tribes. It was a Chinese-dominated area, parts of which were subject to Chinese officials and soldiers. It was also a barbaric backwater which, in the late fifteen hundreds, gave no suggestion that it would rise to become any serious threat to the Ming Dynasty (1368 to 1644), which had arisen centuries before and driven out the Mongol Yüan rulers. The Mongol elites had, over the course of a century, lost their martial interests and inclinations and begun to quarrel among themselves. The Chinese rebel Zhu Yuanzhang was able to drive them from China and established himself as Hungwu, the first Ming emperor.

But just as the Yüan had grown effete, so in time did the Ming, and by the time of the Jurchid rise China was a deeply troubled and weakened country, not nearly the power it had been when, under the Chin Dynasty, it resisted the Mongols for so long. In fact, some scholars have gone so far as to say that the Ming Dynasty "committed suicide."[1]

Like the Mongols, the Manchus owed much of their rise to the foundation established by one man: Nurhachi (1559–1626) of the Nuchen, that group of Jurchids who had established the Chin Dynasty over China some four hundred years before. In 1599 he began to unify the seven Jurchid tribes, accomplishing this by 1606. His rise began as the result of a Chinese frontier commander's meddling in Jurchid politics: the commander backed the loser in a squabble and provoked the winner, Nurhachi, to revenge himself upon the Chinese for the death of his father and grandfather at their hands in 1584. Nurhachi had at that time a small following, a mere one hundred thirty men. By 1613 he commanded forty thousand.

It was a poor time for the Chinese to provoke difficulties among the nomads beyond the wall. Droughts and famine had caused rebellions in the north and Japanese pirates were preying on the Chinese coasts. The Chinese provocation of Nurhachi, which led to the rise of the Manchus over the course of a generation, was only one of many causes of the Ming demise; it prompted one scholar to remark that the rise of the Manchus might be considered an "indirect" cause of the Ming fall.[2] Indirect or not, however, the Manchus took and ruled China for 260 years.

There were echoes of the Mongol organization into tumens of both the military and civil populations, although the Manchu arrangement was somewhat different. In 1601 Nurhachi began the division of his subjects into "arrows," or *niru*. Each "arrow" was of three hundred warriors and their households. Five of these "arrows" made a battalion and ten battalions a "banner," or *gushi*. At first there were four banners: red, white, blue and yellow. In 1615 the number was raised to eight (the extra four were the same colors except with red borders; the extra red banner had a white border). As ethnic Chinese were captured or subjugated in the lands north of the wall they too were pressed into service under new banners; however, they were generally regarded as inferior or subservient to the Manchus proper.

As was usual with Asiatic nomads, the Manchus fought as mounted archers and were known for their skills in handling both bow and horse. With this naturally came the use of stratagem: ambush, feigned flight, spies and thorough reconnaisance. Their armor was largely fabric, made of several layers of cloth stitched one over the other to make a flexible, light and arrow-proof protection. This bemused one nineteenth-century writer,[3] but is borne out by ceremonial suits of such armor in Beijing's Forbidden City. As discussed in earlier chapters, the efficacy of fabric armor has been demonstrated. Contemporary engravings made after the Manchu conquest of China suggest, however, that light cavalry preponderated—as with steppe armies. The Manchu light horsemen are shown with no armor, simply wearing the usual trousers and long, belted coat (it is their round hats with narrow, sharply turned-up brims which are distinctive). They ride small, steppe-style ponies and carry bows and quivers well stocked with arrows.

Nurhachi had established a small state centered in the town of Laochung and he built a palace there in 1587. He was a popular ruler for his fairness and because he kept order, and so managed to unify five of the Manchu districts from his base. This done, he took Yalukiang Province to the east and annexed it to his territories. As he grew in power, however, seven of his neighboring kinglets banded against him, much as the various Mongol and Tatar leagues had done in opposition to the rise of Temujin in Mongolia centuries before. These petty kingdoms raised an army of thirty thousand men divided into three columns and advanced to meet Nurhachi and his Jurchids.

Nurhachi's men were outnumbered and considerably distressed, but their leader chose his ground carefully, not only protecting his flanks but seeing to it that the field was muddy and prepared with obstacles. Bujai, King of Yehe, was thrown from his saddle and killed while Mingan of the Khortsin Mongols became enmired and escaped without his saddle. Bujai's death and Mingan's flight unsettled the confederates, who broke and fled, the Jurchids in pursuit. Four thousand, it is said, were killed during their flight. Having survived this threat, Nurhachi became yet more powerful; in response to the attack he marched against the Kingdom of Hada and annexed it. He followed this by seizing the kingdom of Hrita and continued gradually bringing the entire area north of China under his control.

Now the Chinese grew alarmed and, in 1615, to set one barbarian against another they supported the Kingdom of Yehe—north of the Great Wall and west of Nurhachi's domain—by sending it both troops and guns. This forestalled any immediate Manchu designs on the Chinese realm, but it did not soften Nurhachi's attitude toward the Chinese, whom he rightly judged to be relatively ineffective opponents. In 1616, in fact, Nurhachi declared himself an emperor. This action was followed by his publication of a list of Seven Grievances against the Chinese, which he used as a justification for the invasion of Liaotung province, an action he had been preparing for two years. The Grievances largely turned on Chinese aid to Yehe. In 1618 he took the city of Chingho and beat the Chinese army. He followed this with the capture of Jienchong, but was forced to withdraw in response to his soldiers' fears that Yehe would attack their homes while they were on campaign.

In 1619 the Chinese sent further troops to Yehe, which Nurhachi attacked anyway, although he was forced to withdraw in haste when he learned of a huge Chinese army marching upon his capital of Hingking. This army was said to have numbered two hundred thousand but it is difficult to believe that such a huge force would have been raised to deal with a mere barbarian beyond the

Great Wall. (Such an army could also have hardly supported itself in the area—or been supported by the government—for any significant time.) The figure is likely the result of later Manchu self-congratulation, though the army was certainly quite large and may well have outnumbered Nurhachi's forces, given as sixty thousand after he drained off every soldier he could from the field and from garrisons to defend his capital. That the Chinese army was especially large, however, is indicated by the fact that Emperor Wanli had to raise taxes against the expense of the campaign and this in turn caused more unrest throughout the country. Furthermore it was this type of unrest which led to revolts and the further internal dissension that, ultimately, the Manchus would use to their advantage.

In any case, a certain Yang Hao was made general in charge of the province of Liaotung and he set out in March 1619, marching in four equal columns toward Nurhachi's capital of Hingking. The Jurchid emperor knew he was outnumbered and likely to be beaten. He was aware, however, that the Chinese were approaching in separate formations, any one of which he could himself outnumber. He decided to move quickly and try to beat the columns in detail. It was risky and would depend upon the sort of speed over distance that only a mounted army could achieve. He first decided to meet the Chinese force advancing from the west.

This force was led by a general named Du Sung, who was just as eager to meet Nurhachi; he travelled thirty-three miles in a single day and crossed the Hwun River in a rush by leaving his supply carts behind him. He lost numbers of men and horses in the crossing. Nurhachi, who outnumbered Du Sung slightly, was not far away. Du Sung, meanwhile, split his forces in two. With thirty thousand he established a camp at Sarhu Hill, while the twenty thousand remaining were sent to besiege Jiefan, forty miles northwest of Hingking.

Nurhachi's fourth and favorite son Abahai took the situation in hand. There were only four hundred Manchu troops in Jiefan and he organized them in an ambush near Sarhu. When the head of Du Sung's troops had passed, these men attacked the column and drove the surprised Chinese into the ford across the river below. The surprise did not last, however, and soon this small force was surrounded by the enemy, who would soon have cut them down. Abahai, however, rushed in at the head of a thousand men to support them while two banners, each of seventy-five hundred men, followed him. Nurhachi then led six banners against Du Sung's camp at Sarhu.

The Chinese replied to the Manchu attack with cannon fire and jingals, heavy muskets mounted on swivels, but without great effect. The firearms of the period were not extremely effective, particularly in the Far East, and they were slow to use as well.[4] When night fell the Manchus are reported as having shot into the camp by the light of torches or lamps the Chinese soldiers had lit, but it seems unlikely the Chinese would have made this error. However that may be, the Manchus eventually rushed the stockade and seized the camp.

Nurhachi set out at once to relieve Jiefan, where Du Sung was conducting the siege. The Chinese general was killed by an arrow in the first skirmishing and his troops fled across the Hwun. All of the important Chinese officers were captured and the fleeing Chinese were pursued for seven miles. One of the four armies had been destroyed.

Ma Lin, the commander of a second army at Sanchakow, heard of the defeat at Sarhu and dug three trenches around the outside of his camp, placing his artillery pieces, oddly, outside the fosses. Meanwhile the commander-in-chief, Yang Hao, worked with Ma Lin by sending two detachments of ten thousand men each to establish camps on hills slightly in front of, and on either side of Ma Lin's. Beyond this, Yang Hao commanded that all three positions put their wagons outside camp as a barrier to cavalry, and that heavy shields be made to protect the men from arrows.

The battle began when Abahai attacked one of the forward camps and took it. Nurhachi himself attacked Ma Lin in the main camp; he seems to have outnumbered the Chinese about two to one, although, as noted, they held a thoroughly prepared position. Nurhachi ordered his men to dismount, doubtless because it was impossible for them to attack the entrenched and wagon-barricaded camp on horseback. Before they could do so, Ma Lin threw caution to the wind and sent his men from the camp in a sally against the Manchus. Nurhachi's men were at first surprsed by the unexpected Chinese charge, but soon banner after banner rushed in to their support and the Chinese were beaten and dispersed—not even supported by their fellows in the remaining camp, whose leader, a eunuch official, declined to send them in. The eunuch escaped by himself from the battle. Ma Lin also escaped, while Chinese allies from Yehe turned back from their approach when they learned the results of the fighting.

When Yang Hao heard the result of the battle he ordered the two remaining armies, those of the south and southwest, to retreat. The latter did so, but the former, under the command of Liu Ting, apparently did not receive these orders and advanced to within fifty miles of Hingking. In response, Nurhachi sent four thousand men to defend the capital and then went on a reconnaisance of Liu Ting's army.

Liu Ting meanwhile fortified his camp and sent out small forces to take some forts and villages. Instead of attacking the camp, Nurhachi created a ruse: he sent a number of Chinese deserters to Liu Ting's camp and these men claimed to be from the army of Du Sung. They informed Liu Ting that Du Sung had already taken Hingking, thus implying that he ought to rush to the city in order to win his share of glory and loot. Liu Ting did not immediately accept the story. Instead, he posed a question: If the city had been taken, why had he not heard any cannon fire?

When Nurhachi learned of the general's reservations he had a number of guns fired off. Liu Ting heard these firings, accepted the story and divided his forces into four columns, two of which advanced as far as Abudaligang, where they were attacked by the right wing of the Manchu army—four banners under Abahai. The left wing, wearing Chinese armor, got into the camp and captured it in the ensuing surprise and confusion. The second and third Chinese armies had been defeated. This action was followed up by a march south, where the remaining force comprised of Chinese infantry and Korean allies was encamped at Chojin. The Chinese were defeated and the Koreans came over to the Manchus.

While things were going well for the Manchus it was in large part due to the doddering governance of the Ming Dynasty. This dynasty had begun vigorously enough with the overthrow of the Mongol Yüan emperors, but with time it had gone into decline. Two emperors in particular—Jiajing (reigned 1522–1566) and Wanli (reigned 1573–1620)—had retired from political life and taken no real part in the governance of the country, which was left to a beauracracy largely controlled by eunuchs, most of whom acted in their own personal interests. Jiajing's reign had also been marked by Mongol raids and Japanese piracy, and the political power of the eunuchs grew especially during Wanli's reign. Wanli was succeeded by Tianqi in 1620, but this emperor entrusted his authority to Wei Zhongxian, who was noted as a particularly evil eunuch. This was corrected in some degree when Wei was replaced by Chongzhen, but this minister was not able to cope with the problems that had arisen under Wanli.

Furthermore, the Manchus were not merely a threat in and of themselves: to counter them, the Chinese were forced to keep a large part of their soldiers in the north so that they were unavailable to quell revolts elsewhere which arose from misgovernment, overtaxation, and hunger following spells of bad weather. And still the Manchus grew in strength, extending their influence into eastern Mongolia. In 1624 the khan of the Khorchin Mongols submitted and his people were organized into banners. By the time of Nurhachi's death in 1626, the Manchus were possessed of an extremely effective military state.

As for the great campaign of 1619, all of the major battles comprising the defense of Hingking took place in a mere five days—an indication of the speed and mobility of the Manchu army. The losses to the Chinese were enormous; the Ming records indicated forty-five thousand dead, among them three hundred officers. Beyond this there were losses in horses, camels, armor, weapons and Chinese cannon. The spoil was said to have been "numbered by the million."[5] A month after these serious Chinese defeats, the Manchus marched against Kaiguen, the northernmost Chinese possession. This city was defended by Ma Lin, who placed men outside each of the four gates, but Nurhachi concentrated his attack upon the east gate and drove them inside. As the Chinese entered, some Manchus followed them through the gate while others used scaling ladders.

In 1621 Hiung Tingbi, a very competent Chinese, was nominated general in charge of dealing with the Manchus. He went to Liaoyang, the capital of Liaotung, and from there, in spite of snowy winter weather he toured the countryside and towns to learn how best to defend the province. Hiung set one hundred and eighty thousand men to guard six important passes located a day's ride from the Manchu capital of Hingking. The men in each division were to support each other if attacked, while patrols were constantly sent out on reconnaisance. The general also established a field army with which he menaced the Manchu state by approaching the border in different places. His strategy was primarily defensive, but it was clever and effective. He rebuilt city walls and encouraged the repopulation of the area. For two years Nurhachi did not raid.

Hiung Tingbi's successes in holding the frontier stable were not enough, however, to secure his position; he was the subject of constant criticism from the eunuchs that he was not aggressive enough and was finally forced to give up command. However, the emperor Tianqi ordered an inquiry into the general's conduct which ultimately exonerated him, and Hiung Tingbi was slated to be reinstated. In the meantime, however, the area suffered under the governance of Yuen Yingtai, a competent civil official who was not really fit to deal with such a difficult military problem.

There had been famine in eastern Mongolia and many Mongols asked to be admitted into the empire, where they could be fed. Yuen Yingtai was concerned lest these Mongols become Manchu clients (the Manchus were, of course, extending their sway over Mongolia) and so he agreed to admit them. The Mongols quickly abused the Chinese among whom they were quartered and these Chinese entered into communication with the Manchus, who they judged might protect them. Nurhachi soon began to use these Chinese as a fifth column in Liaotung; he had designs upon the city of Liaoyang, and his opportunity was excellent: Hiung Tingbi was still under house arrest while his tenure of command was being examined, the Chinese army had largely withdrawn and the peasantry was unhappy with Yuen Yingtai.

March 1621 also saw a Manchu advance against the frontier city of Shenyang (later, Mukden). This city was prepared for a siege; a network of fosses had been dug around it and a palisade was constructed that encircled the defenses. Inside were guns, shields and thousands of soldiers. The commander, a certain Shu Hien, was less than capable, however.

The outset of the siege was marked by a basic nomad tactic: ambush. Shu Hien spotted a small party of Manchu scouts and led a pursuit of them with a thousand cavalry. These scouts in turn led the Chinese past an ambush, though Shu Hien, to his credit, was able to keep his men in hand during the retreat. The Chinese kept turning about to keep the Manchus at bay and in this way got back to Mukden only to find that the bridge over the moat had been destroyed by Chinese deserters whom Nurhachi had sent into the city before investing it. There was a sally from the city to rescue the Chinese, but the force was beaten, its leader killed and the city taken. An army sent to the relief of Mukden was attacked at a ford on the Hwun River and many of the soldiers drowned. A second army was defeated, with three thousand killed. In 1625 Nurhachi established the city as his new capital; the Manchu state was moving its capital ever closer to China.

And still the Chinese persisted in delivering their forces to the Manchus piecemeal: a third relieving army of ten thousand under Tung Jungkwei camped on a bank of the Hwun and was joined by an additional three thousand soldiers under a local official. He led his men across a bridge to the far bank to establish a camp, but was suddenly attacked before the work was done. The official himself was killed while the remnants of his men fled back across the river to Tung Jungkwei's camp, which was then quickly surrounded by Manchus outnumbering the Chinese three or four to one.

The Chinese used cannon against the Manchus with good effect, but eventually they ran out of powder and the Manchus were able to approach their camp and shoot arrows into it by the thousand. Tung Jungkwei and a few others rushed from the camp to die fighting while the balance of the Chinese retreated to Liaoyang. Yuen Yingtai was now in the unhappy position of having to defend the provincial capital itself from direct assault. He flooded the moats and advanced against the Manchus only to be beaten back to the city. There was hard fighting between the Chinese and the Manchus, but the Manchu left wing managed to scale a part of the wall, unseen due to smoke from the Chinese cannon. Fighting persisted all night, but by morning the city was taken. Yuen Yingtai went to the tower over the main gate and set it afire, killing himself. Many other officials committed suicide too, though many others accepted the "queue," or Manchu pigtail.

Those who submitted to the Manchus shaved their heads as a sign of loyalty and braided the hair at the back of the head into a pigtail—a sign of submission throughout China from the final conquest

to the fall of the dynasty in 1912. In fact, as the Manchus marched
into the city through the west gate they were greeted with calls of
"Long live the Emperor." The people wore their fancy clothes and
there was music, incense and banners. It may have seemed to the
Chinese of Liaotung province that the Manchu star was in the ascen-
dant and that the Ming Dynasty had run its course. The capture of
Liaoyang marked the final conquest of the territory of Liaotung. The
loss was as much the product of pointless and self-destructive political in-fighting as of Manchu arms. It had previously been shown
that Chinese forces, if competently led, could hold the frontier.

Holding Liaotung was, however, a challenge for the Manchus as
well. The Chinese soon grew restive under the Manchus, whom they
regarded as barbarians, and Nurhachi shifted people from one city
to another, even resettling coastal dwellers inland.

Meanwhile some sense had prevailed at the Chinese court and,
after the fall of Liaoyang, Hiung Tingbi was reinstated as general of
the province. The eunuchs still did not care for him, however, and
saw to it that he had no army. Nevertheless, he went to the Liao
River, where he learned that the Chinese commander there, Wang
Huajun, had divided his forces and put them into six camps. Hiung
Tingbi knew that they would be defeated in detail before they could
support one another, because the Manchus struck so quickly and
could cross the frozen Liao. He argued for a single concentrated
army with patrols to scout throughout the area. Wang ignored the
advice.

The Manchus did, of course, cross the river as Hiung had predicted. They attacked a village to which Wang sent two troops in
support. The commander of one, Duagung, reckoned that he could
not prevail and promptly deserted to the Manchus. Nurhachi hurriedly sent him to the town of Kuangning before his desertion was
known to the Chinese. It was here that Wang himself commanded
and Duagung was known as his lieutenant. The Chinese traitor got
into the city and induced panic by announcing that the Manchus
would attack at any time and that everyone should look to his own
safety. Wang was shaken by the news and galloped off with a pair of
servants. The town, deprived of its commanders through treachery
and flight, was easily taken; Duagung himself opened the gate for the
Manchus when they came.

Wang fled to Hiung Tingbi's camp, but the general commanded only five thousand men and could do nothing for him. Hiung burned his stores and guarded the rear of a trail of a million Chinese who fled south of the Great Wall.

There followed a period of four years during which the Chinese seem to have recaptured a good bit of their territory west of the Liao, though, predictably, it was taken from them again. The recapture of territory was, as might now be expected, as much the result of machinations in Beijing as of Manchu prowess. The recaptured territories were competently governed by Taotai Chunghwan, who was replaced, however, at the instigation of the eunuchs, by a certain Gao Di, who determined that the border should be moved further south. Nurhachi moved into the territory obligingly vacated by the Chinese, taking towns along the way until he came to Ninghwan, which was held by the former governer Taotai Chunghwan, who was determined to stand fast.

The Manchus besieged Ninghwan and tried to dig holes through the city walls, in spite of the defenders' shooting arrows and heaving rocks down on them. Taotai, however, had something even more effective: a European cannon, which he ordered used against the attackers. It is supposed to have made a bloody trail a mile long through the Manchu ranks, killing several hundred of them. The Manchus nonetheless attacked again after three days, but were driven back again and forced to lift the siege.

The disappointment of failing to take Ninghwan literally mortified Nurhachi, who sickened. Taotai, by contrast, enjoyed promotion to General of the East. Nurhachi, meanwhile, visited a mineral spring at Chingho and, still distraught at the failure to take Ninghwan, he died outside of Mukden on the return trip in September 1626. He was succeeded by his fourth and favorite son, Abahai.

Abahai followed his father's lead in renewing the Manchu attack upon Ninghwan, still defended by Taotai. Like his father, however, he was unsuccessful and developed a great hatred for the Chinese general. Taotai's success led, predictably, to his removal from office at the eunuchs' behest, but the Ming Emperor Tanqi soon died and his successor, Chongzhen, the last Ming emperor, reinstated him.

In 1627 the Manchus conquered Korea and two years later conducted their first great raid south of the Great Wall. In 1629 Abahai determined to strike directly at Beijing by first passing through Mongol territory, where the way was easier. Four banners went through Dungan Pass north of Beijing while four other banners with Mongol auxiliaries passed through Lungjing gwan pass to the northeast. All banners rejoined beneath the walls of the city of Hanjunwang, where they were joined by numbers of Chinese deserters, a telling sign of common unwillingness to die for the Mings. The Manchus then advanced, taking a pair of cities and defeating, as usual in detail, a series of separate Chinese forces.

In response to the incursion, Taotai rushed to Beijing with all the men he could gather. Abahai advanced to Nanhaidsu, south of Beijing, and used it as his base. He attacked the Ming capital, but was unable to best Taotai, who stood with his men outside the Shaho Gate. All the same, Abahai gained something: Taotai was executed upon the testimony of two eunuchs who, as captives of the Manchus, had heard he was to betray the city. It was, of course, untrue. The eunuchs had merely been fed a lie by the Manchus, but all the same it resulted in the general's death. This was followed by an attack upon one of the Chinese camps outside Beijing by Manchus dressed as Chinese under Chinese banners.

Still Abahai could not take the city and so lifted the siege, taking a number of towns on his withdrawal. One of these cities was Yungping, where he installed his brother Amin in command of five thousand men to hold that town and others they had taken, such as Lanchow. A huge Chinese army soon advanced upon Lanchow to besiege it, and the Manchu defenders fled to Yungping, where Amin unaccountably panicked. He gathered all of the garrisons under his command, executed all Chinese soldiers who had come to him as deserters and fled north to Mukden without protecting his rear. Few of his men survived the flight.

Amin was tried and found guilty of sixteen capital crimes, but due to his position he was spared execution. Instead he lost all property and was condemned to life imprisonment. His officers received lesser, though severe, sentences. Abahai was, of course, perfectly aware that the murder of the Chinese followers was a particularly dangerous move because it alienated the very people he wished to encourage to desert, and the disastrous retreat would not make them any more attractive to other outside followers like the Mongols who, in nomad fashion, hitched their wagons to men and tribes they viewed as winners.

The Manchu menace had even provoked the Chinese to agree to Portuguese military aid under Captain Gonsalvo Teixera Correa, but the Western force was dismissed without seeing action because of the opposition of Canton merchants. These feared that if the Portuguese were successful with their European cannon and firearms, they would be given trade concessions at the merchants' expense.

In 1631 the Manchus cast their first large cannon, a piece named "The Heavenly-Aiding, Awe-Inspiring Great General." They had already captured numbers of Chinese cannon, called "red-coated" after the Chinese custom of painting cannon red. They soon put the "General" to work in an attack on the Chinese fort at Doliang Ho, east of Kingchow. There the general Dsu Dashow was building a fort to command the area and allow him to control the frontier. The Manchus marched west from Mukden, crossed the Liao and were joined by their Mongol auxiliaries. Though the Chinese camp was not yet completed, Abahai thought it better to invest it than storm it. The "General" was set up to command the road approaching the fort. The siege lasted two months, during which the Manchus beat off Chinese relief armies until Dsu Dashow, close to starvation, surrendered, pretending to desert to the Manchus. The wily general suggested that he be sent to Kingchow, where his family was, to work there as a Manchu agent. Once there, however, he showed his true Chinese loyalties again.

Meanwhile the Mings were saddled with rebellion as well: the rebel Li Zicheng had control of the upper Han Valley by 1633. The son of a prosperous peasant, Li offered to protect the poor from Ming overtaxation. Another rebel arose as well: Zhang Xianzhong, known because of his cruelty as "The Yellow Tiger."

And still things continued apace for the Manchus: 1635 was the year they took the name "Manchu" and it was in this year too that they finally incorporated Mongolia into their empire. 1636 saw them put down a Mongol revolt in the Kwewha Chung area, west of the Yellow River, and this was followed by a winter raid into Shansi Province through Mongolia, with two more to follow in the summer and fall of 1637. These paths through Mongolia were important since the town of Shanhaiguan, where the Great Wall met the sea, was too well defended to allow the Manchus entry into China by that route, no matter how inept the Chinese defense.

The Manchus struck through Mongolia again in 1638 in two columns under the leadership of two of Abahai's brothers, Dorgon and Yolo. Yolo defeated a small Chinese force under Wu Ahung, the governor of Ki and Liao (now northeastern Chihli and part of Liaosi), while Dorgon pierced a decrepit section of the Great Wall and passed into the interior. The columns joined each other at Tungchow not far from Beijing and then marched to Chochow, where they divided, traveling by separate roads in eight columns. The Manchus encountered only a small Chinese force which had already suffered casualties fighting with rebels and they had no difficulty defeating them. They then set a rearguard to slow the approach of any Chinese troops and afterward dissolved into numerous parties to better and more thoroughly ravage the countryside.

The Chinese, meanwhile, were becoming less and less able to deal with the Manchu threat. They had lost many armies and a great deal of prestige, and several provinces were in open revolt. The Manchus had the natural advantage of the fast raider: they could strike when and where it favored them, and be fairly assured of success. And the more they did so, the more they weakened their opponent and made their own successes more likely.

Further raiding into China followed, including in 1639 the siege of Kingchow. The outer city was taken through the treachery of Mongols in Chinese service, but the inner city, or citadel, held out under its energetic commander. Meanwhile a relieving army was sent forth under Hung Chungchow, now governor of Ki and Liao, and eight generals. Though Hung was prudent enough not to divide his forces and to advance cautiously, he had the bad luck to have second to him Jang Yolin of the Board of War, whose job was plainly to spy on him. This fellow maneuvered and provoked Hung into sending part of his army as an advance guard toward the Manchus while leaving his stores defended by another division in the rear. The Manchus swept into these interior lines and took the provisions after beating the defenders. Without provisions the advance guard was forced to retire, as the Manchus knew it would be, and they harried it and ambushed it so that, while it began the retreat in good order, it was in a shambles by the time it reached the safety of the fort of Tushan.

A second march from Tushan to Ninghwan resulted in the complete destruction of the army. Kingchow then fell. After this the Manchus razed Shungshan and Tushan, effectively putting Wu Sangwei, commander of Ninghwan, on the very Chinese border.

Meanwhile, in 1641, the rebel Li Zicheng took Liaoyang and began to attract many followers; by 1643 he had control of the provinces of Hunan and Shansi, and the Ming Dynasty was viewed, properly, as in sharp decline. Li Zicheng went on to capture Kaifeng and Xian, China's ancient capital, and the Mings were unable to field a decent army against him; the dynasty was expected shortly to fall. Li Zicheng marched upon Beijing to announce the start of a new dynasty and Emperor Chongzhen hanged himself from a tree in a garden of the Forbidden City.

Upon his arrival, the court by and large accepted Li Zicheng as the new emperor, although things did not quite work according to plan. The Manchus were shortly to be given one more opportunity to serve their own interests at the expense of the Chinese.

Wu Sangwei, governor of Ninghwan and commander of the last effective Chinese force in the north, wavered in the matter of declaring his loyalty to Li Zicheng. Upon reflection he reckoned that he himself could take Beijing, with Manchu help. The Manchus were happy to oblige. Wu opened the frontier to them, and a combined Chinese-Manchu army marched, in 1644, upon the capital. Li Zicheng's army was defeated and the city taken. When thanked for their help, however, the Manchus declined to retire and, seizing the opportunity, took control of the capital. They established the Ch'ing Dynasty with Abahai's minor son, Shunzhi, as their first emperor. Wu Sangwei was forced into accepting a position as their subordinate: he was made governor of Szechwan and Yunan, where he ruled for a number of years almost independently until he was asked to disband his army. He declared himself emperor in 1678, but then was defeated and killed. Zhang Xianzhong, the "Yellow Tiger," meanwhile created his own state in the southwest with his capital at Chegdu, but it too fell to the Manchus—as did the rest of China shortly.

The Manchus' ultimate success, while due in part to their tactics of speed and their opportunistic strategy, was clearly as much the product of the internal divisions of the Chinese Empire, and their unprecedented success in maintaining themselves in power was due to their lack of interests elsewhere—in sharp distinction to the Mongols, who controlled vast territories outside China.

NOTES
1. René Grousset, *The Empire of the Steppes*, trans. Naomi Walford, New Brunswick, NJ, Rutgers University Press, 1991.
2. J.A.G. Roberts, *A History of China*, Vol. I, Stroud, UK, Phoenix Mill, 1996, p. 200.
3. The Reverend John Ross described the rise of the Manchus in a nineteenth-century work entitled *The Manchus or The Reigning Dynasty of China, Their Rise and Progress*, London, F. Paisley and R. Parlane, 1880. He had obviously read some expression in Chinese which he translated as "mailed men," but is clearly unhappy with the expression. In a footnote he adds: "From what I can learn, this mail consisted of many folds of cotton sewed one above the other, between ten and twenty folds, making the garment arrow-proof" (p. 10).
4. Two hundred years later, Frederick II of Prussia expected his musketeers to hit a five-foot by ten-foot target at 100 yards only 60 percent of the time. Peter Young, *The Fighting Man: From Alexander the Great's Army to the Present Day*. London, Orbis Publishing, 1981.
5. Ross, *Rise and Progress,* op. cit.

Conclusion

The steppe warriors had a run of thirty-five centuries, but it could not continue indefinitely; in time, firearms were no longer inferior to the bow and, furthermore, they had always taken a good deal less skill to master. Moreover, a mounted man is a large target for the musketeer or rifleman; if the man is hit he is out of the fight and if his horse is hit that is hardly less serious from the standpoint of mounted archery. A series of volleys by soldiers trained to countermarch, or a few cannon blasts from field artillery, could disperse a squadron of horsemen.

Gunpowder severely restricted the usefulness of cavalry, as Napoleon recognized when he said, "It is the business of cavalry to follow up the victory, and to prevent the army from rallying." Napoleon states plainly that the cavalry's task is not to win a victory, but to exploit it. As firearms improved, it would not even do that. During the American Civil War the most effective cavalry functioned as mounted infantry (like the dragoons of half a century earlier), using the speed of the horse for movement, but dismounting to fight. By the First World War the cavalry had been superseded even in its scouting role by the airplane. In the end, technology—gunpowder—rendered cavalry obsolete and removed the threat of the steppe warrior, who only fought mounted. The struggle between nomad and settled man had finally been decided in the latter's favor.

But until this happened the tough man on the tough, shaggy pony with his recurved bow and string of remounts was an unequaled threat to his settled neighbors. He was obedient to his chiefs, apt at tactical maneuver on the battlefield, armed with an extremely effective weapon, able to cover great distances quickly and tough and indifferent to killing. For centuries settled people struggled to contain the inroads of these nomads, be they Scythians, Huns, Avars, Magyars, Mongols, Turks or Tatars. From the military standpoint their names and races are unimportant: the descriptions from Herodotus and Ammianus Marcellinus to Guillaume Le Vasseur de Beauplan might be of the same man. In a sense, it *is* a description of the same man.

It was a description of a warrior who, like a phenomenon of nature, did not differ across time. Not so his opponents: the Persian differed sharply from the Roman and the Roman from the Frank and the Frank from the Arab. All were distinct not only in language (as some steppe people were) but in the myriad ways in which their civilized, city-centered cultures were—clothing, religion, myths, manners, arts and architecture, to mention only a few differences. But on the steppe, where existence was reduced to its very basics and where, to survive, the same tools had to be used, the same animals herded and the same migrations made, differences were leveled and the steppe warrior—no matter what his specific origin—was recognized as a pure and almost invariable type.

In the face of this almost natural force, certain of the settled peoples displayed the marks of their exposure in the field of military techniques. This might be expected because it is for the most part in the military field that the nomad excelled. The Byzantine cataphract was armed like a well-equipped Hun, recalling the Huns who had served for so long in the Roman armies of the East and West. Under the Tatar Yoke, Russian armies came to resemble Mongol ones: the men were all mounted and armed with the bow, the right wing having precedence as it did in the Mongol armies, for shamanistic reasons. One can imagine these Russians in their Tatar equipment riding south with Toktamish to fight Timur of Samarkand, or later fighting the Kipchak Tatars themselves. Still later, Polish light horsemen were equipped like the Tatars they fought; they were armed with the bow, the saber and a light, long-shafted battle-axe.

Centuries earlier the Khwarezmian Shah Muhammad II had faced Chinggis Khan, and while he did so with a smiliar army, he was completely unsuccessful. Muhammad faced difficulties that Chinggis Khan did not: a certain amount of internal disunity caused by ill-will between his subjects and his army, and the need to defend territory against an attacker who might appear anywhere. Furthermore, he could not depend upon walls to protect his subjects in view of the Mongols' new-found skill at siegecraft, stemming from their conquests in China. Their ability to take cities and menace concentrations of settled people gave the Mongols a wide field for the calculated use of terror against a civil population, something that Muhammad, fighting a defensive war, could not retaliate with even if he had had the stomach for it. It was not enough, at least in his case, to fight with the same weapons and techniques. Unity, terror and freedom of movement tipped the scales in favor of the nomads.

Oddly perhaps, the greatest military influence upon the West from the steppe was the adoption of shock combat from horseback, a sideshow really to the main aspect of steppe warfare: mounted archery. This was a legacy from the Sarmatian tribes to the wandering German nations as they sojourned upon the steppe before eventually establishing their own kingdoms in Western Europe. These Germans had wandered from Scandinavia to the Black Sea steppe, and during their two hundred years there had learned from the Sarmatians. While not strictly a steppe people, they had become horse warriors fighting with the lance and wearing armor, carrying their families and belongings in wagons while on the march. Their heavy mounted warfare, borrowed from the steppe, was an early stage in the development of the knight and this reliance upon close combat with lance and sword by an armored horseman, often upon an armored horse, persisted for nearly a thousand years.

The fully armored Western knight is the Sarmatian's direct descendant and he fought as the Sarmatians had done centuries earlier, until he was marginalized in the fifteeth century by the crossbow, the handgun and by disciplined infantry armed with the pike. Why this was not the principal steppe approach is clear: it is not generally as effective in open country, and this has been shown empirically. In battles across the centuries Western knightly armies were consistently outmaneuvered and shot to pieces; a thundering charge cannot be delivered against an opponent who will not stand to receive it.

Still, despite the evident superiority of the steppe warrior over most of his settled adversaries, Europe, at least, never suffered actual conquest from the steppe. The Mongols, it seems, might have done this except for their internal political troubles. But the steppe warrior was the product of his environment, shaped by it and therefore suited to it. It follows, then, that he was limited by it. Consider that a steppe army needs a great number of horses, at least two and more commonly three for every man. An army might easily have a hundred thousand horses as well as herds of cattle or flocks of sheep to feed the men, and these animals need a great deal of grass. In Hungary, where the steppe extends into Europe, there may be enough, but farther west there may not. Certainly a horde could feed its animals from granaries instead, but after conquest it would be difficult to maintain the number of horses to which they were accustomed.

This is not to say that the conquest of Europe in the thirteenth century was not eminently possible, only that it may have presented more difficulties than are generally recognized. Aside from its geographic location, which, from the Mongol perspective, was on the remote fringe of the Eurasian landmass, Europe also had many mountain ranges, forests, valleys and rivers, all of which tended to restrict somewhat the movement of cavalry armies. Medieval Europe was also more commonly furnished with castles and walled cities than were the other areas the Mongols roamed: Asia and the Middle East. This was a result of the more general militarization of European society compared with those elsewhere.

Even though the steppe warriors as a group were better fighters than the individualistic and honor-obsessesed knights of medieval Europe, the latter might still have appeared as dangerous foes, particularly when they operated from castles in hilly and forested terrain. So while the Mongols had shown themselves more than capable of dealing with any of these obstacles, the combination of them may have rendered Europe less attractive as a target. One may suppose that when Batu no longer had the support of Karakorum (and its imperial tumens) he must have judged the conquest of Europe, like the reoccupation of Hungary, too risky.

The greatest security for the settled nations was neither in the adoption of mounted archery (though this clearly helped preserve the Egyptian Sultanate) nor in building walls. The best hope for the nations troubled by the steppe lay in the greatest weakness of the steppe warriors themselves: their states, nations, polities or empires were extremely unstable. Left quite to themselves, steppe states inevitably broke apart, usually after a generation.

While the Chinese from time to time had to bear up under steppe overlords for longer periods, even then a second aspect of the steppe nomad came into play: his cultural malleability. Mongols in China were quickly sinicized, Mongols in Persia quickly became Persian. While it is true that the Golden Horde, or Kipchak Khanate, dominated Russia for more than two hundred years and never adopted Russian culture because it was able to remain on the steppe, even these Mongols eventually broke into smaller khanates that the Russians could deal with.

Moreover, as firearms improved, gunpowder nullified the threat these people presented even in the short run, so that long-term issues about the persistance of their states or their assimilation into conquered societies became immaterial. Then it was the nomad who was on the defensive, surrounded by societies who could be indifferent to him, or who might exploit his land according to their whims. Technology had given the upper hand to those societies he had preyed upon since those days so long ago when he first thought to shoot from horseback. In the end, like earlier nomads, the last of the Tatars spent their time living and raiding on the fringes of settled states—not occupying them.

ACKNOWLEDGEMENTS

I would like to thank the Detroit Institute of Arts and Beth Garfield for permission to reproduce *Ardashir fighting Bahman*, the Frick Collection of New York and Kate Gurlow for permission to reproduce Rembrandt's *The Polish Rider*, The Bibliotheque Nationale de France for reproductions from Guillaume Le Vasseur De Beauplan's *Description de L'Ukranie*, and archaeologist Michael Bishop for permission to reproduce his drawings of late Roman helmets and of the cataphract from Dura Europas, as well as his opinion that it probably represents a Persian.

Special gratitude also goes to the staff of the Graduate Library of the University of Michigan for help in locating materials and microfilms, and to Sarpedon editor Donn Teal for his painstaking scrutiny of the manuscript.

Finally, I would like to thank everyone who encouraged me in this project: my parents John and Joanne for their enthusiasm, my old friend and cheerleader Steven Crow, who was always ready to help without complaint, and Beth Macnee, musician, nurse and equestrienne who is good as gold and taught me about horses.

Select Bibliography

Alef, Gustave. "The Battle of Suzdal in 1445: An Episode in the Muscovite War of Succession" and "Moscovite Military Reforms," in *Rulers and Nobles in Fifteenth-Century Muscovy*. London: Variorum Reprints, London 1983.

Alexandrescu-Dersca, Marie-Mathilde. *La Campagne de Timur en Anatolie (1402)*. London: Variorum Reprints, 1977.

Allsen, Thomas T. *Mongol Imperialism: The Policies of the Grand Qan Mongke in China, Russia, and the Islamic Lands, 1251–1259*. Berkeley: University of California Press, 1987.

Amitai-Press, Reuven. *Mamluks and Mongols: The Mamluk-Ilkhanid War, 1260–1281*. Cambridge, UK: Cambridge University Press, 1995.

Arabic Archery: An Arabic Manuscript of About A.D. 1500—A Book on the Excellence of the Bow and Arrow and the Description Thereof. trans. and ed. N.A. Faris and R.P. Elmer. Princeton: Princeton University Press, 1945.

Ayalon, David. *The Mamluk Military Society, Collected Studies*. London: Variorum Reprints, 1979.

"Battle on the River Kalka, The," from the Novgorodian Chronicle, in *Medieval Russia's Epics, Chronicles, and Tales*, trans. Serge A. Venkovsky. New York: Meridian Books, 1963.

Bear, Fred. *The Archer's Bible*, rev. ed. Garden City, NY: Doubleday 1980.

Beeler, John. *Warfare in Feudal Europe, 730–1200*. Ithaca and London: Cornell University Press, 1994.

Beauplan, Guillaume Le Vasseur de. *La Description d'Ukranie*. Ottawa: Les Presses de l'Université d'Ottawa, 1990.

Berchem, Denis van. *L'Armée de Dioclétien et la Réforme Constantinienne*. Paris: Imprimerie Nationale, for the Institut Français d'Arché-

243

ologie de Beyrouth, 1952.

Bonaparte, Napoleon. *The Military Maxims of Napoleon,* trans. G.C. d'Aguilar. New York: Da Capo Press, 1995.

Boyle, John Andrew. *The Mongol World Empire, 1206–1370.* London: Variorum Reprints, 1977.

Burns, Thomas S. *Barbarians Within the Gates of Rome.* Bloomington and Indianapolis: Indiana University Press, 1994.

Bury, J.B. *History of the Later Roman Empire,* Vol. I. New York: Dover, 1958.

———. *The Invasion of Europe by the Barbarians.* New York: Russell and Russell, 1963.

Chambers, James. *The Devil's Horsemen.* New York: Atheneum, 1975.

Chevalier, Pierre. *A Discourse of the Original, Countrey, Manners, Government and Religion of the Cossacks with Another of the Precopian Tartars, and a History of the Wars of the Cossacks Against Poland.* London: printed for Hobart Kemp, 1672.

Clausewitz, Carl von. *On War,* trans. and ed. M. Howard and P. Paret. Princeton, NJ: Princeton University Press, 1976.

Cocceianus, Cassius Dio. *Roman History,* trans. E. Cary. New York: G.P. Putnam's, 1927.

Contamine, Philippe. *War in the Middle Ages.* Oxford, UK, and New York: B. Blackwell, 1984.

Clausewitz, Carl von. On War, M. Howard and P. Paret, trans and ed., Princeton University Press, Princeton, NJ, 1976

Collins, L.J.D. "The Military Organization and Tactics of the Crimean Tartars During the Sixteenth and Seventeenth Centuries," in *War, Technology and Society in the Middle East,* ed. V.J. Parry and M.E. Yapp. London: Oxford University Press, 1975.

Comnena, Anna. *The Alexiad,* trans. E.R.A. Sewter. Hammondsworth, UK: Penguin Books, 1982.

Dalairac, François-Paulin. *Polish Manuscripts: or The Secret History of the Reign of John Sobieski, the III of That Name, King of Poland.* London: printed for H. Rhodes, 1700.

Davis, R.H.C. *The Medieval Warhorse, Origin, Development and Redevelopment.* London: Thames and Hudson, 1989.

Dean, Bashford. *Helmets and Body Armor in Modern Warfare.* New Haven, CT: Yale University Press, 1920.

Delbrück, Hans. *Medieval Warfare,* 3 vols., trans. W.J. Renfroe, Jr. Lincoln and London: University of Nebraska Press, 1990.

Discovery of Muscovy, The. From the collections of Richard Hakluyt.

London: Cassell and Co, 1904.

Dunigan, James F. *How to Make War*, 3rd ed. New York: William Morrow, 1993.

Eberhard, Wolfram. *Conquerors and Rulers: Social Forces in Medieval China*. Leiden, Netherlands, E.J. Brill, 1965.

Einhard. "Life of Charlemagne," in *Two Lives of Charlemagne*, trans. Lewis Thorpe. Hammondsworth, UK: Penguin, 1969.

Ewart, J. Cossar. "The Multiple Origin of Horses and Ponies," in *The Smithsonian Institution Annual Report, 1903–1904*.

Fletcher, Joseph. "The Mongols: Ecological and Social Perspectives," in *The Harvard Journal of Asiatic Studies*, 46:1.

Foley, Vernard, G. Palmer, and W. Soedel, "The Crossbow," in *The Scientific American*, January 1985.

Fulcher of Chartres. *A History of the Expedition to Jerusalem, 1095–1127*, trans. Frances Rita Ryan. Knoxville: University of Tennessee Press, 1969.

Garlan, Yvon. *La Guerre dans l'Antiquité*. Paris: Fernand Nathan, 1972.

Gesta Francorum et Aliorum Hierosolimatanorum, trans. and ed. Rosalind Hill. London: Thomas Nelson and Sons, 1962.

Gibbon, Edward. *The Decline and Fall of the Roman Empire*. New York: Random House.

Giovanni di Plano Carpini. *The Story of the Mongols Whom We Call the Tartars*, trans. Erik Hildinger. Boston: Branden Books, 1996.

Gonzalez de Clavijo, Ruy. *Clavijo, Embassy to Tamerlane, 1403–1406*. New York: Harper and Brothers, 1928.

Grant, Michael. *The Army of the Caesars*. New York: Scribners, 1974.

———. *Constantine the Great*. New York: Scribners, 1994.

Grousset, René. *The Empire of the Steppes*, trans. Naomi Walford. New Brunswick, NJ: Rutgers University Press, 1991.

Haidar, Mirza Muhammad. *A History of the Moghuls of Central Asia, Being the Tarikh-I-Rashidi of Mirza Muhammad Haidar, Dughlat*, trans. E. Dennison Ross. London: Curzon Press; New York: Barnes and Noble, 1972.

Halperin, Charles J. *The Tatar Yoke*. Columbus, OH: Slavica Press, 1986.

———. *Russia and the Golden Horde*. Bloomington: Indiana University Press, 1987.

Hansen, Victor D. *The Western Way of War: Infantry Battle in Classical Greece*. New York: Alfred A. Knopf, 1989.

Heather, Peter. *Goths and Romans*. New York: Oxford University Press,

1991.

Heberstein, Sigismund von. *Das alte Russland*. Zurich: Manesse Verlag, 1985.

Herodotus. *The Histories*, trans. Aubrey de Selincourt. Hammondsworth, UK: Penguin Books, 1972.

Howarth, Henry H. *A History of the Mongols*. London: Longmans, Green, 1876.

Howarth, Patrick. *Attila, King of the Huns*. London: Constable, 1994.

Ischboldin, Boris. *Essays on Tatar History*. New Delhi: New Book Society of India, 1963.

Johnson, Douglas L. *The Nature of Nomadism: A Comparative Study of Pastoral Migrations in Southwestern Asia and Northern Africa*. Chicago: University of Chicago Press, Department of Geography, Research Projects, 1969.

Juvaini, Ala-ad-Din Ata-Malik. *History of the World Conqueror*, translated from the text of Mirza Muhammad Qazvin by John Andrew Boyle. Manchester, UK: Manchester University Press, 1958.

Kalusk, Ludvik. "*Les Armures des Timourides, des Aqqoyunlus et des Shirvanshahs*," in *Timurid Art and Culture, Iran and Central Asia in the Fifteenth Century*, ed. Lisa Golombek and Maria Subtelny. Leiden (Netherlands), New York, and Cologne: E.J. Brill, 1992.

———. *A History of Warfare*. London: Hutchinson, 1993.

Keegan, John. *The Face of Battle*. Hammondsworth, UK, and New York: Penguin, 1987.

———. *The Mask of Command*. London: Cape, 1987.

———. *A History of Warfare*. London: Hutchinson, 1993.

Kehren, Lucien. *Tamerlan*. Paris: Payot, 1980.

Laskowski, Otton. *Sobieski, King of Poland*, trans. F.C. Anstruther. Glasgow, UK: Polish Library, 1944.

Leeuwen, Carel van, Tatjana Emeljanenko, and Larisa Popova. *Nomads in Central Asia*. Amsterdam: Royal Tropical Institute, 1994.

Levanoni, Amalia. *A Turning Point in Mamluk History*. Leiden (Netherlands), New York, and Cologne: E.J. Brill, 1995.

Lewis, Archibald R. *Nomads and Crusaders, A.D. 1000–1368*. Bloomington: Indiana University Press, 1991.

Lot, Ferdinand. *L'Art Militaire et les Armées du Moyen Age*. Paris, 1944.

Maenchen-Helfen, Otto. *World of the Huns*. Berkeley: University of California Press, 1973.

Marcellinus, Ammianus. Books 14–31, trans. Walter Hamilton.

Hammondsworth, UK: Penguin, 1986.

Marco Polo. *The Travels of Marco Polo the Venetian*, Marsden translation, ed. Thomas Wright. New York: AMS Press, 1968; reprint of 1854 Bohn edition, London.

Marshall,Christopher. *Warfare in the Latin East*. Cambridge and New York: Cambridge University Press, 1991.

Maurice (Byzantine Emperor). *Strategikon: A Handbook of Byzantine Military Strategy*, trans. G.T. Dennis. Philadelphia: University of Pennsylvania Press, 1984.

Mayer, A. *Mamluk Costume*. Geneva: Albert Kundig, 1952.

McEwen, Edward, Robert L. Miller, and Christopher A. Bergman. "Early Bow Design and Construction," in *The Scientific American*, June 1991.

Morgan, David. *The Mongols*. Oxford, UK, and Cambridge, MA: Harvard University Press, 1986.

Muir, William. *The Mameluke or Slave Dynasty of Egypt*. Amsterdam: Oriental Press, 1968.

Munyatu'l-Ghuzat: A 14th Century Mamluk-Kipchak Military Treatise, trans. Kurtulus Oztopcu. Cambridge, MA: Harvard University Press, 1989.

Novgorodian Chronicle, in *Medieval Russia's Epics, Chronicles, and Tales*, trans. Serge A. Venkovsky. New York: Meridian Books, 1996.

Oman, C. *A History of the Art of War in the Middle Ages*, 2 vols. New York: Burt Franklin, 1959.

Oman, C.W.C. *A History of the Art of War*. New York: G.P. Putnam's, 1898.

Paterson, G. "The Archers of Islam," in *The Journal of the Economic and Social History of the Orient*, Vol. IX, Parts I–II (November 1966).

Payne-Gallwey, Ralph. *The Book of the Crossbow*. New York: Dover, 1995; reprint of 1903 edition.

Perry, John. *The State of Russia Under the Present Czars*. London and Edinburgh, Thomas Nelson, Ltd; reprint of 1716 edition.

Plutarch. *Lives*, Vol. III, trans. Bernadotte Perrin. London and New York: Loeb Classical Library, 1916.

Political and Military Institutes of Tamerlane, The, Recorded by Sharfuddin Ali Yezdi, trans. James Davy. New Delhi: Idarah-I Adabiyat-I Delli, 1972.

Procopius. *History of the Wars*, Book I, trans. H.B. Dewing. Cambridge, MA, and London: Harvard University Press, 1953.

Ratchnevsky, Paul. *Genghis Khan, His Life and Legacy*, trans. Thomas N. Haining. Oxford, UK, and Cambridge, MA: Basil Blackwell Ltd, 1991.

Roberts, J.A.G. *A History of China*, Vol. I. Stroud, UK: Phoenix Mill.

Ross, John. *The Manchus or The Reigning Dynasty of China, Their Rise and Progress*. London: F. Paisley and R. Parlane, 1880.

Royal Frankish Annals, in *Carolingian Chronicles*, trans. Bernard Walter Scholtz and Barbara Rogers. Ann Arbor: University of Michigan Press, 1970.

Sadeque, Syedah Fatima. *Baybars I of Egypt*, trans. George Cumberlege. New York: AMS Press, 1980.

Secret History of the Mongols, and Other Pieces, trans. Arthur Waley. London: Allen and Unwin, 1963.

Sinor, Denis. "The Inner Asian Warriors," in *The Journal of the American Oriental Society*, October 1981.

Smail, R.C. *Crusading Warfare*. New York: Cambridge University Press, 1956.

Snodgrass, Anthony M. *Arms and Armour of the Greeks*. Ithaca, NY: Cornell University Press, 1967.

Spaulding, O.L, H. Nickerson, and J.W. Wright. *Warfare: A Study of Military Methods from the Earliest Times*. Washington, DC: The Infantry Journal, 1937.

Sulimirski, Tadeusz. *The Sarmatians*. Southampton, UK: Thames and Hudson, 1970.

Tamerlane, or Timur the Great Amir, trans. Ahmed Ibn Arabshah and J.H. Sanders. Lahore, India: Progressive Books, 1976.

Thompson, E.A. *A History of Attila and the Huns*. Oxford, UK, and Cambridge, MA: Blackwell, 1996.

Thorau, Peter. *Lion of Egypt*, trans. P.M. Holt. London and New York: Longman,1992.

Vernadsky, George. *The Mongols and Russia*. New Haven and London: Yale University Press, 1953.

Webster, Graham. *The Roman Imperial Army*, 2nd ed. London: Adam and Charles Black, 1979.

Young, Peter. *The Fighting Man: From Alexander the Great's Army to the Present Day*. London: Orbis Publishing.

Index

249